REORIENTING MODERNISM IN ARABIC AND PERSIAN POETRY

Reorienting Modernism in Arabic and Persian Poetry is the first book to systematically study the parallel development of modernist poetry in Arabic and Persian. It presents a fresh line of comparative inquiry into minor literatures within the field of world literary studies. Focusing on Arabic–Persian literary exchanges allows readers to better understand the development of modernist poetry in both traditions and in turn challenge Europe's position at the center of literary modernism. The argument contributes to current scholarly efforts to globalize modernist studies by reading Arabic and Persian poetry comparatively within the context of the Cold War to establish the Middle East as a significant participant in wider modernist developments. To illuminate profound connections between Arabic and Persian modernist poetry in both form and content, the book takes up works from key poets including the Iraqis Badr Shakir al-Sayyab and Abd al-Wahhab al-Bayati and the Iranians Nima Yushij, Ahmad Shamlu, and Forough Farrokhzad.

LEVI THOMPSON is Assistant Professor of Persian and Arabic Literature in the Department of Middle Eastern Studies at the University of Texas at Austin. His articles have appeared or are forthcoming in the *Journal of Arabic Literature, College Literature, Middle Eastern Literatures, Alif: Journal of Comparative Poetics*, and elsewhere.

CAMBRIDGE STUDIES IN WORLD LITERATURE

World Literature is a vital part of twenty-first-century critical studies. Globalization and unprecedented levels of connectivity through communication technologies force literary scholars to rethink the scale of literary production and their own critical practices. As an exciting field that engages seriously with the place and function of literary studies in our global era, the study of world literature requires new approaches. Cambridge Studies in World Literature is founded on the assumption that world literature is not all literatures of the world nor a canonical set of globally successful literary works. The series will highlight scholarship on literary works that focus on the logics of circulation drawn from multiple literary cultures and technologies of the textual. While not rejecting the nation as a site of analysis, the series will offer insights into new cartographies – the hemispheric, the oceanic, the transregional, the archipelagic, the multilingual local – that better reflect the multiscalar and spatially dispersed nature of literary production. It will highlight the creative coexistence, flashpoints, and intersections of language worlds from both the Global South and the Global North, and multiworld models of literary production and literary criticism that these have generated. It will push against existing historical, methodological, and cartographic boundaries and showcase humanistic and literary endeavors in the face of world-scale environmental and humanitarian catastrophes.

In This Series
SARAH QUESADA
The African Heritage of Latinx and Caribbean Literature

ROANNE L. KANTOR
South Asian Writers, Latin American Literature, and the Rise of Global English

LEVI THOMPSON
Reorienting Modernism in Arabic and Persian Poetry

REORIENTING MODERNISM IN ARABIC AND PERSIAN POETRY

LEVI THOMPSON
The University of Texas at Austin

CAMBRIDGE
UNIVERSITY PRESS

CAMBRIDGE
UNIVERSITY PRESS

Shaftesbury Road, Cambridge CB2 8EA, United Kingdom

One Liberty Plaza, 20th Floor, New York, NY 10006, USA

477 Williamstown Road, Port Melbourne, VIC 3207, Australia

314–321, 3rd Floor, Plot 3, Splendor Forum, Jasola District Centre, New Delhi – 110025, India

103 Penang Road, #05–06/07, Visioncrest Commercial, Singapore 238467

Cambridge University Press is part of Cambridge University Press & Assessment, a department of the University of Cambridge.

We share the University's mission to contribute to society through the pursuit of education, learning and research at the highest international levels of excellence.

www.cambridge.org
Information on this title: www.cambridge.org/9781009164474

DOI: 10.1017/9781009164467

First published 2023

A catalogue record for this publication is available from the British Library.

Library of Congress Cataloging-in-Publication Data
NAMES: Thompson, Levi, author.
TITLE: Re-orienting modernism in Arabic and Persian poetry / Levi Thompson, University of Colorado, Boulder.
DESCRIPTION: Cambridge ; New York, NY : Cambridge University Press, 2023. | SERIES: Cambridge studies in world literature | Includes bibliographical references and index.
IDENTIFIERS: LCCN 2022030711 (print) | LCCN 2022030712 (ebook) | ISBN 9781009164474 (hardback) | ISBN 9781009164450 (paperback) | ISBN 9781009164467 (epub)
SUBJECTS: LCSH: Arabic poetry–20th century–History and criticism. | Persian poetry–20th century–History and criticism. | Modernism (Literature)–Arab countries. | Modernism (Literature)–Iran. | Comparative literature–Arabic and Persian. | Comparative literature–Persian and Arabic. | LCGFT: Literary criticism.
CLASSIFICATION: LCC PJ7561 .T46 2022 (print) | LCC PJ7561 (ebook) | DDC 891/.551309112–dc23/eng/20220822
LC record available at https://lccn.loc.gov/2022030711
LC ebook record available at https://lccn.loc.gov/2022030712

ISBN 978-1-009-16447-4 Hardback

Contents

Acknowledgments *page* vii
Note on Transliteration xi

Introduction: Mapping a Modernist Geography in Arabic and Persian Poetry 1

PART I CRAFTING A MODERNIST GEOGRAPHY ACROSS ARABIC AND PERSIAN POETRY

1 Formal Connections, Literary Criticism, and Political Commitment 27

2 Travel Forms: Arabic Prosody, Craft, and Nīmā Yūshīj's Persian New Poetry 48

PART II IMAGINING NEW WORLDS

3 Aḥmad Shāmlū's Manifesto and Proto-Third World Literature 73

4 Badr Shākir al-Sayyāb between Communism and World Literature 97

PART III AFTERMATH: MODERNIST ENDS IN ARABIC AND PERSIAN POETRY

5 Honoring Commitments: ʿAbd al-Wahhāb al-Bayātī's Existential Trials 123

6 Winter in the Modernist Garden: Furūgh Farrukhzād's Posthumous Poetry and the Death of Modernism 143

Conclusion: Reorienting Modernism 165

Notes 171
Bibliography 208
Index 224

Acknowledgments

Many people and institutions assisted me in writing this book. Most recently, the College of Liberal Arts at the University of Texas at Austin provided me with research funding and other resources to complete and edit the book. I am fortunate to have been warmly welcomed by my new colleagues in the Department of Middle Eastern Studies at UT as a global pandemic continued to upend plans and complicate lives. I am particularly grateful to my Department Chair, Na'ama Pat-el, for making my family's transition to UT and Austin possible, first of all, and practicable as well, and to colleagues in the literature and culture track at UT's DMES: Karen Grumberg, Avigail Noy, Jeannette Okur, Nahid Siamdoust, and Babak Tabarraee. Thanks are also due to the Department of Asian Languages and Civilizations at the University of Colorado Boulder, where I began working on the manuscript during the summer of 2019. When he was Department Chair and after, Matthias Richter advocated for me throughout my time in Colorado and unconditionally supported me even when he did not have to. I will remember my time at CU fondly because of him, the office administrators, and many members of the faculty there: Jackie Coombs, Asuka Morley, Keller Kimbrough, Antje Richter, Katherine Alexander, Evelyn Shih, Rahul Parson, Clarence Lee, Terry and Faye Kleeman, Janice Brown, Karim Mattar, John Willis, Hilary Falb Kalisman, and Naseem Surhio. I am much obliged to Naseem, a fellow southwest Virginian who stepped in – also during the pandemic – to take over the lease on my apartment up the sublime Boulder Canyon and teach my courses as a Visiting Assistant Professor so I could take advantage of a significant junior leave that allowed me to make major progress on the book once more in Providence, Rhode Island.

I had already completed substantial portions of the research found here as the Artemis A. W. and Martha Joukowsky Postdoctoral Fellow in Gender Studies at Brown University's Pembroke Center. Taking part in the 2017–2018 Pembroke Seminar on "The Cultures of Pacifism" convened by Leela Gandhi remains the highlight of my intellectual experiences, and I am thankful for her guidance and that of other mentors at Brown: Bonnie Honig, Ken Haynes, and Elias Muhanna. I traced out the trajectory of the work found here while writing my dissertation at the University of California, Los Angeles, and any success I now enjoy I owe to the interventions of my committee members, Nasrin Rahimieh, Domenico Ingenito, and Michael Cooperson. Nouri Gana, my advisor, deserves all the credit for getting me to think comparatively across contexts, and I thank him for continuing to support me over the many years that have now passed since I was a student in Los Angeles.

Several colleagues from other institutions aided me along the way, primary among them Kamran Rastegar, whose comments on the draft of this monograph for Cambridge were the perfect combination of supportive and corrective. I cannot thank him enough, and I also found pointed and useful the input from the anonymous reviewer. Orit Bashkin took time out of her packed schedule when visiting the University of Colorado to offer advice on publishing the book; I greatly appreciate the valuable guidance she continued to give me as the process moved ahead. Stephen Sheehi has remained supportive throughout my career, and I am so glad he is now holding down the fort at the College of William and Mary, where I received my BA. Thanks also to Roger Allen, Joseph Lowry, Heather Sharkey, and Paul Cobb who all assisted me during my MA in Arabic and Islamic Studies at the University of Pennsylvania. Other friends and colleagues without whom I would not have been able to complete this book include Pelle Valentin Olsen, Qussay Al-Attabi, Kevin Jones, Huda Fakhreddine, Fatemeh Shams, Amir Moosavi, Justine Landau, Amr Taher Ahmed, William Granara, David Hirsch, Shir Alon, Nasia Anam, Rob Farley, Suleiman Hodali, Michelle Quay, Sina Rahmani, Sahba Shayani, Ken Shima, and Rawad Wehbe.

Most recently, I have benefitted immensely from discussions with colleagues studying the trajectories of the Persianate during the modern period, including Maryam Fatima, Alexander Jabbari, Samuel Hodgkin, Mehtap Özdemir, Aria Fani, C. Ceyhun Arslan, and Fatima Burney, who is probably the person most responsible for getting the book published with this series. I am indebted to Fatima for extending an invitation to give a lecture on the material found in here at the Multilingual Locals and Significant Geographies: For a New Approach to World Literature European Research Council-supported project convened by Francesca Orsini at the School of Oriental and African Studies, University of London, in the summer of 2019. I am furthermore grateful to Francesca and her co-editor Debjani Ganguly for supporting my initial book proposal and shepherding it through the process at Cambridge University Press. At Cambridge, I would also like to thank Ray Ryan, whose faith in the book helped immensely during the final stages, as well as Edgar Mendez and Joshua Penney, both of whom alleviated difficulties with the intricacies one faces when publishing a first monograph.

I would not have been able to access the Arabic and Persian texts necessary for completing this research without the help of the many language teachers I have been privileged to study with other the years. I fondly recall beginning my Arabic studies with Annie Higgins. In the fall of 2004, amidst a sea of future military intelligence, CIA, and international aid organization recruits, "Tahani" gave us neophytes a window into an Arab culture that was at once unexpected by the majority of my peers and necessary for our full appreciation of the disconnect between the post-9/11 United States' media representations of Arabic and Arabs and the realities of Arab hospitality, present and past. John Eisele and Olla Al-Shalchi also taught me Arabic at William and Mary, and I am honored to now be Olla's colleague at UT. My thanks also to my other Arabic instructors, Jamal Ali, Ismail Poonawala, Laila al-Sawi, Heba Salem, Nadia Harb, Dina El-Dik, Ahmad Abd Al-Hameed, and many more. I am happy to have also had the chance to study Persian for many years with several instructors, beginning with Pardis Minuchehr at Penn, then Latifeh Hagigi at UCLA, and Mehrak Kamali and his colleagues at the University of Wisconsin-Madison's Arabic, Persian, and Turkish Language Institute summer program.

I owe some special recognition to Elliott Colla and Max Weiss, who have shown me over the past few years that there is still some enjoyment to be found in academia. I appreciate their unjudgmental and constant friendship in an academy I find mostly strict, staid, and stressful.

A few parts of the book have previously appeared elsewhere. Early versions of sections from the Introduction, Chapter 2, and Chapter 5 first were published in "Re-Orienting Modernism: Mapping East-East Exchanges between Arabic and Persian Poetry," *Alif: Journal of Comparative Poetics*, no. 40 (2020): 115–138. Brief material included in Chapter 4 was also published in "An Iraqi Poet and the Peace Partisans: Transnational Pacifism and the Poetry of Badr Shākir al-Sayyāb," *College Literature* 47, no. 1 (2020): 65–88. Chapter 3 significantly updates and expands my book chapter "Until a Shirt Blossoms Red: Proto-Third Worldism in Aḥmad Shāmlū's *Manifesto*," *Persian Literatures as World Literature*, eds. Mostafa Abedinefard, Omid Azadibougar, and Amirhossein Vafa, in the Literatures as World Literature series, ed. Thomas Oliver Beebee (New York:

Bloomsbury Academic, 2021): 171–190, and Chapter 5 also incorporates short parts of the article "A Transnational Approach to ʿAbd al-Wahhāb al-Bayātī's ʿUmar al-Khayyām," *Transnational Literature* 11, no. 1 (2018): 1–14. My thanks to the Department of English and Comparative Literature at the American University in Cairo, Johns Hopkins University Press, Bloomsbury, and the Flinders Humanities Research Centre for allowing me to reuse this material.

I will never be able to express the appropriate amount of gratitude to my wife, Emily Drumsta, and son, Adam Gregorian Thompson, for the joy they have brought to my life throughout the tumultuous period of change, both geographically and professionally, during which I wrote this book. I am lucky to have a strong network of support at home that makes undertaking a task like this not only possible but even manageable, at least once you get started. I hope that one day Adam might find what I have done here inspiring and be motivated to undertake something just as daunting, or harder.

Note on Transliteration

I use the *International Journal of Middle East Studies* (*IJMES*) transliteration chart for Arabic and Persian, with the slight modification of rendering *tāʾ marbūṭah* as "*ah*" (like in "*marbūṭah*") instead of "*a*" when not in construct state and instead of "*ih*" at the end of words in Persian along with dropping "al-" from Arabic surnames following the first instance. Additionally, I use a superscript "*v*" to represent the silent Persian *vāv* (و) that sometimes follows "*khā*ʾ" (خ). Readers who do not know Arabic or Persian are welcome to ignore the diacritical marks, which generally signify either emphasis or aspiration and, in some cases, such as with "*s̱*" (ث) versus "*s*" (س) in Persian, distinguish two different letters with the same pronunciation from one another. I transcribe most of the poetry in the book and therefore depart at times from the *IJMES* system. For instance, when a Persian long *vāv* is clearly short due to the meter of a poem, I have transcribed it "*u*" instead of "*ū*." *Iqlāb*, a silent *nūn* followed by a *bāʾ* not addressed by the *IJMES* system, occurs once in my transcriptions. I have indicated it as "*ṃ*."

Introduction
Mapping a Modernist Geography in Arabic and Persian Poetry

Myth is already enlightenment, and enlightenment reverts to mythology.
—Max Horkheimer and Theodor Adorno, *Dialectic of Enlightenment*[1]

In 1922, just a few years after the shocks of the Great War, a new literary movement emerged from the ashes. The man who announced the birth of this new movement, which came to be called modernism and would eventually find its way into all corners of the globe, had studied foreign language in high school. He later expanded his investigations of his own language in the interests of his craft to include a thorough examination of the tradition that preceded him. Critics initially rejected his innovations because, despite their roots stretching back into canonical works of the premodern period, they challenged current literary standards as well as what topics were fit for proper literature. As his modernist style developed over the years, younger followers took up his innovative approaches to earlier literary forms along with the revolutionary integration of ancient mythic themes into his work to directly address the contemporary moment in his own society and the broader world. Thoroughly steeped in the tradition of the culture that produced him, he became the voice of a generation, and his work came to set the standard for the modernists that followed. He was called Nīmā Yūshīj.

In 1922, independent of the modernist rumblings that quickly turned into a roar in Europe during the interwar years, the Iranian poet ʿAlī Isfandiyārī (who took the pen name Nīmā Yūshīj; d. 1960) laid the groundwork for modernist poetry in Iran with his revolutionary long poem *Afsānah*, or *Myth*.[2] Like T. S. Eliot (d. 1965), whose *The Waste Land* first appeared in the same year, Nīmā found inspiration both in the mythic past and from the work of foundational figures of French modernism such as Charles Baudelaire (d. 1867) and Stéphane Mallarmé (d. 1898). Like Ezra Pound (d. 1972), whose edits shaped the final version of *The Waste Land*, Nīmā directed his call for poetic innovation to the coming generation of poets, declaiming "*Āy shāʿir-i javān!*" ("O Young Poet!") in the introduction to *Afsānah* before laying out his new conception of what poetry could be. Like James Joyce (d. 1941), whose monumental *Ulysses* was first published in its entirety in 1922, Nīmā pushed the boundaries of language due to his status as an outsider to the Iranian literary establishment in Tehran. And like Marcel Proust, who passed away in 1922 but not before the first volume in English translation of his *In Search of Lost Time* came out, Nīmā explored the central role of memory and experience in creating a literature appropriate to the modern age. However, unlike these Western modernists, Nīmā built his modernist project on a foundation anchored in a local tradition that Western modernism only drew on superficially. While Eliot's *The Waste Land* could not have existed without the death and rebirth myth of the ancient Mesopotamian deity Tammūz or the "Shantih shantih shantih" mantra of the *Upanishads*, the poem remains in many ways a specific response to a certain moment in British history after the War, a strange mix of local and global, universal and particular. In the same way, Nīmā's *shiʿr-i naw* ("New Poetry," as modernist poetry came to be called in Persian) developed out of the interplay of the global movement of modernism and more local, regional developments that lay outside the bounds of European influence.

Nīmā's modernism, like that of his well-known Western modernist counterparts, finds its foundation within the literary past of what many Westerners have referred to since the early twentieth century as "the Middle East."[3] The primary argument of this book proceeds from this fact and can be summed up in a reformulation of Horkheimer and Adorno's provocative assertion about myth and enlightenment's dialectical relationship in which one is never without the other – and otherwise neither could exist. In light of the similarity between the connections across modernism in the "East" and the "West" and those that link myth and enlightenment, I propose that *the East is already modernist, and modernism reverts to the East*. By relocating our modernist center to an "Eastern" geography, I argue for a new way of looking at modernist poetic developments within the region and across the border between the Arabic- and Persian-speaking worlds. Considering modernism from this relativist perspective shows how Arabic and Persian poetries form a significant modernist geography within the broader movement of modernism.[4]

Reorienting Modernism in Arabic and Persian Poetry uses comparative analysis to study the work of Arab and Iranian modernists transnationally. Its chapters take up their poetries' lateral relationships with each other; that is, the links between Arabic and Persian poetry that lay outside or even challenged Western influence during the colonial, decolonial, and postcolonial periods. By focusing on lateral transactions between Arab and Iranian poetry during their modernist periods, from roughly 1922 to 1967 in Iran and 1947 to 1967 in the Arab world, I show that we cannot simply understand Persian and Arabic modernisms to be the results or reflections of Western interventions or influence, but rather as parts of a transnational dynamic of poetic exchange that deserves a place in wider discussions about the overall spread of literary modernism. I focus for the most part on poets from Iraq and Iran, the two countries where modernist poetry in Arabic and Persian, respectively, first took root.

My argument works at two levels. First, I demonstrate that Arab and Iranian modernist poetries are linked in terms of both poetic form and content, including their similar innovations on the prescribed forms of Arabic prosodic science and use of myth in both traditions. Second, building on the connections I locate at the first level, I illustrate how these two poetic traditions come together, both through their formal connections and their use of symbols, as a transnational response to the globalizing and homogenizing forces that followed in the wake of Western colonialism and that took new forms during the first decades of the Cold War. Reading Arab and Iranian modernisms as parts of a transnational phenomenon helps us better understand the development of both movements as well as challenge Eurocentric models of literary dynamism and change. By using this transnational approach, this book ultimately questions the efficacy of hermetic, single language studies of Arabic and Persian literatures and an earlier scholarly proclivity for tracing Western influences on their poetry.[5]

In what follows, I first address what I mean by the relativist perspective – not one of philosophical relativism – taken in this book by going back to the beginning of the twentieth century and Albert Einstein's special theory of relativity. I connect the genesis of this idea to the broader modern Zeitgeist in which Einstein lived, one aimed at producing synchronicity and simultaneity across place and time. Following my discussion of Einstein and relativity, I transition briefly into the work of several Arab and Iranian philosophers who looked to their situation in relation to the West as backward, underdeveloped, too late, or suffering from "Westoxification." Engaging with these ideas, I posit that a phenomenon I refer to as a "transnational unconscious" led to similar changes across Arabic and Persian poetries during the twentieth century, and I link this transnational unconscious with a Foucauldian "attitude of modernity" that Arab and Iranian modernist poets took on. At this point, I lay out the theories I will be working with to build my argument throughout the book. Here, I engage with recent literary critical work on transnationalism, planetary and/or global modernism, and polysystem theory as well as the comparative study of Arabic and Persian literatures. Finally, the introduction ends with a detailed chapter outline.

A Special Theory of Relativity

This book works from what I am calling a relativist perspective, a way of looking at Arabic and Persian modernist poetries not only as they relate to Europe but rather as they relate to each other. To do this, I approach these poetries in a way quite similar to how Albert Einstein (d. 1955) was looking at the world around him in 1905 when he published his special theory of relativity. Thinking with Einstein helps us do several things, because the revolution in scientific thought that he inaugurated marks one of several possible beginnings to the modern age. Other shifts in thought we might consider as modern beginnings in the West could be Charles Darwin's theory of evolution, Karl Marx's illumination of the realities of capital accumulation and growth, Friedrich Nietzsche's philosophical declaration of the death of God, or Sigmund Freud's journey into the human psyche, all of which contributed to and reflected the modern moment Einstein lived in.

From this perspective, the concept of being modern is tethered to a certain moment in time. Recently, scholars have challenged us to unshackle the idea of being modern from these time constraints. Huda J. Fakhreddine proposes as much in her 2015 book *Metapoesis in the Arabic Tradition*, where she suggests that we work to uncouple the word "modern" from history when applying it to Arabic literature.[6] Susan Stanford Friedman advocates for the same approach in her 2015 book, *Planetary Modernisms*, where she issues the challenge to "rethink *modernity* and *modernism* outside the long twentieth century, outside the post-1500 temporal frame commonly understood as the *period* of the *modern* in its stages from early to late."[7] And, as Robyn Creswell has recently asserted, Syro-Lebanese poet Adūnīs (*nom de plume* of ʿAlī Aḥmad Saʿīd Isbir; b. 1930) likewise locates a "deep and authentic" Arabic poetic modernism during the era of the Abbasid Caliphate (r. 750–1258) in his *Dīwān al-shiʿr al-ʿarabī* (*Anthology of Arabic Poetry*).[8] I agree with these scholars that we ought not limit the concept of being modern to a specific time in history. However, I think it is productive to think also in terms of the relationship among modernism (as an artistic movement with a particular history), modernity (as an event in time), and a notion of being modern that is disengaged from time.

In approaching modernity as an event, I am drawing on Tarek El-Ariss's treatment of "the Arab encounter with Europe" in his book *Trials of Arab Modernity*, with which he "challenge[s] the reading of modernity (*ḥadāthah*) as innovation (*iḥdāth*) in relation to tradition, and anchor[s] it instead in the notion of event (*ḥadath*) or events (*aḥdāth*), which also means incidents, trials, and episodes."[9] While modernity certainly plays host to seemingly endless innovations, we cannot limit innovation to some specific time in history. I therefore find it useful to also think with El-Ariss now as we return to Einstein and the particular events that led to the special theory of relativity.

In the summer of 2019, Peter Galison, Professor of the History of Science and Physics at Harvard, appeared on an episode of the popular radio show and podcast *Radiolab* to discuss the relationship between the world around Einstein and the genesis of his theory. The episode poses the question of whether or not Einstein's genius was innate, the product of his environment, or some combination of the two. Providing evidence for the second possibility in this list, Galison brings our attention to the changes going on in Europe during Einstein's life: the introduction of trams, electric motors, networks of clocks, the telegraph, trains. With the development of the train, Galison's interviewer Pat Walters explains that "for the first time in human history, *you could be in several different times at once*."[10] Elsewhere, Galison suggests that it is highly likely that these technological developments, and particularly the need for coordinating clock times across vast distances for the purposes of train scheduling, led Einstein to think about relativity across time and space. "Einstein," Galison tells us, "must also have had coordinated clocks in view while he was grappling with his 1905 paper, trying to understand the meaning of distant simultaneity. Indeed, across the street from his Bern patent office was the old train station, sporting a spectacular display of clocks [. . .]."[11] Time, Einstein noticed when thinking about how to synchronize two clocks in different places, is relative in relation to the place of the observer. This simple yet prodigious realization led to the article "On the Electrodynamics of Moving Bodies," which "became the best-known physics paper of the twentieth century, and [Einstein's] dismantling of absolute time is its crowning feature."[12] Overturning Isaac Newton's (d. 1727) concept of an absolute time – a time independent from space – Einstein's theory ushered in a new moment of modernity that would inaugurate the atomic age.

If we separate being modern as Adūnīs and Fakhreddine understand it from modernism and modernity, then we might still locate modernity and modernism within a certain time period, one in which theoretical innovations like Einstein's were quite literally changing our perceptions of reality and expanding the realm of possibility. Although I do not believe that being modern should be limited in time, my treatment of modernism and modernity in this book is connected to a particular moment in history when our experience of the real and the possible changed. People in the early twentieth century could not only "be in several different times at once," but space itself was also changing. "All distances in time and space," Martin Heidegger (d. 1976) observes in an essay written after the atomic bombs, "are shrinking. Man now reaches overnight, by plane, places which formerly took weeks and months of travel [. . .] . Distant sites of the most ancient cultures are shown on film as if they stood this very moment amidst today's street traffic."[13] I look to these shrinking distances, these ruptures in space-time, as constitutive features of a shared experience of modernity, one that moves across cultural and geographic contexts and brings disparate peoples, places, and things into new relations with each other faster than ever before.

Before moving on from Einstein's theory, it is worth mentioning that he rejected the links his contemporaries drew between the special theory of relativity and modern art. For instance, responding to a draft paper by Paul M. Laporte titled "Cubism and the Theory of Relativity," Einstein wrote, "Now, as to the comparison in your paper, the essence of the Theory of Relativity has been incorrectly understood in it, granted that this error is suggested by the attempts at popularization of the theory."[14] And the theory was indeed popular, especially once Einstein won the 1921 Nobel Prize in Physics, which he received in 1922. "While the celebrated physicist has been evolving his shocking theories of the course of natural phenomena," art critic Thomas J. Craven (d. 1969) wrote in *The Dial* in 1921, "the world of art has suffered an equivalent heterodoxy with respect to its expressive media. This revolt has sprung from the conviction that the old art is not necessarily infallible, and that equally significant achievements may be reached by new processes and by fresh sources of inspiration."[15] Further afield, Roman Jakobson (d. 1982) recalls the Russian Futurist poet Vladimir Mayakovsky's (d. 1930) interest in Einstein's theory as a precursor to immortality. "I'm absolutely convinced," Mayakovsky told Jakobson, "that one day there will be no more death. And the dead will be resurrected. I've got to find some scientist who'll give me a precise account of what's in Einstein's books. It's out of the question that I shouldn't understand it."[16] While I do not want to make direct connections between Einstein's work and subsequent changes in the creative arts, I do want us to consider the general milieu within which Einstein's special theory of relativity and modernist poetry developed, a world in the grip of rapid and unprecedented technological advancement.

By linking space and time together, Einstein's special theory of relativity changes not just the way we think about the world, but also how we might act in it. Einstein's modern moment spans two events: coming up with the special theory of relativity in 1905 and the United States dropping atomic bombs on Hiroshima and Nagasaki in 1945, events that only became possible with Einstein's new way of looking at things. It is within this same span of time that the modernist movements in Arabic and Persian took root, emerging in parallel with Einstein's theory in answer to a changing world.

The early twentieth century push toward standardization, simultaneity, and synchronicity was not limited to European train stations but was part and parcel of Western imperial projects across the globe; it was the logical outcome of an enlightenment need to categorize and control. The subjects of this book dealt with these changes in their poetry in much the same way Einstein engaged them with his theory. This is not, therefore, a study focused on the conflicts of West versus East, imperialist versus colonial subject, or even tradition versus modernity. Instead, this book tells a story about the way the world might look if regarded from a different perspective and seeks out connections where enlightenment thought would have us make distinctions.

Imagine a modernist map as a Mercator projection with the Arab world and Iran in the center. The border between Iraq and Iran sits at the middle. With this new map, the amount of deformation increases as we move out from this central point, thereby mirroring a relativist perspective on the world. The outsize proportion of Greenland or northern Europe or Canada in comparison to the center of our map might represent for us the huge amount of attention given to the Global North in modernist studies, but by focusing on the area where the Arabic and Persian speaking regions meet, I will attempt to change this balance. This relativist perspective is thus quite similar to what Jessica Berman has termed "the transnational optic," which "seeks to unsettle our assumptions about the European nexus of modernism and its national spheres of literary activity while highlighting the nonnormative dimension of the text as it operates both locally and globally."[17] From this reorientation of perspective in space, I turn our attention to the 1953 royalist coup d'état against democratically elected Prime Minister Muḥammad Muṣaddiq (Mohammad Mosaddegh; d. 1967) in Iran in the middle of this book's timeline. These are *Reorienting Modernism*'s focal points in space-time, the center of the relativist perspective from which it looks out on the world.

I want us to sideline the West in order to investigate the profound connections linking Arabic and Persian modernist poetries. I likewise encourage us to address modernism from this relativist perspective so we can highlight continuities rather than ruptures within Arabic and Persian poetry across the premodern and modern periods. On the one hand, instead of depending on the juxtaposition of "modernity as innovation in relation to tradition,"[18] we should think about how Arab and Persian modernists retained elements of tradition in their poetry while still speaking to their contemporary moment. Shengqing Wu, for example, complicates the tradition-modernity paradigm in the Chinese context in a similar way. Her conception of "modern archaics" "emphasize[s] the conflicted and contested nature of the formulation of modern culture while highlighting each aspect's mutually transformative power. To think in terms of modern archaics is to think dialectically without privileging the critical category of modernity or replicating the traditional/modern antithesis."[19] On the other hand – here drawing again on Einstein's theory as a revolution in the human perspective on the world – if we look to modernity as an event, like El-Ariss does, we can contribute to "unsettl[ing] European modernity's imagined homogeneity."[20] Modernity, this book likewise confirms, is not Europe's alone.

By this I mean two things. First, *Reorienting Modernism* locates connections across the globe, across cultures, languages, and continents, within the experience of modernity by considering modernity as an "attitude" one takes to the things happening in the world around oneself. This "attitude" plays a significant role in the creation of what I refer to as a "transnational unconscious" in the twentieth century. By using a single standard for how an individual might envisage the self as modern, we can do away with the concept of a modernist center and periphery because the reaction to a perceived experience of being modern becomes our object of investigation instead of modernity itself. We can then turn our attention to the "shrinking distances in space and time" that modernity brings about as it is tied up with the processes of synchronicity, simultaneity, and standardization. Second, this book also argues that the East has always already been a part of European modernity, whether as a geographic location and collection of people against which Westerners defined themselves as modern or due to the inextricable links between cultures that the processes of globalization produce.

Consider, for instance, the words of J. Robert Oppenheimer after he witnessed the first explosion of an atomic bomb: "Now I am become death, the destroyer of worlds," from the *Bhagavad Gita*.[21] In thinking about the East as an essential actor in the elaboration of modernity, I am also engaging with Wendy Laura Belcher's concept of "discursive possession." This "new model of transcultural intertextuality . . . enables us to recognize how Europe's others were not merely an ingredient of European representations, not merely the exploited subjects of the European gaze, but also *producers of discourse* that has co-constituted European representations."[22] As creators of their own visions of the modern world, the poets we will read in this book participated in the same discourse of modernity that Einstein did at roughly the same moment in history.

The Transnational Unconscious and the Attitude of Modernity

In the face of such military might as a nuclear bomb, it is easy to understand the feelings of backwardness that plagued many thinkers from the part of the map we are putting at the center of our study. While Oppenheimer's thoughts may have drifted eastward as he contemplated the first atomic mushroom cloud, the technology used to produce this bomb was developed in the West, the beneficiary of hundreds of years of colonization and exploitation. As colonial projects came to an end and modern nation states emerged in their place, the dominant position of the West vis-à-vis formerly colonized nations weighed heavy on the minds of intellectuals like Ṭāhā Ḥusayn (d. 1973), Constantine Zurayk (Qusṭanṭīn Zurayq; d. 2000), Sadik al-Azm (Ṣādiq al-ʿAẓm; d. 2016), and others in the Arab world along with writers and thinkers in Iran, such as Aḥmad Fardīd (d. 1994) and Jalāl Āl-i Aḥmad (d. 1969). In the Arab world, Ḥusayn called for the Europeanization of Egypt in his *Mustaqbal al-thaqāfah fī Miṣr* (*The Future of Culture in Egypt*);[23] Zurayk sought to understand the reasons for the 1948 loss of Palestine in *Maʿnā al-nakbah* (*The Meaning of the Disaster*);[24] and al-Azm launched a scathing critique of the Arab failure against Israel in the Six-Day War in *al-Naqd al-dhātī baʿda al-hazīmah* (*Self-Criticism After the Defeat*).[25] To the east, "[m]odern Iranians, according to Fardid, were living under the symbolic contamination of foreign influence, which remained as yet on the *collective unconscious* level. He promoted a kind of rebuttal to this foreign influence, which involved the purging of 'inauthentic' elements."[26] And it was Fardid who coined the term "Westoxification" that Āl-i Aḥmad popularized with his book *Gharbzadagī* (*Westoxification*).[27]

These thinkers and their self-reflective and self-criticizing work were responding to what I call a "transnational unconscious." There has been relatively little scholarly attention paid to this phenomenon, but we find a useful reflection in the foreword to a 2009 edited volume titled

The Transnational Unconscious: Essays in the History of Psychoanalysis and Transnationalism. "There may be such a thing as a national consciousness," Akira Iriye and Rana Mitter tell us, "but not national *un*consciousness. Since psychoanalysis deals with the unconscious, it must by definition be considered a transnational scholarly discipline."[28] Writing from the decaying heart of US empire, I am motivated to seek out such modes of thinking and being that exist outside national identifications. The concept of a transnational unconscious offers one way of working beyond or outside, even against, the nation.

Furthermore, we can easily admit that the experience of modernity – the shrinking of distance and time brought about by technological advances, the possibility of total annihilation due to human actions, not Divine ones, and so on – engenders a shared way of thinking about existence in individual psyches that spreads across and through invented national borders. In the case of the Arabic-speaking world and Iran, the focus of this book, a shared transnational unconscious developed across geographic and linguistic borders due to parallel experiences of modernity in the decolonial and postcolonial context. I do not think we ought to limit this transnational unconscious to the region of the world I study here, for elements of it might well have extended yet further, perhaps even to the West. Instead, the transnational unconscious brings the subjects of this study together beyond the formal and thematic interrelationships of their poetry.

This transnational unconscious led to the creation of Arabic and Persian modernist poetries and developed alongside a particular "attitude of modernity." Michel Foucault suggests that modernity be considered "rather as an attitude than as a period in history." This observation marks El-Ariss's starting point in his investigation of modernity from the perspective of affect theory in his book, *The Trials of Arab Modernity*. El-Ariss clarifies in his quotation of Foucault that "attitude" means a "bodily posture."[29] I agree, but I think we ought to think of this "attitude of modernity" to be a mental posture as well. That is, to use Foucault's words, an "ethos" of action and a "task" that Arab and Iranian poets worked to complete as modern nation states and notions of citizenship came to replace colonial ways of being.[30] At the same time, and precisely because of the continued ramifications of their colonial pasts, these poets grappled with a politically committed transnational *consciousness* driven by decolonization and the growth of Third World solidarity movements. These two transnationally shared modes sometimes existed in concert and sometimes at odds with one another, thus defining the parameters of modernist poetry (culturally and politically; formally and thematically) across these two literary contexts.

A Theoretical Map for Arabic and Persian Modernist Poetry

I focus on Arabic and Persian modernist poetry not only because of the similar experiences of decolonization and modernization that shaped these modernists' experiences and poetry, but also because of the deep interconnections of poetic form and theme they share. These interconnections existed beyond the scope and beneath the radar of Western modernism, helping us overcome literary analytical approaches based on a paradigm of influence and focused on the role of Western poetry in non-Western poetic contexts.

We are instead here going to *reorient* modernism, to put the region frequently referred to as the Middle East at the center of the modernist movement and see the whole map differently. I place the poetry of Iranian modernists like Nīmā into a comparative conversation with modernist poetry in Arabic so we might start to understand the role that transnational dynamics of poetic exchange had in the wider development of a "planetary" modernist movement.[31] My focus here will be Arabic and Persian poetry because in these two traditions we find a deep reserve of shared formal, thematic, and mythic foundations for modernist poetry. Poets in both traditions went back to these foundations while they took similar innovative approaches to the system of Arabic prosody that undergirds metrical analyses of both Arabic and Persian poetry.

Although we cannot deny the role Western modernism played in the movement's dissemination across the globe, I am not so much interested in tracing lines of influence from West to East, something that has already been done – and done well – by scholars like Muhsin al-Musawi, M. M. Badawi, and Salma Khadra Jayyusi in the Arabic tradition, and Ahmad Karimi-Hakkak and Kamran Talottof in the Persian, among many others. I am instead interested in investigating literary exchanges that went on beyond the bounds of Western influence, something that is hardly done in English scholarship on modern Arabic and Persian literatures except for one recent study by Kamran Rastegar in his 2007 *Literary Modernity between the Middle East and Europe*.[32]

Rastegar's book provides some waypoints for the comparative study of Arabic and Persian together, and his approach to modernity and the complicated relationship that exists among modernity, ideology, and politics is refreshing. "Speaking of modernity," he writes, "is not unlike speaking of the divine – the concept adheres through a faith in its object, but nonetheless is continually contested by divergent interpretations, different narratives."[33] He goes on to challenge what he sees as the "reified category" of modernity prevalent in academia, something that derives from what he considers to be "the overpoliticization of literature."[34] Rastegar's comments on this "overpoliticization" guide my own critical framework. I thus understand literature and politics as parts of a discursive system in dialectic flux. Rastegar likewise argues against using a simple dichotomy of traditionalism and modernism in literary criticism and points out that "postcolonial scholars have tended to emphasize questions of ideological and political orientation and influence, in evaluating modern literatures." Due to the prevalence of this approach, there has been "an overemphasis of the centrality of these issues to the aesthetic dimension of the innovation of literary practices in the modern period, as well as to the understanding of changes to the practice and value of reading."[35] Overall, Rastegar's comparative study of Arabic and Persian prose provides a practical model for my own project to read these two literatures transnationally, though I focus on a later period and on poetry rather than prose.

Additionally, *Reorienting Modernism* employs this transnational paradigm of understanding to bring the global and the local together. I use such an approach to highlight the deep connections between Arabic and Persian modernist poetry, looking at how they are linked at the levels of texts (the poetry itself) and contexts (nation states' parallel accretions of political power in Iran and the Arab world after the colonial period). Such a transnational approach to literature, Paul Jay explains, "has productively complicated the nationalist paradigm."[36] Moreover, by taking account of how "minor" literatures interact with each other, we can challenge the usual binary models of center-and-periphery that have defined previous analytical approaches to literary production. However, even when approaches using such models are critical of the center, as Françoise Lionnet and Shu-mei Shih clarify in *Minor Transnationalism*, "Critiquing the center, when it stands as an end in itself, seems only to enhance it; the center remains the focus and the main object of study."[37] Along the same lines, Jay "argue[s] that the center-periphery model for the study of globalization [. . .] needs to be complicated."[38] Continuing in this vein, Barbara Fuchs adds that "[t]ransnationalism offers great opportunities to transcend monolingual and formal categories of analysis, taking us beyond the national literature and replacing the inert vectors of 'transmission' or 'imitation' through which literary studies have managed these connections in the metropole."[39] Although I take account of the center-periphery relations with Europe that contributed to the genesis of Arabic and Persian modernist poetry, this book's focus on the lateral connections of these two poetries not only endorses the transnational approach but also puts it into practice by studying literatures less-commonly taught in the Western academy. *Reorienting Modernism*, then, represents the combination of theory and practice modernist studies needs to confront the field's usual Western framework. Friedman recognizes this problem when she writes:

> As a field in general, modernist studies is insufficiently planetary to fulfill the promise of what Douglas Mao and Rebecca L. Walkowitz have termed 'the transnational turn' in the field. Whether adhering to a canonical modernism, a Jamesonian "singular modernity," the modernity of a Wallersteinian "world-system," or a Deleuzian "minor" or "alternative" modernity, the field has insufficiently challenged the prevailing "Western" framework within which studies of modernity and modernism are conducted.[40]

Friedman proposes as an alternative a "planetary turn" in modernist studies currently developing from the "work of a community of scholars challenging canonical modernist studies, pushing the field in new directions by focusing on other modernisms in non-Western parts of the world."[41] Still, Arabic and Persian literatures are conspicuously absent from her list of recent work in this direction, and they have as of this writing yet to make serious inroads into Columbia University Press's Modernist Latitudes series, which is supposed to "pay particular attention to the texts and contexts of those latitudes (Africa, Latin America, Australia, Asia, Southern Europe, and even the rural United States) that have long been misrecognized as ancillary to the canonical modernisms of the global North."[42] *Reorienting Modernism* intervenes to fill this gap in the scholarship on global modernisms.

It does so by first locating a formal and thematic basis for doing comparative work across the Arabic and Persian poetic contexts. I begin with the fact that Arabic and Persian poetry shared the same prosodic rules for more than a thousand years. Likewise, the Arab and Iranian modernists dealt with this shared prosodic tradition in the same way, despite the linguistic divide separating them, Arabic being a Semitic language and Persian an Indo-European one, like English. In terms of content, the modernists I read reinvigorated local mythic traditions, drawing on a shared trove of pre-Islamic myth, where we find Tammūz and the Phoenix – the same symbols of death and rebirth that animated Western modernism. (For instance, Tammūz is the same god of death and rebirth whose story lies at the heart of T. S. Eliot's *The Waste Land*.) But other ghosts haunt the poetry of the modernists in this book: the martyred mystic al-Ḥusayn ibn Manṣūr al-Ḥallāj (d. 922), the purported author of the *Rubāʿiyyāt* quatrains ʿUmar Khayyām (d. 1131), the cataloger of famous Sufi saints Farīd al-Dīn ʿAṭṭār (d. 1220), and a host of other heroes and poets from the premodern era. Our comparative approach crosses not only the linguistic border between Arabic and Persian but also a chronological one between the modern and premodern eras.

Working comparatively across these borders from our relativist perspective helps us to treat Arabic and Persian modernist poetries on their own terms, and not as mere receptacles, recipients, or testing grounds for Western modernism. This is all the more so if we are willing to direct our attention away from the novel (which has so far been the main focus of studies on world literature) and factor in so-called traditional literary genres such as poetry. If modern Arabic is mentioned at all as a part of world literature, it is usually to address the novels of Nobel Laureate Najīb Maḥfūẓ (Naguib Mahfouz; d. 2006) or the frequent engagements with al-Ṭayyib Ṣāliḥ's (Tayeb Salih; d. 2009) 1966 novel *Season of Migration to the North* in Comparative Literature departments. The Persian case is yet more dismal if we limit our discussion to literature from the modern period. For the most part, Western scholars have only paid scant attention to modern Persian literature as world literature with the exception of Ṣādiq Hidāyat's 1937 novel *Blind Owl*, from which I might note Michael Beard's study of the book as a "western novel."[43]

But the novel form came relatively recently into both the Arabic and Persian literary spheres. Poetry, on the other hand, has long been the most prestigious type of literary production in both contexts. Therefore, I am also taking a side in the debate that was in the New Left Review in the early 2000s between Franco Moretti and Efraín Kristal about developing literary canons for "peripheries."[44] Challenging Moretti's mode of canon formation and its focus on the novel, Kristal goes to the Spanish American literary context, a so-called periphery, "where poetry *does* matter."[45] I contend that despite the marginal position of poetry in twentieth century literature after the rise of the novel, any significant change in Arabic or Persian literary history must pass a litmus test in their poetic traditions. Furthermore, I argue that the cross-linguistic, transnational connections of Arabic and Persian poetic production constitute a *significant modernist geography* within what we have been calling – for better or worse – the realm of world literature.

"One of the problems with current theories of world literature is that the term 'world' is insufficiently probed and theorized," Karima Laachir, Sara Marzagora, and Francesca Orsini begin the abstract of their well-timed article "Significant Geographies: In Lieu of World Literature."

Taking issue with current ways of thinking about world literature, including market-based ones[46] and the concept of a literary world-system,[47] they offer a new model for literary study that works "'from the ground up' and employs multilingualism and location/locatedness to *resist the urge to flatten* world literature and make it monologic." Instead, they suggest "the notion of 'significant geographies' as a way of ensuring sensitivity to the richness and plurality of spatial imaginings that animate texts, authors, and publics in the world."[48] In further defining what they mean by the phrase "significant geographies," they explain, "[W]e mean the *conceptual, imaginative*, and *real* geographies that texts, authors, and language communities inhabit, produce, and reach, which typically extend outwards without (ever?) having a truly global reach [. . .] . 'Significant geographies' underlines how 'the world' is not a given but is produced by different, embodied, and located actors."[49] Finally, significant geographies allow us to explore Arabic and Persian modernist poetries from the relativist perspective I introduced earlier. "[T]he term 'significant geographies,'" Laachir, Marzagora, and Orsini add, "introduces a certain relativism, but it is a relativism that issues not from the macro- or meta-categories chosen by the critic/scholar but from the texts and authors; it is a point-of-view relativism based on historically concrete actors. What geographies are significant to *them*?"[50]

For my purposes, I consider the "world" of the "world literature" we will engage with in this book to be a horizon of possibility, a geographical imaginary, and a dynamic space of exchange all at once. That is, I conceive of the possible future worlds birthed within the poetry my subjects wrote, worlds that in turn shape their part of the world as a significant modernist geography. Likewise, I will focus on the Arab and Iranian worlds, both of which are themselves modern inventions on the one hand and – to some extent – geographical realities on the other. Hence, the areas where Arabic and Persian modernisms developed make up a geographical imaginary we can bring to significance within modernism more broadly. Rather than attempting to seal off our investigations from the realities of globalization and the unequal political and economic relationships engendered by colonialism and imperialism, I readily admit to the imbalanced power dynamic of the West versus the rest. However, instead of merely recognizing the impact Western influence had on non-Western literatures, I suggest looking to lateral literary exchanges that took place beyond the bounds of the West's literary reach in order to better understand vibrant local modernist traditions on their own terms and as participants in and creators of a significant modernist geography. Such a "comparative perspective," Berman argues, "brings previously marginalized languages and literatures into view and shuttles among the variety of locations, temporalities, languages, and histories of modernism" to "dismantle the sway of a universal modernist canon, complete with the mythology of its inward turn or its disassociation from politics."[51] By also taking a page from Dipesh Chakrabarty's *Provincializing Europe* and resituating my critical lens to what are generally seen as the margins of modernism, I further trouble our current understanding of modernism as a movement that began in Europe and diffused across the world.[52] Instead, I show that reorienting our focus to minor traditions and looking to lateral connections in local modernist form and content calls into question Europe or the West more broadly as the single source of the modernist movement.

Nīmā's poetic innovations as well as those of his followers in Iran and their contemporaries from the Arab world invite consideration from this new relativist perspective within comparative literary studies. By working against a Eurocentric model of poetic change and analyzing close formal and thematic links between Arabic and Persian modernist poetry, I not only re-map the history of modernist poetic development between two Eastern traditions, but also invite a reorientation of modernist studies more broadly. *Reorienting Modernism*'s planetary approach to the growth of modernism is thus inspired both by Friedman's *Planetary Modernisms* and Aamir Mufti's *Forget English!* While we must of course account for the role Western modernism played in the changes Arab and Persian poets introduced to their respective projects, this book highlights foundational modernist innovations that occurred outside, or alongside, explicit Western influence. These innovations include the retention of several elements of premodern poetic form based in the Arabic prosodic tradition, such as the continued presence of the Arabic metrical foot in both Arabic and Persian modernist poetry during the early decades of their growth. I argue that these metrical connections, along with references to the same mythic and religious traditions in both Arabic and Persian modernist poetry, constitute a noteworthy instance of unity among literary traditions in the Global South and a way for us to map a significant modernist geography that spans the border between Iraq and Iran.

If in doing this work I am reifying the East as a category against the West, I do so with a purpose: to set the West aside, however briefly, so that we might investigate other significant geographies that have contributed to the development of modernism. I admit up front that bracketing the West off is an impossible endeavor, and readers will notice throughout the book that we will often find ourselves bringing the West back in for the sake of comparison. However, this is but a secondary interest of mine, and our focus will remain for the most part on East-East (you might call them South-South or minor or Third World or Global South) exchanges, connections in form and theme that manifest either outside or beside Western modernist influence on Arabic and Persian modernism.

Furthermore, this book seriously addresses the implications of Friedman's "planetary turn" for studying Arabic and Persian literatures. "[S]tudies of non-Western modernisms in the late nineteenth and early twentieth centuries," she tells us, "have provided in-depth examinations of how these modernisms wrestle with and maintain considerable independence from Euro/American modernisms."[53] Regrettably, many critical approaches to Arabic or Persian modernisms often situate these movements in relation to European poetic developments rather than in relation to local developments across languages. To work against this trend, I also draw on Mufti's recent work, where he explains that world literature as it is currently conceived emerges out of practices informed by European Orientalism.[54] I propose looking to East-East literary exchanges, such as those we find between Arabic and Persian, as one way we might forget English.

But how exactly are we supposed to forget about English, and what sort of planetary model could we use to analyze the exchanges that go on in East-East literary networks lying beyond the reach of Western modernist metropoles? It's not enough to simply notice the similar changes in Persian and Arabic modernism because we could easily just look to Europe, trace the contrails of influence moving from West to East, and be done with it. We could also chalk the resemblance of these Eastern modernisms up to parallel engagements with European modernism and style them merely the result of trends in top-down globalization. Alternatively, we have Lionnet and Shih's model of "transnationalism from above" versus "transnationalism from below." The first is driven by a globalizing economy increasingly subservient to capitalism: homogenizing, totalizing, and flattening. Transnationalism from below, on the other hand, is "the sum of the counterhegemonic operations of the nonelite who refuse assimilation to one given nation-state."[55] Lionnet and Shih's formulation of these two categories is indeed useful, but the systemic workings of the approach remain undertheorized, at least within the context of Cold War cultures and the time period we will be working with in this book.[56]

One way to bolster our theoretical framework of analysis for East-East literary exchanges is to understand literature(s) as part of a set of systems, a dynamic grouping Itamar Even-Zohar (b. 1939) calls a polysystem. "The idea that semiotic phenomena," Even Zohar explains,

> i.e. sign-governed human patterns of communication (such as culture, language, literature, society), could more adequately be understood and studied if regarded as systems rather than conglomerates of disparate elements has become one of the leading ideas of our time in most sciences of man. Thus, the positivistic collection of data [. . .] has been replaced by a functional approach based on the science of *relations*. Viewing them as systems made it possible to hypothesize how the various semiotic aggregates operate. The way was subsequently opened for the achievement of what has been regarded throughout the development of modern science as a supreme goal: the detection of the laws governing the diversity and complexity of phenomena rather than the registration and classification of these phenomena.[57]

The reorienting I am arguing for here aims at just such a goal: to delineate the hows and whys (i.e., the "laws") behind the interconnection of Arabic and Persian modernist poetry, both of which have mainly been "registered and classified" within the context of national literary productions defined either by or against European imperialism and colonization. By considering Arabic and Persian modernist poetry transnationally, I suggest a move beyond previous studies based on cataloging instances of European influence and local response. This reorientation draws on polysystem theory, which provides us the tools to account for multiple nodes of connection and disconnection among various literary systems. Even-Zohar points out how students of literature, when confronted with a reality in which two literary systems exist among one community, generally limit themselves to one out of convenience, though "how inadequate the results are cannot be overstated."[58] (The problem is particularly acute in modern studies of Arabic and Persian literatures, and in academic approaches to the Global South more generally, to say nothing of an unfortunate focus on Anglophone literature [whether original or in translation] in the field of postcolonial studies.)

I do not mean to say we ought to collapse Arab and Iranian poets into a single literary community juxtaposed against Europe. Instead, I suggest that we think of the planetary movement of modernist poetry as a systemic whole made up of smaller systems (English, French, Arabic, Persian, etc.) that continually transact with each other – while also, of course, accounting for the power dynamic of the colonial relationship. Even-Zohar explains that "with a polysystem one must not think in terms of *one* center and *one* periphery, since several such positions are hypothesized."[59] The polysystem allows us to create a model of literary study that challenges the notions of center and periphery created by colonial relationships and opens up the possibility of dynamic engagement between a group of unstable, changing systems that can, and often do, operate in concert beyond or even against colonial states in spite of the unequal power relations at work.

The transnational approach for reorienting modernism I use here focuses on the dynamism of the polysystem and develops out of modernist thought itself. Adūnīs, the most prominent of the Arab modernists, argues convincingly for us to consider modernism as a dynamic response to a static past, and the parallels between his thought and Even-Zohar's theory of the polysystem are striking. Adūnīs's monumental study of Arab culture, *al-Thābit wa-l-mutaḥawwil: baḥth fī al-ibdāʿ wa-l-ittibāʿ ʿinda al-ʿarab* (*The Static and the Dynamic: A Study of Innovation and Imitation among the Arabs*) explores the relationship between two distinct systems in Arabic literature, one static and linked to religious orthodoxy (the past) and the other dynamic and directed toward new possibilities (the future).[60] Although polemical, Adūnīs's conception of the relationship between the static and the dynamic within Arabic literary history parallels Even-Zohar's usage of the same categories in his theory of the polysystem, which also favors dynamic, diachronic approaches to how literary systems function and interact.

In engaging with the texts I read in this book as dynamic parts of a literary polysystem, I show how modernist poetry grounded in a shared reserve of myth and symbol brought the Arabic and Persian literary traditions together at a time when political vicissitudes worked to define the boundaries of imagined communities in distinct nation states.[61] Moreover, there are also implicit transnational links between the Arab and Iranian modernists, whom I approach as members of one of Lionnet and Shih's "minor-to-minor networks that circumvent the major altogether."[62] For these reasons, I earlier posited that a transnational unconscious and a particular "attitude of modernity" brought on by similar experiences of Western colonial intervention developed concurrently across the Arab world and Iran and also within Arabic and Persian modernist poetry. Because there were rarely any direct contacts between the leading figures in Arabic and Persian poetic modernisms, *Reorienting Modernism* addresses the formation of this transnational unconscious by looking first at the features shared within their poetry.

Chapter Outline

Chapter 1 offers preliminary information about poetry for readers unfamiliar with the Arabic and Persian contexts by showing how the constituent parts of poetic verse work in Arabic and Persian modernist poetry. While composing this chapter, I was inspired by a quote from Talal Asad: "The modern nation as an imagined community is always mediated through constructed images."[63] Reminding us of Benedict Anderson's "imagined communities," Asad adds that these imagined communities are "always mediated through constructed images," an idea I take as a starting point for my investigation of poetry as craft at the moment of the modern nation state's birth. While politicians, nationalists, and rulers (and, yes, often former colonizers too) imagined the forms new nation states would take, the modernist poets we are here interested in were working with poetic forms to put forth their own imaginaries, frequently in opposition to nationalist imaginary communities. This first chapter starts with a section on the Egyptian Marxist Louis Awad's (Luwīs ʿAwaḍ; d. 1990) radical modernist project, where I lay out the transnational roots of Arabic poetry from the premodern period to the twentieth century before explaining the intricacies of Arabic prosody. In the second section, I detail how I represent poetic meters throughout the rest of the book and discuss the history of prosodic science across Arabic and Persian. Next, I cover critical approaches to modernist poetry in the two contexts before moving into a long section on the history of literary commitment, its philosophical foundations, and the role it played in Arabic and Persian poetic criticism. I end by suggesting a way out of the debates that took shape around literary commitment and offer further details on my balancing of formalist and contextual analytical approaches to Arabic and Persian modernist poetry.

Chapter 2 turns to several of the early modernist poems Nīmā Yūshīj wrote in Persian in the 1920s and 1930s. The chapter's title, "Travel Forms: Arabic Prosody, Craft, and Nīmā Yūshīj's Persian New Poetry," gives an idea of the book's focal points at this early stage. Having just addressed the building blocks of Arabic and Persian poetry in Chapter 1, I begin applying formal analysis to Nīmā's poetry, tracing how he deals with premodern Arabic prosodic norms in his modernist Persian poetry. I also introduce an Arabic rhetorical device, *muʿāraḍah* contrafaction, into my reading of these early modernist poems. In consideration of Nīmā's incorporation of premodern formal and thematic elements into his New Poetry, I argue that he *sublates* the past into the present in his poems.[64] Throughout, I compare Nīmā's process of sublation with the Pahlavi dynasty's fabrication of a national myth by reformulating the Iranian past in their attempt to institute modernity in Iran. Part one of the book treats poetry as a craft, and poetic forms as real, physical things (whether as they come together in spoken sounds or ink on a page) in order to engage with the images that construct national imaginaries in a material way.

Part II of *Reorienting Modernism*, "Imagining New Worlds," might recall to us those famous lines from Lebanese poet Khalīl Ḥāwī's (d. 1982) 1957 poem "The Bridge," in which the persona imagines its own body as a bridge to a "new East" emerging "from the caves of the East, from the swamp of the East."[65] In the chapters of this part, I compare two poetic projects that were involved in some way with Communist solidarity movements in Iraq and Iran and imagined alternative Eastern futures following World War II. In Chapter 3, I look to how the Iranian Aḥmad Shāmlū (d. 2000) imagines the future of what would eventually come to be called the Third World in his second collection of poetry, *The Manifesto* (1951). Shāmlū's committed poetry reaches beyond the borders of Iran in a bid to build solidarity with, for instance, a Korean soldier fighting against the United Kingdom and United States in the Korean War (June 25, 1950–July 27, 1953).

However, Shāmlū's idealism was cut short in 1953 only weeks after the Korean War ended, when these same imperial powers staged their coup against Mohammad Mosaddegh on August 15–19. Therefore, Part II locates the axis around which this book's timeline rotates. The 1953 coup represents a momentous turning point not just for local politics but also for cultural production. Shāmlū tempered his political engagement following the coup, and the Iranian Left suffered a general malaise from which it never recovered. Likewise, for poets across the border in Iraq, the coup left a lasting impression.

Accordingly, Chapter 4 addresses the impact the coup had on the poetic project of perhaps the most well-known Iraqi modernist poet, Badr Shākir al-Sayyāb (d. 1964). His political positions underwent a monumental shift after his experiences witnessing the coup firsthand in Iran. Chapter 4, "Badr Shākir al-Sayyāb between Communism and World Literature," traces the effects this political shift had on Sayyāb's view of his own poetry and the worlds he imagined within it. Sayyāb was a card-carrying Communist prior to the coup, but afterwards he began to support a nationalist politics informed by Western Liberalism. The changes his poetry underwent thus offer a useful point of comparison with Shāmlū's committed project.

The third and final Part, "Aftermath: Modernist Ends in Arabic and Persian Poetry," picks up with where modernist poetry went in the uncertain years following the coup. Chapter 5, "Honoring Commitments: ʿAbd al-Wahhāb al-Bayātī's Existential Trials," examines the courses modernist Arabic poetry took in Iraq following Sayyāb's premature death in 1964. Bayātī (d. 1999) was a well-known poetic rival of Sayyāb who remained affiliated with the Communist Party even after the difficulties Communists had to grapple with during the late 1950s following the coup and the nearly simultaneous revelations about the realities of Joseph Stalin's authoritarian rule following his earlier death in March 1953. I take up the existential crisis Bayātī faced as the hopeful possibilities decolonizing nations had imagined in the 1950s became more and more limited in the face of rising totalitarianism. Despite the changing political situation in the region, modernists continued to use the same techniques in the 1960s that their predecessors had employed. Consequently, I examine Bayātī's use of *taḍmīn* poetic quoting in his poetry as yet another method of sublating the premodern poetic tradition into modernist poetry, seeking out continuities in the Arab and Iranian modernists' approaches to form over time.

Likewise, in Chapter 6, "Winter in the Modernist Garden: Furūgh Farrukhzād's Posthumous Poetry and the Death of Modernism," I analyze Farrukhzād's (d. 1967) innovative approach to Nīmā's earlier prosodic experiments. I also spend more time linking Farrukhzād's late modernist poetic project with Western modernist poetry. I do this purposefully in an attempt to provincialize European poetic modernism and consider instead the significant links in poetic form and theme that may indeed have been more important for the development of modernism in the Arab and Iranian contexts. However, Western poetic influence plays a significant role in the ways Arab and Iranian modernists approached poetry. I address Farrukhzād's poetry not just in terms of local poetic connections but also of those she forged with Western modernist poetry. In so doing, I look at how Farrukhzād's poetic persona might be understood as a *flâneuse*, the female Iranian counterpart to Charles Baudelaire's Parisian poetic persona. I furthermore undertake a lengthy analysis of the close associations between Farrukhzād's late poetry and T. S. Eliot's *The Waste Land*, thereby bringing our transnational study of Arabic and Persian modernist poetry back into conversation with Western modernism. Finally, I suggest that we mark one possible end of poetic modernism in Iran with Farrukhzād's 1967 death, which unfortunately pairs well with Israel's 1967 defeat of the Arabs in the Six-Day War, a traumatic event resulting in changes significant enough to literary production to finish this study in the Arab world. In the short Conclusion that follows, I go back over the key points of my argument and look briefly at some other modernist ends in Arabic and Persian poetry. I also review the formal and thematic analyses from throughout the book and the undeniable links between Arabic and Persian modernisms as the foundation of a significant geography within the broader movement of modernism during the mid-twentieth century.

In making transnational links between Arab and Iranian modernist poetry, I draw on a wide variety of thought, both from the literary traditions in question and from the West. It would be short-sighted to simply deny the influence of Western philosophy and poetry in the growth of Arab and Iranian modernism, just as I would merely be extending orientalist biases were I to ignore local intellectual approaches to these movements. And rather than bracketing Western influence – a fruitless endeavor as Western modernism played an undeniable role in the development of Arabic and Persian modernist poetries – I explore where these poetries sit relative to their pasts, to the West, and to modernism as a planetary phenomenon.

A Reoriented Modernist Cartography

Nīmā and his Iranian followers' modernist poetry, along with that of their neighbors in the Arabic modernist movement, lay at the heart of planetary modernism due to their geographical beginnings in the Fertile Crescent, the wellspring of the mythic imaginary that even defined Western modernist poetry. Arab and Iranian poets have much to tell us if we want to understand modernism as a whole and its various iterations across the planet. Although Arabic and Persian modernism emerged out of these poets' engagements with Western thought and poetry, they also carried out a project of speaking laterally across their poetic traditions – often far removed from Western poetic influence, especially with regard to the tradition of Arabic prosodic science shared between them. In their poetry they negotiated, on the one hand, Western colonialism and an increasing familiarity with Western poetry and, on the other hand, the continued influence of Arabic prosodic science and premodern poetic themes.

With its analytical focus on the transnational links between modernist Arabic and Persian poetry, this book brings together recent critical trends that attempt to reevaluate the relationship of these poetries with the contexts of their composition. By investigating the emergence of modernism in both traditions and dealing with their parallel development of content and form, I analyze how Arabic and Persian modernisms transacted with each other across national borders to create a significant regional space within the broader modernist movement. I account for lateral transactions between these two modernist traditions to argue that if we employ a transnational paradigm of understanding, we can call into question the West's location at the origin of the modernist movement and establish Arabic and Persian poetries as the creators of a significant modernist geography.

PART I

Crafting a Modernist Geography across Arabic and Persian Poetry

CHAPTER 1

Formal Connections, Literary Criticism, and Political Commitment

حطّموا عمود الشعر

- لويس عوض، بلوتولاند

Break poetry's back!

—Louis Awad, *Plutoland*[1]

"*Ḥaṭṭimū ʿamūd al-shiʿr*" – thus began Louis Awad, the Egyptian writer and Marxist, in the introduction to his 1947 collection of experimental poems, *Plutoland*. "Break poetry's back!" he commands his readers. With these three words he called out for revolutionary change in the world of Arabic letters. For more than a thousand years, *ʿamūd al-shiʿr*, poetry's back, had provided the formal base of Arabic poetry and those poetries it interacted with. The *ʿamūd al-shiʿr* aided poetry's oral transmission by combining a monorhyme and any one of sixteen standard poetic meters. Arabic is a language largely made up of three-letter word roots, and the root *ʿayn–mīm–dāl* in the word *ʿamūd* has to do with propping up or supporting something.[2] From this root, we get words like *ʿumdah* (support; prop), *ʿimād* (buttress; pole; pillar), and *ʿamūd* (pole; post; column). The phrase *ʿamūd faqrī* means vertebral column, and I borrow from this usage of the term in my translation of Awad's imperative. By ordering his readers to break out of the traditional metrical mold, Awad is calling for nothing less than an attack on poetry's shape upon the page and its structure in the mind, not to mention the formal features lying at the core of Arabic poetry.

Earlier critics of Arabic poetry conceived of the poem as a tent held up by a central pole, the *ʿamūd*.[3] But, as Fakhreddine explains, the phrase *ʿamūd al-shiʿr* (which she translates literally as "the tent pole of poetry" and figuratively as "the accepted conventions of poetry") only entered the critical tradition *after* the advent of the *muḥdath* (pl. *muḥdathūn*) movement, a group of premodern "modernist" poets who composed their poems during the first centuries of the Abbasid Caliphate (r. 750–1258).

In her approach to the *muḥdathūn* modernizers and in parallel to Friedman's argument in *Planetary Modernisms*, Fakhreddine argues that "the term 'modern' should be understood as *a literary term*, rather than an historical one."[4] She then goes on to explain how critics such as al-Āmidī (d. ca. 897), al-Qāḍī al-Jurjānī (d. 1001), and al-Marzūqī (d. 1030) developed a critical framework for *ʿamūd al-shiʿr* by contrasting the poetry of the *muḥdath* poets (modernists such as Abū Tammām [d. ca. 845/846], Bashshār ibn Burd [d. ca. 783/784], and Ibn al-Rūmī [d. ca. 896/897 or 889]) with the poetry of the *qadīm* (ancient, pre-Islamic, or "old" poetry).[5] The premodern critics held in high regard poets who conformed to the rules of *ʿamūd al-shiʿr* that the critics themselves had standardized. For instance, al-Āmidī, who coins the phrase "*ʿamūd al-shiʿr*" in *al-Muwāzanah* (*The Balance*), tells us that the "more moderate" *muḥdath* modernist al-Buḥturī (d. 897) "follows the methods of the ancients and does not depart from the accepted conventions of poetry (*ʿamūd al-shiʿr*)."[6]

But when Awad issues his order to "break poetry's back" in 1947, the meanings of *ʿamūd al-shiʿr* and *muḥdath* that he has in mind have shifted. We find him lumping together Abū Tammām with al-Buḥturī as poets who both conform to the same *ʿamūd al-shiʿr* he intends for his audience to break. "Our generation reads [Paul] Valéry [d. 1945] and T. S. Eliot [d. 1965]," he declares, "and we do not read al-Buḥturī or Abū Tammām."[7] In Awad's understanding, *ʿamūd al-shiʿr* represents the entire Arabic poetic tradition, from the earliest pre-Islamic odes to the occasional poetry of the Egyptian poet laureate Aḥmad Shawqī (d. 1932), and he considers the original *muḥdathūn* to be as traditionalist as the rest.

For Awad, the tradition of Arabic poetry ends with Shawqī. As we venture into the first lines of his introduction, we find him announcing the death of "Arabic" poetry – the quotation marks are Awad's. "'Arabic' poetry has died (*la-qad māta al-shiʿr 'al-ʿarabī'*). It died in 1932. It died when Aḥmad Shawqī died. It died an everlasting death. It's dead."[8] If Arabic poetry is dead, what is left to break? And why does Awad put Arabic in scare quotes? Who killed Arabic poetry?

By the time Awad was writing, the foundations of Arabic poetry had been tried, tested, shaken, and even broken as Arabic literary culture developed over the ages and spread across a vast swath of West Asia, North Africa, and Andalusia – to say nothing of the worldwide movement of Islam, which carried with it the Arabic language in the Qur'ān. Awad's declaration of Arabic poetry's "death" is both highly ironic and hyperbolic, as he envisions a future full of possibilities for poets still writing in Arabic but striking out into new poetic realms. In fact, later in his introduction, he reneges, poetry has not died, but Arabic poetry has. The truth of the matter is that Arabic poetry's back (*ʿamūd al-shiʿr al-ʿarabī*) was not broken during our generation. Rather, it was broken in the tenth century: the Andalusians broke it. The truth of the matter is that Arabic poetry did not die during our generation. Rather, it died in the seventh century: the Egyptians killed it.[9]

As it turns out Arabic poetry did not die with Shawqī in 1932. According to Awad, Arabic poetry was dead on arrival in Egypt because the poetry Arabic speakers in Egypt composed was different than that of the ancient Arabs, different than that of the poets in Arabia, Iraq, or Syria. As Arabic literature spread across West Asia and throughout the southern Mediterranean, it began a process of transaction with other cultural contexts and their literatures, which resulted in an ongoing dynamic relationship between the Arabs and the cultures they came into contact with. Arabic poetry may have remained Arabic because it was composed in the Arabic language, but it was no longer purely Arab. "We can certainly say that Arabic poetry in Egypt did not die, for it was never even born there," Awad elaborates, and hence the scare quotes he puts around "Arabic."[10] Moving on to Andalusia, where the Arabs arrived in the eighth century, new poetic forms like the *muwashshaḥāt* with their mixed-rhyme stanzas and the *zajal*, which incorporated colloquial language, appeared as Arabic literary forms mixed with local Christian and Jewish cultural production.[11] Looking to these changes, Awad shows his readers that *ʿamūd al-shiʿr* had already been broken centuries ago as Arabic literature traveled with the Islamic conquests (*futūḥāt*), came into contact with other traditions, and developed through its interactions with them.[12]

With *Plutoland*, titled after the (former) planet that Clyde Tombaugh (d. 1997) had only recently discovered in 1930, Awad wanted to force Arabic poetry into the outer limits of its possibilities by adopting European styles wholesale, giving up the older Arabic meters, revolutionizing rhyme schemes, exploring the possibilities of prose poetry, and elevating colloquial Arabic poetry to the same level of literature written in "standard" Arabic, *fuṣḥā*. This last suggestion did not sit well with contemporary Arabic critical tastes, and so Awad's call to "break poetry's back" and the experimental poetry that followed in *Plutoland* found no receptive audience at the time. Even today, traditional poetry based on *ʿamūd al-shiʿr* remains popular across the Arab world.

Still, despite the continued resilience of traditional forms, Arabic modernist poetry eventually found its place, and Awad's introduction reveals the difficulties the new modernists faced. He situates the new generation of poets who came after Shawqī, which includes himself, against those who came before. "The battle, then," he tells us, "is a biological one. A battle between the young and the old (*maʿrakah bayna al-shabāb wa-l-shuyūkh*)."[13] More than this, however, the young generation's willingness to engage with European poetry opened up new poetic vistas before it, just as the Andalusian poets invented new poetic forms out of the cultural mixing they experienced in premodern Europe. "The Europeans," Awad writes admiringly, "have understood how to reject the ancients (*al-qudāmā*), and they have renewed life (*jaddadū al-ḥayāt*) with innovative melodies."[14] He further argues that the new generation of Arabic poets must do the same thing with their tradition by giving up the premodern monorhyme, going beyond the standard sixteen Arabic poetic meters, and focusing on the unity of the entire poem rather than single lines.[15] By turning to earlier instances of cultural contact that went on between the Arabs and others, first in Egypt and later in Andalusia, Awad highlights the foundational role intercultural transactions had for the development of Arabic literature and makes the case for his generation's contemporary engagement with European literature. Although *Plutoland* may not have successfully instigated the poetic revolution Awad wanted, his introduction locates the primary impetus for Arabic poetry's development at the margins of the Arab world in its interactions with other cultures, languages, peoples, and places: first in Egypt, then Andalusia, and finally the Europe of Valéry and Eliot.

But Arabic modernism was not simply a product of European modernism. In the very same year that Awad published *Plutoland* in Egypt, a new generation of Iraqi poets had already begun exploring new poetic avenues with their compositions of what they came to call *al-shiʿr al-ḥurr* – literally "free verse" – though it still followed many premodern rules. (Let me be clear from the outset: Arabic free verse is anything but free, and although European poetic developments may have played a part in its growth, it remains absolutely grounded on premodern Arabic prosodic structures.) While *Plutoland* was largely ignored in Egypt as too radical, the Iraqi modernist pioneers Nāzik al-Malāʾikah and Badr Shākir al-Sayyāb found an audience that responded favorably to their free verse.[16] By 1950, the Arab modernist poets had gained a foothold in Iraq. The Iraqis provided a theoretical and formal basis for their poetry that remained rooted in the Arabic tradition. They changed the shape of the poem on the page by making the poetic foot (still based on the feet of premodern Arabic poetry) the basis of their poetic rhythms rather than the entire line. Because they did not call for their contemporaries to completely break away from *ʿamūd al-shiʿr*, their poems provided the first models for the new poetry that soon followed them in other Arab countries. This new poetry shared much in kind with developments happening across the border (both geographic and linguistic but – importantly – not prosodic) in Iran, where some poets also stopped depending on the entire premodern poetic line in favor of the poetic foot, repeated or not as necessary in each line.

The remainder of this chapter consists of three sections providing preliminary information about the modern Arabic and Persian poetic traditions necessary for understanding the rest of the book. Readers unfamiliar with the intricacies of Arabic prosody will benefit from the first of these, a short section that explains the history of Arabic prosody as a science as well as my method for representing the different meters that we will come across later in the book. Those not well versed in Arabic criticism about modernist poetry will find in the second section an introduction to some of the salient issues that emerged in the middle of the twentieth century. Finally, in the third and last section I cover debates about political commitment in modern Arabic and Persian literatures. These three sections will provide us with the analytical tools we need for reading the poetry in the chapters to follow. I end the chapter with a brief conclusion where I suggest a way out of the commitment debates and discuss my literary-critical frame.

The Rules of Prosody (*ʿArūḍ*)

To better understand what exactly the Arabic and Persian modernists do to distinguish their poetry from what came before, we now turn to the first scientific analysis of Arabic prosody, which al-Khalīl ibn Aḥmad al-Farāhīdī (d. between 777 and 791) undertook in the eighth century. In the introductory material to an edition of *Kitāb al-ʿarūḍ* (*The Book of Prosody*) by the grammarian ʿAlī Abū al-Ḥasan al-Rabaʿī (d. 1029), the German Arabist Stephen Wild tells the traditional myth of how al-Khalīl came up with a way to illustrate Arabic metrical patterns with symbols.[17] The story goes that al-Khalīl was walking through the market in the southern Iraqi city of al-Baṣrah (Basra) when the rhythms of the blacksmiths' hammers inspired him to derive a method describing the various metrical patterns that existed in Arabic poetry. The elements of this system are worth outlining now because I use them to represent metrical feet in some of the Arabic and Persian poetry that comes later when such formal analysis aids in our understanding of the poems. Al-Khalīl's system is based on varied combinations of moving (*mutaḥarrik*; that is, "followed by a vowel") and quiet (*sākin*; "not followed by a vowel") letters that combine into *taf'īlāt* (s. *taf'īlah*), metrical feet, which then come together in regular patterns to create the *bayt* (a line of poetry; pl. *abyāt*). These sub-units combine into *awzān* (s. *wazn*), or meters. The technical term for this science of Arabic prosody is *al-'arūḍ*, a word that refers to the perfect versions of the *awzān*, which are also called *buḥūr* (s. *baḥr*), or seas, in their ideal forms.[18] Wild specifically mentions two items in his discussion of al-Khalīl's system: his use of the Arabic letters *fā'* - *'ayn* - *lām* – the three root letters from the verb *fa'ala* ("do"; the noun form is *fi'l*, or "verb") – to represent the feet that make up poetic meters and his creation of the two-part classification system of either moving or quiet letters. Below, I take recourse to al-Khalīl's patterns for metrical feet to display how the Arab and Iranian modernists went about changing the regular number of feet per line that had formally defined premodern Arabic and Persian poetry.

As a brief introduction to how al-Khalīl's metrical representations look, the *ṭawīl* (long) meter, in its ideal form (*baḥr*), looks like this, with " //" representing the caesura between the two hemistichs in a line:

fa'ūlun mafā'īlun fa'ūlun mafā'īlun // fa'ūlun mafā'īlun fa'ūlun mafā'īlun

These feet can also be represented by a system of long (¯) and short (˘) syllables like this, with " /" indicating the separation of feet and " //" the caesura:

˘ ¯ ¯ / ˘ ¯ ¯ ¯ / ˘ ¯ ¯ / ˘ ¯ ¯ ¯ // ˘ ¯ ¯ / ˘ ¯ ¯ ¯ / ˘ ¯ ¯ / ˘ ¯ ¯ ¯[19]

In the chapters to come, I use both systems when describing the metrical elements of poetry in the interests of clarity for readers unfamiliar with the Arabic system, along with plenty of explanation about why the meter matters in cases where it does.

The Persians also applied the Khalīlian system of analysis to their poetry after the Arabs invaded the Sasanian Empire (r. 224–651) during the Islamic conquests in the seventh century. In the aftermath, Middle Persian, the official language of the Sasanians, reemerged with a vocabulary inundated with Arabic words. This language is now called New Persian, or just Persian. Although New Persian kept many features of Middle Persian grammar, Middle Persian prosody disappeared. Mary Boyce writes that Middle Persian verse is "governed evidently by stress, without regard for quantity, and the number of unstressed syllables varies from line to line. And there is no rhyme."[20] Although New Persian poetry retains its qualitative origins in the actual sounds of its prosody, after the Islamic conquests it was analyzed according to the quantitative *ʿarūḍ* patterns of the Arabs, with necessary additions of new terms into the system describing the realities of Persian verse.[21] Despite these differences in prosodic origins, ever since the ninth century Arabic and Persian poetries have looked quite similar in terms of their shapes on the page. Two-hemistich lines arranged in columns with a monorhyme at the end of each line and a single meter that repeats throughout are standard in poetry in both languages. I therefore also use al-Khalīl's model for representing metrical feet in my discussions of Persian poetry, fully knowing that the qualitative reality of Persian metrics is not thoroughly captured by it.

Finally, although the story of how al-Khalīl came to create his system is probably apocryphal, his derivation of a way to describe phenomena that already existed but had yet to be explained remains an admirable scientific achievement. Mirroring al-Khalīl's technique of creating the science of *ʿarūḍ* from an existing body of poetry, I build my theoretical model for understanding Arab and Iranian modernist poetry as part of a shared, transnationally significant geography by starting with the constituent elements of modernist poetry in either tradition: changing the shape of the poem upon the page from columnar monorhymes to lines of varying length with different or irregular rhymes; using ancient myth to symbolically talk about the present; and dealing with Western colonial and imperial influence in verse form.

Despite the continued presence of premodern Arabic metrics in both Arabic and Persian modernist poetry, the twentieth century clearly witnessed a sea change in the wake of the innovations the modernist poets made in both contexts. These changes rang in a new era but also preserved the richness of the poets' respective poetic traditions. Working in and around the period of European colonial domination and influence, Arab and Iranian poets grappled with the weight of an age-old tradition anchored in the Arabic prosodic science that had moored the analysis of both Arabic and Persian poetry for centuries. While the chapters to follow do not plumb the depths of the metrical changes the modernists made – for a number of other scholars have already undertaken such studies[22] – the story about the invention of the science of Arabic prosody parallels my own analytical approach to the poetry in this book. Like al-Khalīl, we begin with form, which grounds our comparative discussion of modernist poetry in Arabic and Persian and links the movements across linguistic and cultural borders. Now, we will explore how Arab and Iranian critics themselves approach modernism as a movement.

The Local Critical Traditions

آخر ما أود أن أقوله في هذه المقدمة، إنني أؤمن بمستقبل الشعر العربي إيماناً حاراً عميقاً. أؤمن أنه مندفع بكل ما في صدور شعرائه من قوى ومواهب وإمكانيات، ليتبوأ مكاناً رفيعاً في أدب العالم.

وألف تحية بشعراء الغد.

- نازك الملائكة، *شظايا ورماد*

> The final thing I would like to say in this introduction is that I truly, deeply believe in the future of Arabic poetry. I believe that it is bursting with all the strengths, talents, and possibilities found within its poets' hearts and will occupy pride of place within world literature.
>
> A thousand greetings to tomorrow's poets.
>
> —Nāzik al-Malā'ikah, *Shaẓāyā wa-ramād*[23]

We begin this section with Nāzik al-Malā'ikah's closing paragraph in the introduction to her second *dīwān* (collection of poetry), which she titled *Shaẓāyā wa-ramād* (*Shrapnel and Ashes*) and published in 1949. She wrote these lines at the beginning of the modernist movement in Iraq, and like Awad before her in Egypt, she sets up a dichotomy between the poets of her generation (along with those of tomorrow) and the poets who came before them. Also like Awad, she considers the traditional *ʿamūd al-shiʿr* too constraining for poetic creativity. Further, she imagines Arabic poetry eventually occupying "pride of place" in the canon of world literature (*adab al-ʿālam*), but only if Arab poets are willing to interact with other cultural and linguistic contexts in order to revivify their language and to develop premodern Arabic forms to better express themselves.[24] If the poets answer her call, she believes that eventually "nothing of the old styles will remain, for meters, rhymes, styles, and schools will all be shaken to their core."[25]

The critic Muhsin al-Musawi translates the name of Malā'ikah's collection as "shreds and ashes," a title which "encapsulates the paradigms of the phoenix oriented ideology, for from ashes there is rebirth; from shreds and fragmentation there will emerge wholeness and life." Further discussing Malā'ikah's collection, he adds, "The redemptive suffering factor coalesces with Babylonian mythology, and inhabits a contemporary ideology of renaissance, affluence, and freedom."[26] *Shrapnel and Ashes*' title, then, marks a moment of self-realization connecting the various factors that contributed to the genesis of Arabic modernist poetry. We are at once dealing with the aftermath of real bombs (the nuclear bombs the United States had recently dropped on Hiroshima and Nagasaki, along with the rest of the destruction from World War II), the "rebirth" from ashes of nations in the formerly colonized world, and the consequent development of a new geographic imaginary that looked to but also beyond and outside the West. This is at the broader, planetary level, and I will continue to deal with the emergence of literary networks across the proto-Third World, the Third World, the Non-Aligned Movement, and the Global South (whatever our preference may be) as we progress through the book. For now, however, we will remain within the local Arab and Iranian contexts to explore what modernism meant to the self-described modernists and their critics at a local level.

Notwithstanding the Arabic poetic modernists' ambition for change that Malā'ikah makes clear in *Shrapnel and Ashes*, the poets whose works I discuss remain faithful to many features of the premodern poetry that Awad challenges them to break away from. While their poems are no longer columnar (*ʿamūdī*) or arranged in two-hemistich lines that all rhyme at the end as the premodern Arabic *qaṣīdah*, or ode, does, the modernists writing in Arabic and Persian initially retain parts of the old poetic meters in their new poetic forms.

Malā'ikah – the other Iraqi modernists like Bayātī, Buland al-Ḥaydarī (d. 1996), Sayyāb, Shādhil Ṭāqah (d. 1974), and more – along with the Persian modernist poets across the border in Iran such as Nīmā, Shāmlū, Farrukhzād, and many others, paid particular attention to the central place of premodern Arabic prosodic forms in their modernist experiments. When we look at their early modernist poetry, we find the older poetic feet still at the center of their rhythms, a phenomenon I explore at length in the chapters to follow. Although their poems continued to depend on premodern Arabic poetic feet, Iranian and Arab modernist poets alike wrested the line of poetry away from the dominant two-hemistich monorhyme to create new poetic forms. These poets and their critics have debated how exactly these changes ought to take shape and how much of the old ought to remain in the new.

Until now, for the most part, literary critics in both traditions have considered these developments to be the result of a political impulse among poets seeking to express themselves more fully in their own verse, beyond the limitations of past poetic conventions.[27] Eric Davis sums up the gist of these arguments when he writes that the poetry of the Arabic free verse pioneers "offered a critique of tradition that went far beyond poetry," concluding that "the Free Verse Movement, as well as all new literary, cultural, and artistic movements [in Iraq], must be seen in *political as well as aesthetic terms*."[28] Also discussing the Arabic tradition, Salma

Khadra Jayyusi (Salmā al-Khaḍrāʾ al-Jayyūsī; b. 1926) offers a nuanced view of the connection between the birth of the free verse movement and the 1948 Palestinian *Nakbah*[29] in her seminal study of modern Arabic poetry, but her ultimate conclusion aligns with Davis's position. She writes:

> The formal beginning of the movement of free verse [she sets this in 1949] must therefore be seen as an artistic phenomenon which succeeded because it was both artistically mature and timely in that it suited the historic and psychological moment in the Arab world [. . .] . Because of the spiritual shock caused by the Palestine debacle of 1948, and the general mental, political and social energy it produced, the new poets were able to imbue their new form with finer poetic qualities and with more contemporaneous attitudes and visions.[30]

Jayyusi theorizes a direct link between the Arab military failure against Israel and the growing independence movements in the Arab world that followed, which in turn encouraged poets to "imbue their new form with finer poetic qualities and with more contemporaneous attitudes and visions."

As just one example of more current criticism in the same vein, Waed Athamneh claims in her 2017 book *Modern Arabic Poetry* that "while poetry has profoundly influenced modern Arab politics, it has also been transformed and reshaped by it. It is thus hard to attempt an understanding of [Arabic poetry] by dropping historical and cultural context in favor of close-reading strategies alone."[31] While I of course agree that we cannot depend on "close-reading strategies alone," I do think that it is worth at least attempting to understand Arabic and Persian modernist poetry as aesthetic projects at a deep level. I therefore pay attention to not only their relationships with premodern forms and themes but also to their transnational interactions in both form and content during the modern period. Athamneh goes on to posit that "an examination of modern Arab politics is essential to understanding the broad, multifaceted, and often complex ways in which modern Arabic poetry has evolved in form, content, and subject matter."[32] The relationship of politics and poetics certainly contributes to the development of modernist Arabic poetry, but what we have here is a case of necessity versus sufficiency. Politics and poetics are necessarily connected in the production of modern Arabic poetry, but this is not sufficient reason to explain why modernist poetry developed the way it did. The issue is limited to neither extratextual context nor the realm of pure aesthetics, but rather crosses both/and.

We find a similar reductive trend in the Iranian critical context, a trend which frequently forces a direct link between the internal aesthetics of modernist poetry and external political developments. The foremost critic of modern Persian poetry writing in English, Ahmad Karimi-Hakkak, explains how the methods Iranian critics used for approaching modernist poetry generated specifically political readings. As a result, "a whole new interpretive culture emerged wherein poetry was read primarily with the purpose of deciphering the poet's political views, its abstractions and ambiguities attributed to a perennial case of absence of freedoms, particularly those relating to free expression of ideas through poetry."[33]

In Iran as well political context defined contemporary critical models for understanding the modernist movement. A "new interpretive culture" used these models dogmatically in its analyses, which sought to unveil the hidden political meanings of poems by "deciphering the poet's political views." In both the Arab and the Iranian critical traditions we therefore find the political spliced with the literary in both directions: Modernist poetic forms change in tandem with political triumph and tragedy, while the critical tradition dealing with that same poetry seeks out the political motivations underlying the texts.

I take up this politicized critical reception of Arab and Iranian modernist poetry in order to better understand the transnational links between the two contexts. While the political impetus behind modernist poetry in each case has received ample critical attention, no studies have analyzed why poetic modernism developed so similarly in both traditions or the reasons behind their corresponding formal innovations and shared thematic content. Using a comparative approach and making connections between these traditions in both form and content, I link them together as the results of not just local and international political phenomena but also a shared transnational modernist imaginary, that constitutes a significant modernist geography. We will begin these formal and thematic investigations in Chapter 2. Before that, however, we will continue to consider how politics links up with poetry in the Arab and Iranian contexts by tracing the courses the concept of literary commitment took within them.

The Commitment Debates: *Iltizām*, *Taʿahhud*, and Poetry

> Ever since [Louis Awad] returned to Egypt at the age of twenty-five, he has been cut off from inspiration. If he wants to write some poetry, he finds he cannot because Karl Marx has finished him off (*ajhaza ʿalayhi Kārl Mārks*). From the myriad colors of death and life, he only sees one. Grass has turned

red before him, the skies red, sand, water, women's bodies, men's words, and even thought itself have turned the color of blood before him. Even sounds, scents, and tastes have turned to red around him, as though the whole universe has been consumed by a terrible fire. He is content to live amidst this fire, for anyone who has seen the chains ripping through the bodies of slaves can think of nothing but red freedom (*lam yufakkir illā fī al-ḥurriyyah al-ḥamrā'*).

—Louis Awad, *Plutoland*[34]

Louis Awad, who we met at the beginning of this chapter, saw himself as something of a prophet heralding a new age of Arabic poetry after Shawqī, a modern poetry for a modern time. Thinking back to this book's Introduction, we find in *Plutoland* another example of Foucault's "attitude of modernity" at work.[35] By the time Awad returned to Egypt from his studies at Cambridge, he tells us that the whole world had "turned red" before his eyes. He and many other Arab and Iranian modernist poets frequently associated themselves with the Communist movements in their own countries. If they did not, these movements just as often claimed them as fellow travelers. Awad and the other modernists, including those who eschewed Communism and affiliated themselves with nationalist trends – though these were not mutually exclusive – thus participated in the debates over political commitment in literature that went on in the Arab world and Iran at the middle of the twentieth century. Awad brazenly takes up the Marxist cause in the above passage, concluding the introduction to *Plutoland* with his declaration that "anyone who has seen the chains ripping through the bodies of slaves can think of nothing but red freedom." He wrote these words in 1947, when Egypt was still governed by a monarchy within a British sphere of influence. It would be another five years before the disillusionment caused by the Palestinian *Nakbah* in 1948 and growing anti-monarchical and anti-imperial sentiment in Egypt led to the 1952 Free Officers Revolution, which overthrew the monarchy and instituted, finally, Egyptian self-rule. Other independence movements would soon follow across the Arab world, including Iraq, as we will see later in my treatment of Sayyāb's life and poetry in Chapter 4.

The year leading up to the *Nakbah* was pivotal in the history of Arabic literature, as during it the esteemed Dean of Arabic Literature Ṭāhā Ḥusayn introduced the French philosopher Jean-Paul Sartre's (d. 1980) literary *engagement* ("commitment") to the readers of his journal *al-Kātib al-Miṣrī* (*The Egyptian Writer*). Sartre's manifesto about the relationship of politics and literature and the necessity of the writer's commitment, which he titled *Qu'est-ce qu'écrire?* ("What Is Writing?" [1947]), set off a flurry of activity in literary circles across the planet as writers struggled to make sense of how literature and politics fit together.[36] The transnational movement of Sartre's theory into Arab literary circles, and later into Iranian ones, occurred alongside the growth of local Communist organizations.

Ḥusayn's engagement with Sartre is but one example of how Western thought can be transformed when introduced into other geographical contexts, and it is a crucial moment in the history of Arabic literature during the twentieth century. In what follows, I present the primary points of Sartre's argument and then trace how debates over commitment developed in the Arab world and Iran before addressing my own approach to the politics of literature.

We might consider all literature to be somehow committed, whether due to the author's explicit commitment of her writing to a political cause or, should we understand literature to be autonomous, its implicit deference to the status quo. I will deal with how we might understand committed literature in detail shortly, but for now Sartre's theory and its movement through Arab and Iranian intellectual circles opens up a number of issues central to the development of modern Arabic and Persian literature. Let us now account for how writers in these contexts understood commitment. To do so, we first need to examine the philosophical background of Sartre's theory of commitment.

"The 'committed' writer," Sartre tells us, "knows that words are action." The committed writer *uses* language; she turns her text into a tool of "disclosure" she then uses to change the world as it is.[37] In this same essay, Sartre makes what Raymond Williams calls an "artificial distinction between poetry and prose"[38] when he writes that the poet, who "refuse[s] to *utilize* language," "withdraw[s] from language-instrument in a single movement. Once and for all he has chosen the poetic attitude which considers words as things and not as signs."[39] Prose, then, functions as a *tool.* Writers, especially politically committed writers, *use* prose to some other purpose, not for the sake of the words themselves.

Prose is, to use the Heideggerean terminology upon which Sartre implicitly relied, ready-at-hand. Sartre's long engagement with Martin Heidegger's *Sein und Zeit* (*Being and Time*, 1927) was foundational for his thought. Sartre's theory of literary commitment, and particularly his distinction between poetry and prose, develops out of Heidegger's categories for understanding objects either in terms of their *Zuhandenheit* (handiness; readiness-to-hand) or *Vorhandenheit* (objective presence; presence-at-hand).[40] Fredric Jameson offers the following by way of defining Heidegger's terms in plain(er) English. For Heidegger, there are "two essential modes of the perception of objects: as *vorhanden*, simply there, inert and disconnected, and as *zuhanden*, or as action latent, tools and instruments lying ready to hand in case of need."[41] As Heidegger himself puts it, "That which is handy (*Das Zuhandene*) is not grasped theoretically at all [. . .] ."[42] To clarify the difference between the two categories: We do not think about the tool itself, only about how we are using it for some other end. Anything we use to some other purpose is not an end in itself and has no *Vorhandenheit* as long as it is working, that is, being used for its intended purpose. Things have *Vorhandenheit* when we contemplate them as singular objects, unrelated to the context within which they might be used. Something that initially had *Zuhandenheit* might break and suddenly lose its handiness, thus becoming unhandy and forcing us to engage with it in terms of its *Vorhandenheit*. "Unhandy things (*Dieses Unzuhandene*)," Heidegger explains, "are disturbing and make evident the *obstinacy* of what is initially to be taken care of before anything else."[43]

Poetry, which according to Sartre "considers words as things and not as signs," is an end in itself, and, consequently, *Unzuhanden*. Poetry requires contemplation. It does not immediately offer itself up for some purpose other than what it is. Poetry is, in Heidegger's terminology, *unhandy*, forcing us to confront it head on, unconnected from any context of use (at least at first). So poetry must initially be thought of as present-at-hand. I agree with Williams and critics like Ṭāhā Ḥusayn and Riżā Barāhinī (Reza Baraheni) that Sartre's separation of prose and poetry is contrived. However, considering poetry as present-at-hand and therefore as an object that requires contemplation is central to my project here and helps us understand what poetry is and does – though I would not exclude prose from working in the same manner.

Modernist poetry, the topic of our present study, is particularly unhandy. Take, for instance, the American literary critic Daniel Albright's description of T. S. Eliot's *The Waste Land* as a "jagged" poem: "you bleed when you handle the jagged edges of *The Waste Land*"; "[t]he edges of [Eliot's] stories are jagged, not carefully filed down."[44] The adjective "jagged" equally applies to the poetry we will engage with in the chapters to come. While I am intent on also showing certain features of continuity between premodern Arabic and Persian poetry and modernist poetry in both contexts, the changes the Arab and Iranian modernists introduced to the shape of the poem on the page are a direct visual representation of and parallel to the modernist "jagged edges" Albright sees in *The Waste Land*.

Furthermore, even if we might disagree with Sartre's distinction between poetry and prose and refuse the neat separation of the two into ready-at-hand and present-at-hand, the issue of politically engaged literature still persists, particularly in the colonial, decolonial, and postcolonial milieu. In fact, the responses of Arab and Iranian critics to Sartre's concept of literary commitment are a significant instance of their transnational interconnection. According to Sartre, committed writers must choose "to reveal the world and particularly to reveal man to other men so that the latter may assume full responsibility before the object which has just been laid bare." Committed writers must therefore make their readers aware of the injustices in the world in order to move them to action. "[T]he function of the writer," Sartre continues, "is to act in such a way that nobody can be ignorant of the world and that nobody may say he is innocent of what it's all about."[45] Sartre's call for social justice resonated with those who had experienced or were still experiencing the effects of European colonialism and the initial fallout of the Cold War, but many local critics opposed the strictures of literary commitment, of directing a work of literature to some purpose beyond itself.

Although Ṭāhā Ḥusayn stood firmly with the exponents of "art for art's sake,"[46] we can locate the introduction of Sartre's theory into the Arabic tradition when he coins the phrase *iltizām al-adīb* (the writer's commitment) in the editor's comments ("*Mulāḥaẓāt*") of the June, 1947 issue of *The Egyptian Writer*.[47] In his article, Ḥusayn translates some sections of Sartre's piece and gives his own position on what Sartre has to say.[48] Ḥusayn takes issue with Sartre's stance on the possibility of writing committed poetry, mentioning that poetry – which was first produced orally and therefore preceded written prose in ancient societies – certainly played a political role in the growth of human civilization. Ḥusayn argues that no matter how poetry relates to language, even if it does approach words as ends rather than means, it would be "absolutely foolish" (*askhaf al-sakhf*) to say that poets have not been committed to changing the world through their work.[49] Naturally, Ḥusayn was later proven correct, as we can count some of the most prominent advocates of literary commitment in the Arab world among the poets.

Iltizām (commitment) quickly came to the fore in Arabic literary discourse after Ḥusayn's introduction of the term.[50] By 1953, when the Lebanese writer Suhayl Idrīs founded the Beiruti literary monthly *al-Ādāb*, commitment had become so central to Arabic literature that he issued a rallying call for it in his first editorial, "*Risālat al-ādāb*" ("*al-Ādāb*'s Mission"). "[T]he kind of literature which this Review calls for and encourages," he proclaims, "is the literature of commitment (*iltizām*) which issues forth from Arab society and pours back into it."[51] Many Arab writers, including but not limited to Louis Awad, Maḥmūd Amīn al-ʿĀlim (d. 2009), and ʿAbd al-ʿAẓīm Anīs (d. 2009) – the proponents of socialist realism in Egypt – as well as the Marxist Lebanese critics Raʾīf Khūrī (d. 1967) and Ḥusayn Muruwwah (d. 1987), took up their pens for the cause of commitment during the years of anti-colonial and budding nationalist movements. Agreeing with Sartre's position on *engagement*, these writers and others championed the transformative power of socialist realism in literature. Commitment defined Arabic literature during the mid-twentieth century, so much so that M. M. Badawi writes, "From the middle of the 1950s onwards commitment, whether moderate or extreme, seems to have been the rule rather than the exception."[52]

The history of commitment in Iran parallels the Arab one, though Sartre's inaugural essay did not play such a central role in early discussions of literary engagement. It did, however, become a topic of debate decades later. Samad Alavi outlines in detail the courses of the commitment debate in Iran, from which I ought to mention a few salient points relevant for comparison with the Arab case.[53] First of all, like *iltizām* in the Arabic critical tradition, the Persian word for commitment, *taʿahhud*, "seems to have entered the lexicon of Persian literary discourse as a calque on Jean-Paul Sartre's *engagement*."[54] Secondly, Iranian writers did not restrict the call for committed writing to prose because poetry had always had a political role in society, as we also find in the Arab world. Finally, although *iltizām* and *taʿahhud* entered the Arab and Iranian literary spheres at roughly the same moment, *taʿahhud* would not reach the fevered pitch that *iltizām* did during the 1950s until much later on, hitting its peak in the late 1970s.[55]

This reflects the different political trajectories of Iran and the Arab nations. In Iran, the Shāh (Shah) Muḥammad Rizā Pahlavī (r. 1941–1979; d. 1980), became more and more despotic until the outbreak of the Islamic Revolution in 1978–1979, and committed writers grew more concerned with the lack of progress on social justice issues in Iran as his rule wore on. In the Arab case, the 1967 loss to Israel in the Six Day War forced writers to reevaluate the role of committed writing, which lost its former luster in the wake of the defeat. Initially, however, Iranian literary commitment advanced along the same lines as it did in the Arab world, the "mainstream"[56] view best outlined in the comprehensive though often polemical analysis of modern Iranian poetry found in Reza Baraheni's *Ṭalā dar mis: dar shiʿr va shāʿirī* (*Gold in Copper: On Poetry and Poesy*).[57] Baraheni's stance on the necessity of committed writing is largely congruent with that of Sartre (other than Sartre's position on poetry, of course) and Suhayl Idrīs. Additionally, Baraheni's thought is quite useful in overcoming the contradictions Sartre finds in poetry's relationship with words. He moves beyond Sartre's denigration of poetry's use of words as ends in and of themselves when he argues, "The only means from which the poet can choose in undertaking the task [of creating a better society and advancing humankind] are words. Words are at one and the same time *the means and the ends* of poetry."[58]

Due to the similar positions critics had on the possibility of committed poetry and the comparable (though not exactly parallel) political situations in the Arab world and Iran, we find many threads strung between commitment debates across the two contexts. Explicit political affiliations likewise tie together a number of the subjects of this study, particularly their progressive politics and Communist sympathies (if not actual membership in Communist organizations). Sayyāb was a card-carrying member of the Party, as was Aḥmad Shāmlū before his affiliation with the Iranian Communist Party (the *Tūdah* [Tudeh]; lit. "The Masses") got him thrown in prison in the early 1950s. Both Sayyāb and Shāmlū would later distance themselves from Communism, Sayyāb moving in a nationalist direction and Shāmlū preferring to remain ideologically free but sympathetic to the Left. Bayātī was affiliated with the Communist Party long after Sayyāb turned his back on it. Nīmā was never a member of the Tudeh, but his poetry was hailed as a Communist rallying call, associated with the Iranian left, and published in Communist journals.[59] Farrukhzād, the youngest of our subjects, remained rather removed from direct involvement in Leftist politics, but she did write poetry challenging Iranian nationalist ideals.[60]

Still, the continual demands that writers commit their work to a cause eventually led the Tunisian writer, intellectual, and statesman Maḥmūd al-Masʿadī (d. 2004) to argue for the necessity of the writer's ideological freedom in 1957 at the third conference of Arab writers in Cairo. His assertion that "no attempt should be made to confine [the writer] within a certain ideology, whether it is Marxist or any other equivalent ideology of the western or eastern variety" met with a "vehemently hostile" reaction from the audience,[61] thus bringing into sharp relief the fault lines of the commitment debates not just in Egypt but the broader region as well.[62] In any case, participants on both sides of the debate over commitment and the writer's freedom acknowledge that art – whether explicitly committed or autonomous – carries with it political meaning.

A Way Out of the Commitment Debates

Remaining with these commitment debates a bit longer, let us now consider the position of one of our modernist poets, Badr Shākir al-Sayyāb, who expressed his exasperation with the call to commitment many times toward the end of his life. Sayyāb's vocal frustration with the restraints commitment placed on literary creativity led him to an insightful observation about T. S. Eliot's poetry that can help us out of the commitment debates.[63] At the 1961 Conference on Modern Arabic Literature in Rome, Sayyāb argued that Eliot, whom Louis Awad had called a *raj'ī* (reactionary) poet years before in an article Sayyāb almost certainly read, was perhaps the harshest critic of capitalist society.[64] "I would not be going too far," Sayyāb ventures, "if I were to say that modern European civilization has faced no deeper or more violent ridicule than that of T. S. Eliot in his poem *The Waste Land, not in everything Communist writers and poets have written* against capitalism's role in said civilization."[65] These brief comments encapsulate the trajectory the commitment debate took in both the West and the region studied in this book during the years after Sartre published his essay. In fact, Theodor Adorno's take on the matter closely parallels later discussions of commitment in the Arab world and Iran.

Adorno's short essay "On Commitment" (1962) helps us out of the contradictions that emerge with Sartre's absolute distinction between committed and autonomous art. Addressing the (apparently) mutually exclusive categories of committed art and "art for art's sake," Adorno explains,

> There are two "positions on objectivity" which are constantly at war with one another, even when intellectual life falsely presents them as at peace. A work of art that is committed strips the magic from a work of art that is content to be a fetish, an idle pastime for those who would like to sleep through the deluge that threatens them, *in an apoliticism that is in fact deeply political*.[66]

Contra Sartre, Adorno calls not for any type of explicit commitment on the part of the writer, but rather addresses the autonomy of art, writing that "any literature which therefore concludes that it can be a law unto itself, and exist only for itself, degenerates into ideology no less. Art, which even in its opposition to society remains a part of it, must close its eyes and ears against it: it cannot escape the shadow of irrationality."[67] The immediate takeaway here is how Adorno's essay exposes a weak point in Sartre's argument – namely, that there must be some authorial intent behind the political impetus of an artwork. By arguing that all art is in some way political, Adorno offers us a way out of the commitment debates. In her engagement of Adorno's critique of Sartre, Jessica Berman explains, "From this perspective, only in *rejecting* transparency and direct relationship to reality can art become politically charged."[68] And even art that does not rise above the level of the fetish still represents a political position in its wanton lack of meaning beyond itself, its being content to be art and nothing else. Now that Adorno has leveled the playing field, bringing all art works together under the umbrella of the political – whether progressive and explicit or regressive and implicit, or some mixture of these – we can ask new, more meaningful questions like: Does some art have *more* political meaning or function *better* politically than other art? The question is no longer one of commitment, but rather of how all art works politically and how well it does so.

In order to address this question of how well art works politically, I find it productive to consider the poetry we will be reading together in light of Jacques Rancière's concept of the aesthetic regime. He explains:

> I call this regime *aesthetic* because the identification of art no longer occurs via a division within ways of doing and making, but it is based on distinguishing a sensible mode of being specific to artistic products. The word aesthetics does not refer to a theory of sensibility, taste, and pleasure for art amateurs. It strictly refers to the specific mode of being of whatever falls within the domain of art, to the mode of being of the objects of art.[69]

Answering the question of how literature becomes political rather than attempting to locate the political motivations of the writer, Rancière clarifies that the "politics of literature is not the politics of its writers. *It does not deal with their personal commitment to the social and political issues and struggles of their times.*"[70] Instead of focusing on the conscious commitment or non-commitment of the writer, Rancière is interested in how "literature 'does' politics as literature."[71] He explains how the intertwining of politics and literature occurs through a process of "dissensus," which is "the essence of politics, [. . .] the demonstration (*manifestation*) of a gap in the sensible itself. Political demonstration makes visible that which had no reason to be seen; it places one world in another [. . .] ."[72] In the end, "[p]olitics, before all else, is an intervention in the visible and the sayable."[73] Thus, the "aesthetic regime" is a politically driven concept which replaces "modernism" in Rancière's vocabulary. By defining art in terms of the aesthetic regime, Rancière highlights a change in how people relate to art in the modern period and looks to how art can "shift the coordinates of what is seeable, sayable, and possible."[74] This redefinition of modernism through the aesthetic regime, which intervenes on the sayable, the possible, and the thinkable itself, results from Rancière's historicization of literature and the human relationship to it in the modern period.

I understand Arab and Persian modernist poetry as just such interventions on the sayable, as Rancière puts it. To return to Awad's modernist manifesto once again as a point of comparison, its concluding paragraph, bathed in Communist red, reflects Awad's attempt to "place one world in another," to intervene on the seeable and the sayable by changing the form of poetry and in turn the world as well. Awad's failed modernist project and the successful one that took off in Iraq just after had to deal with the highly influential force of European poetic modernism, the coalescing of Third World consciousness, and the growing presence of Communist ideology and local nationalist movements of the mid-twentieth century. Like much previous scholarship on modernist Arabic and Persian poetry, I too look to poetry's relationship with politics. However, whereas many studies have conceived of this poetry as a reflection of society and therefore as a way to understand the truth of an external political reality, I consider modernist poetry as inherently political in its demonstration of the "gaps in the sensible" through its negotiations of contemporary political and social phenomena and attempts to offer its own interventions on the seeable and sayable.

I am primarily interested in modernist poetry's internal aesthetics: its formal make up, its intertextual links with the past, and the new worlds it makes manifest. In striking a balance between text and context while always paying attention to the role that form plays in defining a poem's content, I am led in part by Cleanth Brooks's rejection of a formulaic dualism in poetic criticism "that the poem constitutes a 'statement' of some sort, the statement being true or false, and expressed more or less clearly or eloquently or beautifully." Because of this dualism, "the critic is forced to judge the poem by its political or scientific or philosophical truth; or, he is forced to judge the poem by its form as conceived externally and detached from human experience."[75] Instead of seeking out some immutable (but, if we are honest with ourselves, wholly inaccessible) truth in a poem or attempting to locate its core "statement," I account for poetry's dialectic relationship with the context of its composition, its creators, and its readers in my analyses. While I am not bound to New Criticism – I balance such an approach in later chapters with biographical and historicist analysis when appropriate – text-based readings help us look beyond earlier scholarly limitations within national paradigms of understanding. Too often modernist poetry in Arabic or Persian has been understood primarily as a type of writing back against the colonizer whether due to its perceived revolutionary posturing, nationalism, or apolitical autonomy that challenges by way of ignoring. While such readings are useful and necessary, they are, again, not sufficient if we want to account for the transnational dynamics of poetic exchange out of which Arabic and Persian modernist poetries emerged or ask how these poetries' transnational poetics (their lateral East-to-East or South-to-South transactions) might also challenge received views of West-to-East (vertical) poetic and political influence – a much thornier problem.

I therefore want to explore how and where Arabic and Persian modernist poetries fit (or do not fit) into broader notions of what world literature is. In this regard, my study also calls into question a number of assumptions about these poetries: they primarily represent nationalist sentiment, they directly result from European colonization and poetic influence, and they violently break away from local poetic traditions. I am thus also guided by Stanley Fish's work on interpretive communities, if only to question some of the "collective decision[s] as to what will count as literature"[76] that have figured into scholarly approaches to modernist poetry in Arabic and Persian and to *persuade* you to read it in a new way.[77] That is, I want us to actually read this poetry as poetry. To do so, I bring formal analysis grounded in the Arabic and Persian rhetorical traditions into broader conversations about transnationalism and literary development, combining the global and the local in my approach to establish the significance of the Arab world and Iran on our map of modernist geographies. We begin our survey of these geographies in Iran in the next chapter with the poetry of Nīmā Yūshīj, who, like Awad, envisioned the modernist movement as a battle between the young and the old.

CHAPTER 2

Travel Forms
Arabic Prosody, Craft, and Nīmā Yūshīj's Persian New Poetry

ای شاعر جوان!

این ساختمان که «افسانه»ی من در آن جاگرفته ست و یک طرز مکالمه ی طبیعی و آزاد را نشان می دهد، شاید برای دفعه اول پسندیده ی تو نباشد و شاید تو آن را به اندازه ی من نپسندی.

> O Young Poet!
>
> This structure into which my *Afsānah* (*Myth*) has been placed, and which demonstrates a natural and free type of conversation, might not appeal to you at first, and you might not like it as much as I do.
>
> —Nīmā Yūshīj, Introduction to *Afsānah*[1]

In the introductory notes to his 1922 long poem *Afsānah* (*Myth*), Iranian poet Nīmā Yūshīj begins by calling out to an unnamed "Young Poet" (*ay shāʿir-i javān*).[2] Addressed to a new generation of Iranian poets, these three words along with the comments and poem to follow were as foundational for modernist Persian poetry as Ezra Pound's command to "Make it new!" and his shepherding of the nascent European modernist movement with his edits to T. S. Eliot's *The Waste Land* were in the West.[3] But Nīmā was not following Pound's lead, as he did not read English. In fact, *The Waste Land* was published in English the same year *Afsānah* was in Persian in Iran, where a significant modernist geography was developing.

Nīmā lays a foundational claim to his own concept of modernism in the Persian context when he tells his young charge, "This structure (*sākhtimān*) into which my *Afsānah* has been placed, and which demonstrates a natural (*ṭabīʿī*) and free (*āzād*) type of conversation, might not appeal to you at first, and you might not like it as much as I do." Nīmā's word choices highlight the central role he attributes to form as well as the generational divide he saw taking shape in the Persian poetic tradition. First, he speaks to a young (*javān*) poet, opposing this poet (and also himself) with the classical poets, whom he later refers to as the "*qudamā*," literally "the ancients." (The Arabic root of the word, *qāf - dāl - mīm*, has to do with being old or coming before.) Second, Nīmā relates the qualities of "natural" (*ṭabīʿī*) and "free" (*āzād*) to describe what he has endeavored to do with the language he uses in *Afsānah*. Implicit in the comment is that older poetry is neither natural nor free, and that his contemporaries who were attempting to revive the old styles remained bound by them. Finally, by choosing to open his remarks with the word *sākhtimān*, Nīmā foregrounds the significance of poetic form as the foundation for modernist poetry to come.

Sākhtimān means many things, among them building, construction, frame, and structure. In describing the style of *Afsānah* through its structure, Nīmā grounds the modernist poetic developments he hoped to introduce to Persian poetry. His choice of *sākhtimān* along with his later use of semantically similar terms such as *bunyād* (foundation) and *banā* (building) as well as the etymologically related verb *sākhtan* (the gerund form; "to build") show how Nīmā conceives of modernist poetry as a structure. Nīmā approaches the "building" of the poem using the terminology of an artisan. We can therefore understand and elaborate Nīmā's poetic process by looking to the words he employs as tools in building what he refers to as the "imaginary edifice" ("*banā-yi khayālī*") that is the poem.[4]

In what follows, we will see how Nīmā's understanding of poetry as craft (*ṣanʿat*) allows him to create a "new poetry" (*shiʿr-i naw*) out of the Persian poetic tradition. This new poetry, however, retains several features also found in premodern Persian (and Arabic) poetry. By investigating how the feet of the Arabic *ʿarūḍ* (Persian *ʿarūż*) make their way into Nīmā's modernist poetry and his dependence on premodern and Islamic myth, I emphasize the profound connections between Persian New Poetry and Arabic "free verse" (*al-shiʿr al-ḥurr*). Using these links as the analytical focus of this chapter, I propose that the techniques Nīmā uses in his poetic craft allow him to sublate the premodern Persian, Islamic, and pre-Islamic past into his New Poetry and that this sublation of the past constitutes a significant manifestation of the shared transnational unconscious that gave rise to modernism and shaped the Arab world and Iran as a significant modernist geography. Moreover, I argue that Nīmā's sublation of the past into his poetry works against the limited vision of the Pahlavi dynasty's (r. 1925–1979) nation-building modernization projects. Nīmā's poetic practice of sublation situates his work within the wider modernist imaginary due to what Eliot terms in his analysis of contemporary European poetry "the historical sense," a method of historical perception that "compels a man to write not merely with his own generation in his bones, but with a feeling that the whole of the literature of Europe from Homer and within it the whole of the literature of his own country has a simultaneous existence and composes a simultaneous order."[5] Nīmā's deep study of premodern Persian poetry gave him this "historical sense" of his place within the Persian tradition while also making him "acutely conscious of his place in time, of his contemporaneity."[6]

The chapter begins with a discussion of poetry and craft in Nīmā's work. I next juxtapose Nīmā's techniques for approaching the transnationally shared Islamic past of the Arab world and Iran with the Pahlavi dynasty's attempts to create a particular version of Iranian history in the interests of their nationalist program. We will see how the Pahlavis' limited concept of modernity contrasts with Nīmā's open engagement of premodern Persian and Arab heritage and culture. At this point, I move into my readings of Nīmā's poetry, beginning with 1922's *Afsānah*, continuing to 1926's "*Qū*" ("The Swan"), and ending with the quintessential modernist poem "*Quqnūs*" ("The Phoenix"), from 1938. With these three poems, we will trace the development of Persian modernist poetry during its first decades. Furthermore, these three poems offer us opportunities to see an Iranian modernist poet's techniques of form and theme in action. With *Afsānah*, we will see how premodern metrical science continues to structure a poem whose persona challenges the continued relevance of the past in the present moment. In "*Qū*," we find a novel modernist approach to symbolism with Nīmā's use of a swan as a stand-in for the poet – a first in Persian poetry. Likewise, we will make an etymological connection between the title character of the poem and the shared linguistic past of the Mesopotamian region. Finally, a close analysis of "*Quqnūs*" will bring together Nīmā's modernist metrics, symbolism, and sublation of the premodern into the modern through the rhetorical technique of *muʿāraḍah* contrafaction. Approaching "*Quqnūs*" with the assistance of the Arabic rhetorical tradition will help us understand the poem's subtle references to the martyrdom story of the mystic al-Ḥusayn ibn Manṣūr al-Ḥallāj (d. 922), a figure central to modernism across the Arabic and Persian linguistic contexts. Overall, the chapter presents an alternative view of what it means to be modern by investigating a modernist poetic project starkly opposed to the modernization programs of the Pahlavi state.

Nīmā's New Poetry as *Ṣanʿat* (Craft)

Nīmā's vision of modernity directly opposes the Pahlavi regime's top-down modernization of Iran. Whereas the Pahlavis sought to cover over the illusory, constructed nature of their state-sponsored modernity, Nīmā's modernist vision revels in the imaginary structures that make it possible, namely, metaphor, simile, and symbolism. Nimaic modernity and Pahlavi modernity both represent returns to and recapitulations of the Iranian past, but Pahlavi modernity followed a path laid out by the Iranian elite toward a set end, a telos that mirrored Western ideologies of secular modernity. Nīmā's modernist vision is decidedly different: rural, natural, and connected to everyday experience, Nīmā's modernity challenges Pahlavi modernity in its openness, its refusal to conform to a singular notion of what modernity might be. Notwithstanding the undeniable influence of Western thought and poetry on Nīmā's literary criticism and poetic style, the innovations he introduced to Persian poetry do not attempt to cover over the Persian poetic tradition or the realities of the Iranian past. Instead, the formal and thematic connections of Nīmā's poetry to the premodern Persian poetic tradition point to his careful, prolonged engagement with the past to revivify it and make it a part of an Iranian future yet to come.

Two terms frequently pop up in Nīmā's literary criticism as he outlines his vision of modernity: *ṭabīʿat* (nature) and *ṣanʿat* (craft). To understand Nīmā's critical process and how it overcomes the problems inherent to the structure of modernity, I place these terms within the context of "the modern" as Bruno Latour defines it. Dealing with Western ideas about modernity in his book *We Have Never Been Modern*, Latour explains that conceiving of oneself as modern is more a matter of faith than an objective reality.[7] Latour posits that "the Moderns" subscribe to what he calls "the modern Constitution," which depends on the neat separation of subject (society) and object (nature). Ultimately, however, this Constitution fails due to the presence of quasi-objects, hybrids that intervene on either side. For Latour, a crisis occurs since "*the proliferation of hybrids has saturated the constitutional framework of the moderns.*"[8] Although he is the preeminent modernist in the Persian poetic tradition, Nīmā's poetics do not fall victim to this crisis and instead recognize and respond to a continuing hybridization of subject and object in a world increasingly ordered along the lines of enlightenment categorization.

Ṭabīʿat sits squarely in the realm of nature, the object. *Ṣanʿat* is the medium through which humans (who occupy the realm of society, or subject) act on nature. However, Nīmā continually works to bridge the artificial divisions proposed by "the modern Constitution" in his approach to poetry as *ṣanʿat*, or craft. Delving deep into Nīmā's poetics, Karimi-Hakkak explains, "On the basis of the implied dichotomy between nature and culture, [Nīmā] rejects the notion that individuals can be separated from their environment."[9] In spurning this dichotomy, Nīmā is at odds with a foundational element of modernity as Latour's "Moderns" conceive of it. Whereas Nīmā elaborates a poetics grounded in a collective experience of society *and* nature, Western political ideologies of modernity – the ultimate results of the enlightenment push for categorization – depend on neat separations, specifically between nature and society, in their elaborations of an administrative, teleological modernity. Consider the two extremes of modern Western political formations, Fascism and Communism – totalizing systems that depend on the complete and total regulation of every part of both society and nature.[10] As Horkheimer and Adorno put it, "Enlightenment stands in the same relationship to things as the dictator to human beings. He knows them to the extent that he can manipulate them."[11] Nīmā instead emphasizes the interconnectivity of subject and object and the hybridity of existence that "the Moderns" seek to overcome. Thus, Nīmā's "attitude of modernity," though informed to a great extent by the Western philosophical tradition, results from his recognition of the insurmountable presence of hybrids, those things that defy the categorization required by "the Moderns."[12]

Karimi-Hakkak argues that Nīmā's modernist poetry overcomes the "artificialities" (*takallufāt*) of premodern and neoclassical Persian poetry through his use of natural diction. In doing so, Nīmā "opposes the simplicity and naturalness of his own descriptions to the artificialities (*takallofat*) which have constrained the old poets in expressing their ideas poetically." *Ṣanʿat* has to do with poetic craft and "relates invariably to the means and mechanisms by which poems are produced."[13] However, *ṣanʿat* and *ṭabīʿat* are not mutually exclusive for Nīmā, since good *ṣanʿat* can also be natural rather than artificial. For Nīmā, the two are closely related in the craft of poetic composition.

I close this section with Nīmā's brief comments on his view of poetry as craft from his 1946 address to the Iranian Writer's Congress.

> In my free poems (*ashʿār-i āzād-i man*) meter and rhyme are accounted for differently, but the hemistichs (*miṣraʿ-hā*) do not shorten or lengthen out of mere flights of fancy. I believe in an ordered lack of order (*man barā-yi bīnaẓmī ham bi*[*h-*]*naẓmī iʿtiqād dāram*). Every one of my words connects to the next one by way of a specific rule (*qāʿidah-'i daqīq*), and for me composing free poetry (*shiʿr-i āzād surūdan*) is more difficult than the other [i.e., composing traditional verse].[14]

As we see here, elements of *sanʿat* suffuse Nīmā's definition of his poetic process. He conceives of himself as a builder using the tools available to him as a poet (his own experience, words themselves, and poetic form). Additionally, Nīmā tells his audience that composing "free poetry" is no simple task for him and is in fact more difficult to do than it would be to compose verse in the traditional style. In what follows, I demonstrate how some of the elements of what Nīmā terms an "ordered lack of order" work within his modernist poems and what these innovations have to tell us about the development of modernist Persian poetry.

Pahlavi versus Nimaic Visions of Modernity: The Craft of Sublation

We now turn to Nīmā's application of *ṣan'at* within his poetry. Nīmā began to lay the foundations of his modernist edifice in 1922, just after Riżā Shāh Pahlavī's (Reza Shah Pahlavi; r. 1925–1941; d. 1944) 1921 coup and the subsequent creation of the *Anjuman-i ās̱ār-i millī* (The Society for the National Heritage of Iran [SNH]), also in 1921 – their founding bylaws were composed in 1922. Talinn Grigor has amply demonstrated in her work how the SNH immediately set about "effectively and shrewdly co-opt[ing] the visual and the spatial into the mainstream of Pahlavi ideology and program" with their plans for a series of archeological and architectural projects, including the "invention of patrimony" by way of constructing a number of mausoleums for important figures from the Persian literary past: Firdawsī (d. 1020), Ḥāfiẓ (d. 1390), Khayyām (d. 1131), and others.[15] In elaborating their plans for these projects, Grigor argues, the SNH's "techniques of cultivating and naturalizing the new parameters of modernity persistently intersected with their anxiety over collective memory, public space, and the cultivation of cultural taste – *all of which were formulated along western lines.*"[16] Contrasting with the SNH's invention of a glorious Iranian past, particularly the pre-Islamic Iranian past, is Nīmā's more open engagement of Persian, but also Arab and Islamic, cultural patrimony. This is not to say that Nīmā's modernism offered nothing new, but instead to highlight how different his modernist project was from the SNH's due to its transnational linking of Western poetic influence with Arabic poetic form. In this section, I demonstrate how Nīmā's modernist poetry comes to be by way of sublating Arabic prosodic norms and Iran's Islamic past into an Iranian modernism at odds with the SNH's myopic view of the past's role in the present.

Nīmā's sublating (in the multiple senses of the German *Aufhebung*: "abolishing," but also "transcending" and "preserving"), rather than co-opting or refashioning, of Iran's cultural past first emerges in 1922's *Afsānah*. Unlike the SNH, which sought to establish a particular version of the Iranian past and its historical and mythic figures in the interests of the new Pahlavi regime, Nīmā challenges a static notion of the past in his poem. In one of its oft-quoted passages, *ʿĀshiq* (Lover) shouts at *Afsānah* (Myth), with whom he is carrying out a dialogue:

> *Ḥāfiẓā! Īn chih kayd u durūgh-īst*
> *ka-z zabān-i may u jām u sāqī-st*
> *nālī ar tā abad bāvaram nīst*
> *kih bar ān ʿishqʾbāzī kih bāqī-st*
> *man bar ān ʿāshiqam kih ravandah-st*
>
> O Ḥāfiẓ, what sort of lie and trick is this
> that comes in the language of wine, goblet, and cup-bearer?
> Despite your moaning on into eternity, I do not believe
> in falling in love with static things
> I am in love with things that are in motion![17]

While Nīmā's Lover here takes the famed premodern Persian poet Ḥāfiẓ to task (in a nod to the neoclassical *bāzgasht* movement in vogue in Persian letters during the early twentieth century), *Afsānah* remains grounded in the Arabo-Persian prosodic tradition. In fact, the above lines are in the *mutadārik* (continuous) meter, a perfectly acceptable premodern meter in the Khalīlian system.[18] Lover's demands for new poetic content that goes beyond tradition and is in motion (*ravandah*) are thus tempered by the retention of the old poetic form as something static, eternal, or permanent, (*bāqī*).[19] The retention of premodern form restrains Lover's outburst that we find in the content, thereby limning the central point of Nīmā's modernist project: the demand for a modernity that sublates (transcends and preserves) elements of the past rather than only abolishes it. Nīmā's juxtaposition of the static (*bāqī*) with something moving (*ravandah*) in these lines directly parallels Adūnīs's conception of the static (*al-thābit*) versus the dynamic (*al-mutaḥawwil*) in his elaboration of Arabic modernism. My English translations of Nīmā's Persian terms is meant to highlight this connection here, though Nīmā's poem predates Adūnīs's intervention by more than half a century.

The Past in the Present of Modern Persian Poetry

Nīmā continued to develop this poetic practice of sublation through the second half of the 1920s to the late 1930s when he wrote "*Quqnūs*" ("The Phoenix"). Birds play a critical role in the poems Nīmā composed as they help him represent his modernist vision. Likewise, birds provide yet another instance of the interconnection of ancient Mesopotamian cultural traditions across the region where the significant geography we are exploring in this book is located. For instance, consider the following summary of scholarship on the translinguistic movement of the words for swan and Phoenix in the classical and premodern Mediterranean and Mesopotamian regions. According to Hellenist and scholar of birds in the ancient world W. Geoffrey Arnott, the whooper swan (Latin name *Cygnus cygnus*) "has a remarkably shaped trachea, convoluted inside of its breastbone; and when it dies, the final expiration of air from its collapsing lungs produces a 'wailing, flute-like sound given out quite slowly.'"[20] The whooper swan's name, *Cygnus* twice over, comes from the Greek *κύκνος*, a word that also went east in the philosophical work of Persian polymath Ibn Sīnā (d. 1037; known as Avicenna in the West), where it still meant swan.[21] Over a century later when it appears in Farīd al-Dīn ʿAṭṭār's (d. 1221) *Manṭiq al-ṭayr* (*The Conference of the Birds*; an account of a mystical quest by a group of birds to discover Being), the *quqnus* has a beak with a hundred holes and sings beautifully. In the story, when the *quqnus* is about to die it collects kindling around itself as it sings a mournful swan song. Finally, it sets itself alight on its pyre and is reborn in the ashes. The story of the premodern Persian *quqnus* mirrors that of the Phoenix in Greek myth, but its name comes from the Greek word for swan. Although I have been no more successful than Muḥāmmad Riżā Shafīʿī-Kadkanī (b. 1939), who recently completed an edition of *Manṭiq al-ṭayr*, in finding the philological link between the Persian *quqnus* and the Greek *κύκνος*, I am convinced that the two birds are connected by their swan song, which each of them sings as death approaches.[22]

In *The Conference of the Birds*, ʿAṭṭār goes on to say that it was the *quqnus* that first taught man how to sing.[23] Acknowledging ʿAṭṭār's account of the *quqnus*'s abilities, Nīmā chooses both the swan (*qū*) – almost certainly a whooper swan – and the *quqnūs* to symbolically represent the poet as he makes his initial interventions in the history of Persian prosody.[24] He does so because their songs announce an ending, a death out of which something new is born that still retains elements of the old.

Nīmā composed "*Qū*" on 20 Farvardīn 1305 (10 April 1926). "The Swan" is a *chahārpārah*, a "four-parter" with an ABAB rhyme scheme in each of its eleven stanzas. In the Khalīlian *ʿarūḍ* system, the meter is a *khafīf* (light) sextameter with lines arranged in a single column rather than in traditional two-hemistich lines.[25] I address "*Qū*" here not because of its traditional metrics, but rather because its content is entirely new to Persian poetry. As Amr Taher Ahmed has pointed out, this is the first time that a poet used the figure of a swan as a symbol for the poet in all of Persian literature, the swan not having been among the animals usually found in earlier verse.[26] In the following lines, Nīmā uses the swan to metapoetically address the act of writing poetry.

It [the swan] goes into a dark lair
With imagination (*khayāl*) as a companion
In a bright line thin as a hair,
It sees things deserving of a swan

But a far-off cloud remains,
The waves keep crashing,
And in this place, no one knows
What images will come apart (*kih chih ashkāl mīshavand judā*).[27]

Nīmā conceives of the swan as poet, which allows him to offer a metaperspective on the act of creating poetry. The swan, like the poet, ventures into the unknown with imagination (*khayāl*) as its only companion, and, also mirroring the poet, it has a special ability to see things others cannot. However, the swan's creative vision is unruly, and, like the poet, it cannot tell what will come of what it sees. In Persian, the final line is *kih chih ashkāl mīshavand judā*, and *ashkāl* (images) might also be understood to mean "forms," hinting at Nīmā's later poetic experimentation and his testing of the formal boundaries of premodern Persian prosody.

Nīmā's swan-as-poet disrupts the history of Persian verse in ways other than the stark novelty of its symbolism just as his continual use of rural, natural scenes also contrasts sharply with the typically urban setting of Persian poetry.[28] By portraying the swan as a solitary figure, the poem implicitly positions the modernist poet as an individual on the margins of society just as Nīmā presented himself as disconnected from the urbane trappings of modernity. Although Nīmā worked as a government bureaucrat in the Archives Division of the Ministry of Finance during the 1920s, he sartorially set himself apart by wearing a traditional robe, boots, and fur hat, completing the look by carrying a knife at his waist. "He needed all that," Karimi-Hakkak explains, "to let his bosses know that he was not like the others. The 'knife at the waist' image, which also surfaces in accounts written by his colleagues, tells of the basic incongruity between Nima's upbringing and the position he now held in the stolid bureaucracy of 1920s Iran."[29] Nīmā thus physically set himself apart from other state bureaucrats in precisely the same way his modernist poetic imagination remained incommensurable with the Pahlavis' construction of a modern nation.

Overall, "The Swan" upends arguments that Iranian poets required new, freer poetic forms to express new, freer poetic content. Rather, we find Nīmā here working closely with the earlier poetic tradition to create something new yet similar, and certainly not breaking away from traditional prosodic norms. Instead, Nīmā places his symbolic intervention on poetic content within a form still based wholly on the prosodic system for description used in premodern Persian poetry, a system that took its analytical terms from the Arabic science of *ʿarūḍ* prosody.

Nīmā's Phoenix Rises (I): Premodern Form and New Poetry

Later in his career, Nīmā innovated on premodern Persian prosody by making the poetic foot (*rukn* – literally a pillar or column – in Persian; *tafʿīlah* in Arabic) the basis of his poetic line. He repeated combinations of feet any number of times in a single line, similar to the method of the Iraqi free verse pioneers Badr Shākir al-Sayyāb, Nāzik al-Malāʾikah, and their followers, but different in that Nīmā often used meters consisting of two different poetic feet (unlike the Iraqi pioneers and against Malāʾikah's prescriptions for Arabic free verse).[30] These experiments with premodern prosodic form emerge most clearly in "*Quqnūs*" ("The Phoenix"), first published in 1938.

Consider how the sublation of premodern metrics into a modern form works in the first ten lines of the poem.

Quqnūs, murgh-i khᵛushkhᵛān, āvāzah-yi jahān,
āvārah māndah az vazish-i bād-hā-yi sard,
bar shākh-i khayzurān,
binshastah ast fard.
Bar gird-i ū bih har sar-i shākhī parandigān.
Ū nālah-hā-yi gumshudah tarkīb mīkunad,
az rishtah-hā-yi pārah-yi ṣad-hā ṣidā-yi dūr,
dar abr-hā-yi mis̱l-i khaṭṭ-ī tīrah rū-yi kūh,
dīvār-i yak banā-yi khayālī
mīsāzad.

The Phoenix, sweet-singing bird, known across the world
made homeless by gusts of cold wind
sits, alone, on
a stalk of bamboo.
The other birds gather around it on every branch.
It composes lost laments
from the tattered shreds of a thousand distant voices,
in clouds like a dark line on the mountain,
the wall of an imaginary edifice, it
builds.[31]

Before I begin my analysis of these lines, a brief note on a translation choice I have made throughout the poem. Informed by the etymological discussion in the previous section, I have chosen to translate *quqnūs* as "Phoenix." However, there is no indication of the bird's gender in the poem. Despite the fact that it ends, as we will see, with the Phoenix's eggs hatching, there is nothing to indicate that the Phoenix laid the eggs (or inseminated them). Hamid Dabashi, who has also translated the poem, in a wonderful Freudian slip renders *quqnūs* as "Sphinx," a mythical figure that is sometimes male, sometimes female.[32] The Persian of the poem cannot help us either, since the language is not gendered, and the pronoun used to refer to the Phoenix ("*ū*") can be masculine, feminine, or neuter. While using the singular "they" appeals to me, the resulting translation would be unwieldy when carried over to English. I have therefore decided to translate "*ū*" as "it" throughout the poem.[33]

To begin our reading of the poem, these opening lines present us with several key features of modernist poetry. First and most obviously, the poem depends on the ancient myth of the Phoenix and the cycle of death and rebirth, so central to the broader modernist movement. Second and not immediately evident is Nīmā's intertextual reference to ʿAṭṭār's *The Conference of the Birds*. We find this extremely refined reference in the rhymes of the first line (*khᵛushkhᵛān; jahān*), the "*ān*'s" of which send us back across the centuries to ʿAṭṭār's own first line about the Phoenix: "*hast quqnus ṭurfah murghī dilsatān // mawżaʿ-ī īn murgh dar Hindūstān*" (The Phoenix is a peerless bird, heart-enrapturing / This bird's abode is Hindustan).[34] Nīmā's "The Phoenix" can thus be read as a contrafaction or an *imitatio*, what's called in Arabic a *muʿāraḍah*, though Nīmā noticeably does not employ the same meter as ʿAṭṭār like we would expect in a traditional *muʿāraḍah*.[35] By engaging the premodern tradition in such a way, Nīmā invites us to consider his new poem in terms of its relationship with the poetry that came before it while also pushing the boundaries of the very same tradition. Including such a complex reference to ʿAṭṭār's original in the first line of the poem emphasizes Nīmā's delicate sublation of the old into the new. This sublation extends to the poem's innovative metrics. "The Phoenix" simply does not look like premodern Persian or Arabic poetries, which follow strict rules of prosody requiring the same number of feet in regular patterns in each and every line.

In order to bring the old into the new, Nīmā does not fully break away from these rules. Instead, he sublates the premodern into the modern by retaining the premodern poetic foot (or, in this case, pairs of feet) as the basis of his metrics. The poem's meter is a version of al-Khalīl's *baḥr al-*

muḍāriʿ (the similar meter). As a reminder, al-Khalīl's system organizes poetry according to the sequences of long and short syllables that make up set numbers of poetic feet (*tafʿīlāt* in Arabic; *arkān* in Persian) in the various Arabic poetic meters, feet that came to be represented by *ad hoc* words created from the three-letter Arabic root *fāʾ - ʿayn - lām*. With this in mind, here is how a prosodist can represent the meter of "The Phoenix" using both the Arabic Khalīlian system and traditional Western scansion (with "¯" indicating a long syllable, "˘" a short, and "/" a separation between poetic feet). (The strikethroughs indicate missing feet. I leave those feet out of the Western scansion.)

mafʿūlu fāʿilātu mafāʿīlu fāʿilun	– – ˘ / – ˘ – ˘ / ˘ – – ˘ / – ˘ –
mafʿūlu fāʿilātu mafāʿīlu fāʿilun	– – ˘ / – ˘ – ˘ / ˘ – – ˘ / – ˘ –
mafʿūlu fāʿilātu ~~mafāʿīlu fāʿilun~~	– – ˘ / – ˘ – ˘
mafʿūlu fāʿilātu ~~mafāʿīlu fāʿilun~~	– – ˘ / – ˘ – ˘
mafʿūlu fāʿilātu mafāʿīlu fāʿilun	– – ˘ / – ˘ – ˘ / ˘ – – ˘ / – ˘ –
mafʿūlu fāʿilātu mafāʿīlu fāʿilun	– – ˘ / – ˘ – ˘ / ˘ – – ˘ / – ˘ –
mafʿūlu fāʿilātu mafāʿīlu fāʿilun	– – ˘ / – ˘ – ˘ / ˘ – – ˘ / – ˘ –
mafʿūlu fāʿilātu mafāʿīlu fāʿilun	– – ˘ / – ˘ – ˘ / ˘ – – ˘ / – ˘ –
mafʿūlu fāʿilātu mafāʿ~~īlu fāʿilun~~	– – ˘ / – ˘ – ˘ / ˘ – –
mafʿūlu ~~fāʿilātu mafāʿīlu fāʿilun~~	– – –[36]

Nīmā's third and fourth lines stop midway through, but the first two usual poetic feet remain unaffected. While this is out of the ordinary, it only hints at the metrical experimentation to come. In line ten, Nīmā ingeniously pushes the meter's limits with the plodding succession of syllables in *mīsāzad*, which means "builds." (*Mīsāzad* is also the indicative third-person singular verb form of the noun *sākhtimān* that we saw Nīmā discuss in his foundational introduction to *Afsānah* at the beginning of the chapter.) The meaning of this verb in combination with the meter encapsulates Nīmā's formulation of poetic modernism in a single word. We might even say this represents modernism as a whole: at the same moment the poet creates something new, he also shakes its foundations. Metrics and content stand at odds with one another, and their dissonance sounds out the inner workings of Nīmā's modernist project, which builds as it breaks away and thereby sublates the old into the new.

Furthermore, the "wall of an imaginary edifice" from line nine is *dīvār-i yak banā-yi khayālī. Banā*, from the Arabic *bināʾ*, means building or structure. I translate it as edifice here because of the dual meanings of this word in English: either a large, stately building or a figurative reference to a system of belief. Nīmā's Phoenix simultaneously tears down and rebuilds the system of Persian prosody, just as the mythical Phoenix is only reborn by destroying itself. The Phoenix thus represents the process behind Nīmā's composition of modernist poetry, which continues the older tradition in a new form born out of its ashes. The meter, therefore, constitutes the *banā* of these lines, which provide the edifice upon which Nīmā's modernist imagination (*khayāl*) is firmly based. We might even understand this modernist *khayāl*, then, as a constitutive element of the transnational unconscious that bridges between the Iranian and Arab modernist poetic movements.

Nīmā's Phoenix Rises (II): Modern and Premodern Themes in a Modernist Persian Poem

After making its imaginative and prosodic interventions at the end of its first stanza, "*Quqnūs*" goes on to explore the limits of its modernist imagination. It paints a mysterious, dark scene punctuated by natural phenomenon like sunlight, crashing waves, and a jackal's howl yet also host to the lonely figure of a peasant. Alone in his hut, he lights a small lamp, while other people pass by in the distance.

> Ever since the yellow of the sun upon the waves
> faded away, and the jackal's howl
> rang out over the shore, and the peasant (*mard-i dihātī*)
> lit a hidden light in his home,
> his eyes reflect red a tiny flame that
> draws a line under night's two wild eyes
> and at far off points (*v-andar nuqāṭ-i dūr*)
> people pass by (*khalq-and dar ʿubūr*).

The motif of the urban passerby is a pivotal feature in modernist poetry, from Baudelaire's direct address to a woman passing on a Paris street in "*À une passante*"[37] to T. S. Eliot's Unreal City in *The Waste Land*'s version of London. "Unreal city / Under the brown fog of a winter dawn, / A crowd flowed over London Bridge, so many, / I had not thought death had undone so many. / Sighs, short and infrequent, were exhaled, / And each man fixed his eyes before his feet."[38] Modern society reordered by capital; poet as witness to an age. In these modernist poems, the poet's keen eye for detail unveils the deeper reality of everyday moments. Nīmā's "*Quqnūs*" is no different. The peasant (*mard-i dihātī*; literally a "village man") and his lamp shining out weakly into the night are contrasted with other people (*khalq*) far away, who do not know or ignore the challenges of the night closing in on the margins of their world. The rhymes of *dūr* (far) and *ʿubūr* (passing) further tie the people up in the distance, sheltering them from the reality the peasant experiences in his countryside solitude.

In these lines, the simple act of lighting a lamp initiates a symbolic mode that would later become the primary critical focus of Nīmā's Iranian readers. As night falls in the wilderness, the peasant's "hidden light" shines out into the darkness, a glimmer of hope in a gloomy scene. The dichotomy of night (*shab*) and day, the sun, daybreak, the cock's crow, etc. represents, for many critics writing about Nīmā, his allegorical representation of a repressive political environment.[39] But when the poem returns to the Phoenix, the binary relationship of night and day (dark and light) shifts and disappears.

> The bird, that rare song, hidden as it is
> rises from where it is perched
> through things tangled up
> with the light and dark of this long night (*bā rawshanī va tīragī-'i īn shab-i dirāz*),
> it
> passes.
> A flame out ahead, it
> sees.

The Phoenix takes off from its perch and flies away, passing through "the light *and* dark of this long night" (*bā rawshanī* va *tīragī-'i īn shab-i dirāz*) to arrive at its ultimate fate, the fire where its end and new beginning meet, bringing life and death together. Night and day collapse into one long night that the Phoenix flies through to reach the fire that will lead to its rebirth.

As the Phoenix struggles to free itself from night, the other birds crowding around it stand in for the human passers-by so familiar to us from Western modernism. The Phoenix, like the poet, bears the burdens of poetic perception, but the other birds in the poem merely deal with basic survival in a barren land. The following lines describe a desolate scene reminiscent of Eliot's *The Waste Land*, though, I must reiterate, Nīmā likely took no direct inspiration from Eliot's poem. The land is "without plants, without air," and the other birds eke out an existence there. The Phoenix's struggle, however, takes place beyond this material world as it fights against existence itself in an attempt to escape from an unending cycle.

Although the Phoenix's death and rebirth are imminent and assured, the poem (mirroring ʿAṭṭār's version of the story) is not hopeful for the new life to come after death. In these next lines, "*Quqnūs*" introduces one of the themes we will trace through Arabic and Persian modernist poetry in this book.

In a place without plants, without air,
the stubborn sun breaks on the rocks,
land and life are nothing special here.
It senses that the hopes of birds like it
are dark as smoke, even if some of their dreams
are like a harvest of fire
sparkling in the eye and in their white morning.
It senses that if its life
passed by like other birds
in sleeping and eating
it would be an unnameable pain.

While the other birds are content to limit their experience of reality to the everyday tasks of sleeping and eating and to only entertain dreams of "a harvest of fire" (*kharmanī za-ātash*), the Phoenix lives for the impending flames. To live like the other birds "would be an unnameable pain" (*ranjī buvad k-az ān natavānand nām burd*) more painful than continuing its struggle.

By basing the poem around the death and rebirth myth, Nīmā interrogates the never-ending cycle through his Phoenix's will to break free of continual returns. Solely political readings of Arabic and Persian modernist poetry fail to account for the pessimism that inheres within this use of myths of resurrection and rebirth because they tend to situate modern history within a sequence of dichotomies: first colonialism versus self-determination, and second authoritarianism versus democracy. On the contrary, Arabic and Persian modernist poetries show themselves to have at their core a constitutional ambivalence about the decolonial moment and the rise of the nation state. This ambivalence is embodied in Nīmā's sublation of premodern symbols like the Phoenix, which remains stuck in the cycle of death and rebirth indefinitely in the same way colonial subjects remain subjects precisely because of the trappings of citizenship the nation state hoists upon them.

The predetermined teleology of the Phoenix's lonely life – and, I would also argue, of the atomized citizen whom modernity has uprooted from her traditional roots – is not one of happy, productive progress. Moreover, we cannot reduce the bird's struggle to politics alone. ʿAṭṭār uses the Phoenix's story to admonish his audience about the inevitability of death: "If you were given all the phoenix's years / Still you would have to die when death appears. / For years he sings in solitary pain / And must companionless, unmated, reign; / No children cheer his age and at his death / His ash is scattered by the wind's cold breath."[40] Nīmā uses the Phoenix because, in combination with the metrical innovations he introduces in "*Quqnūs*," it embodies the modernist poet's individual experience.[41] The Phoenix hopes to break free of the cyclical system it is stuck in though its end is already known. Nīmā's continued reliance on and sublation of premodern Arabic prosodic forms represent this conflict in the way his poetry only seems to break away from its precursors while actually remaining closely bound up with them.

The first part of the final stanza reads,

> That mellifluous bird (*ān murgh-i naghz-khᵛān*)
> in that place glorified by fire – (*bar ān makān za ātash-i tajlīl yāftah*)
> now turned into a hell – (*aknūn bih yak jahannam tabdīl yāftah*)
> keeps blinking, its sharp eyes, (*bast-ast dambidam naẓar u mīdahad tikān*)
> darting around, (*chashmān-i tīzbīn*)
> and from over the hill,
> suddenly, it unfurls and flaps its wings
> from the depths of its heart it lets out a cry, burning and bitter,
> its meaning unknown to other passing birds.

Just as Nīmā's Phoenix remains within the thrall of the traditional Phoenix narrative, the "new" poetic forms in "*Quqnūs*" sublate certain features of the premodern poetic foot due to the overwhelming importance of the Arabic *ʿarūḍ* for Nīmā's metrics. The final stanza begins with four tightly knit lines, rhyming ABBA. The "B" lines also include a *radīf* (or 'refrain'), an entire word which follows the rhyme letter.[42] The combination of the *radīf* with a two-letter rhyme (*yāʾ* and *lām*; "*īl*") further ties lines 38 and 39 together. Moreover, Nīmā employs a *tarṣīʿ* (a rhetorical technique somewhat like isocolon)[43] with the words *tajlīl* and *tabdīl*, both nominalizations of Arabic verbs in the same pattern, to accentuate the parallel structure of the lines.

The extended *tarṣīʿ* isocolon of *tajlīl yāftah* and *tabdīl yāftah* limns the transition that occurs between the two lines because of their exactly equivalent metrical weight. Through their metrical and sonic balance, they represent the nexus of the poem and move the scene from the Phoenix's song and preparation for the imminent fire to the immolation. In line 38, though the fire is not yet lit, we learn that the spot the Phoenix is in has been "glorified by fire" already. The Persian past participle *yāftah* indicates that the *tajlīl* (glorifying or exaltation) has happened there before, thus representing the continual repetition of the Phoenix's cycle of life and death. *Tajlīl* also has to do with the Divine, as in the Arabic phrase often said after the name of God, *ʿazza wa-jalla* (the Mighty and

Glorified). The holy fire (*ātash*) of line 38 is doubly antithetical to the hell (*jahannam*) of line 39.[44] In line 38, the fire is a Persian word related to divine glorification; in line 39, the place transforms into a hell with "*jahannam*," an Arabic loan-word. The fires of *ātash* and *jahannam* are further differentiated by their respective functions in Zoroastrianism and Islam, and the poem plays on their contrasting symbolism. Whereas *jahannam*'s fire is an eternal punishment, the Zoroastrian *ātash* purifies with its ashes and is related to the old Iranian divinity Ahura Mazda.[45] The combination of formal parallelism with the rhetorically charged opposition in religious meaning between the lines marks their transitional nature.

Nearing its end, the poem lingers on the miseries forcing the Phoenix toward its death. After years of suffering and pain, it cries out "from the depths of its heart," but the other birds do not understand the meaning of its cry. Considering the metapoetic thrust of the poem introduced in the first stanza's juxtaposition of meter and meaning, the end of the poem continues to elaborate on the conceit of poet-as-phoenix. The poet suffers just like the Phoenix, and the poem itself represents the Phoenix's mournful cry. Again, "*Quqnūs*'s" intertextual connection to ʿAṭṭār's poem brings out the close links between the Phoenix and the poet, who both live on after death in what they create out of their pain: "What other creature can – throughout the earth – / After death takes him, to himself give birth?" ʿAṭṭār sardonically asks.[46]

Modernist Spirits: The Past and the Present in Nīmā's "The Phoenix"

The final stanza of *Quqnūs* brings together a number of other premodern Persian poetic themes beyond its obvious reference to ʿAṭṭār's Phoenix story in yet another demonstration of how Nīmā approaches modernist poetry as craft. The interconnection of heaven and hell in lines 38 and 39 constitutes a subtle reference to the Persian mystical tradition, bringing us back to the beginnings of Islamic mysticism and the story of Ḥallāj. We find faint traces of Ḥallāj's passion[47] in "*Quqnūs*." While Nīmā's innovative development of Arabic prosody functions as the keystone in the modernist edifice he constructs for the poem's form, his subtle gestures to the Sufi tradition situate the poem's content within the broader movements of modernism in the Islamic, and particularly the Arabic-speaking, world.[48]

As the Phoenix prepares for death it sits steadfast on its funeral pyre, looking out at the surrounding birds who do not understand the meaning behind its swan song. The scene indirectly recreates Ḥallāj's execution in

922 CE by the order of the Abbasid Caliphate. The range of connections between Nīmā's Phoenix and Ḥallāj is quite broad, but it will suffice here to mention only a few of the links between the two in order to further elaborate how intertextuality operates in the background of "*Quqnūs*'s" content. First of all, ʿAṭṭār's Phoenix looms large as Nīmā's primary reference, and it was ʿAṭṭār who popularized Ḥallāj in the Sufi tradition when he "included a relatively long biography of [Ḥallāj] at pride of place, the very climax, of his *Taḏkerat al-awliā*ʾ [*Biographies of the Saints*]." Additionally, ʿAṭṭār's account "contains motifs that would become associated closely with Ḥallāj in Persian poetry, such as fearless self-sacrifice, eagerness to ascend the gibbet and die in order to return to God, and celebration at his own bleeding and the approach of death."[49]

Because of these motifs, Ḥallāj also proved a popular figure among the Arab Tammūzī (that is, Adonisian) poets, including Bayātī, Adūnīs, and Ṣalāḥ ʿAbd al-Ṣabūr (d. 1981). "In the Arab lands," Reuven Snir tells us, "in which [Ḥallāj] was less renowned than in those areas influenced by the Persian mystical tradition, he has recently gained fame and recognition, especially among poets who tend to highlight his social message."[50] As an Arabic-speaking native of the Persian Fārs province, Ḥallāj thus moves transnationally through both Arabic and Persian modernism, and many modernists looked to Ḥallāj's ministry and martyrdom for inspiration. For instance, Ḥallāj's suggestion that believers forego the *ḥajj* pilgrimage to Mecca, instead build a Kaaba in their own homes, and then donate the money saved to the poor appealed to their sensibility for social justice, however anachronistic applying the concept to Ḥallāj's life and work might be. Carl Ernst writes that it was in fact Ḥallāj's above suggestion that led to his death sentence under the Abbasid Caliphate, though "the legend of Hallaj has obscured both his life and his death." Ernst goes on to explain that ʿAṭṭār's narration of Ḥallāj's life popularized the story of "his public utterance of the daring statement 'I am the Truth' (*ana al-haqq*), a brazen claim to divinity," which supposedly riled political and religious authorities and resulted in his execution.[51] In any case, Ḥallāj serves as a symbol of revolt against state-sponsored violence across modernist Persian and Arabic poetries. The Abbasid state intended its inscription of violence onto Ḥallāj's body to serve as a warning by making him and his ideas taboo. Legends about him include gruesome recountings of how the Caliphate tortured and dismembered his body: flogging, amputating limbs, crucifying, beheading, and finally burning his corpse to ashes.[52] In the end, however, their plan backfired because memories of Ḥallāj have persisted until today.

In "*Quqnūs,*" Ḥallāj's inversion of Islamic ritual and belief resonates with Nīmā's mixing across boundaries, especially the reversals of heaven and hell in lines 38 and 39, as "Ḥallāj is also renowned for having identified closely with and glorified Satan."[53] The final lines of the poem closely parallel Ḥallāj's execution on the gibbet, the burning of his corpse, and the collection of his ashes, which possessed magical properties.[54] Purification through immolation and unification with the Divine thematically connects ʿAṭṭār's entry on Ḥallāj to the Sufi tradition. The same theme is famously found in the story of the moth and the flame also canonized in ʿAṭṭār's *Manṭiq al-ṭayr.*[55] Annemarie Schimmel gives an account of Ḥallāj's take on the theme.

> Ḥallāj describes the fate of the moth that approaches the flame and eventually gets burned in it, thus realizing the Reality of Realities. He does not want the light or the heat but casts himself into the flame, never to return and never to give any information about the Reality, for he has reached perfection. Whoever has read Persian poetry knows that the poets choose this story of the moth and the candle as one of their favorite allegories to express the fate of the true lover.[56]

Although the story of candle and moth can be traced throughout the mystical poetic tradition in Persian, Schimmel notes that the "classic quotation in the Persian lyric tradition is probably Ḥāfiẓ's verse:

> Fire is not that about whose flame the candle laughs –
> fire is what is thrown into the moth's harvest!"[57]

The Phoenix's dirge in "*Quqnūs*" echoes this line of Ḥāfiẓ, and we can tease out more threads tying Nīmā's poem to the premodern Persian poetic tradition by comparing their vocabulary. Ḥāfiẓ's line is, "*ātash ān nīst kih bar shuʿlah-'i ū khandad shamʿ / ātash ān ast kih dar kharman-i parvānah zadand.*"[58] Retracing our steps to an earlier point in "*Quqnūs,*" we find in lines 30–32, "their dreams / are like a harvest of fire / sparkling in the eye" ("*umīdishān / chūn kharmanī zi ātash / dar chashm mīnamāyad*"). The word "harvest" (*kharman*) recalls Ḥāfiẓ's verses, especially once we consider how the poem continually reaches back to earlier poetry for inspiration. In Ḥāfiẓ's line, the moth's harvest is fire, a metaphor for the mystical annihilation of the self in the Divine. "*Quqnūs*" depends on this same theme. The other birds can but dream about a "harvest of fire / sparkling in the eye." The Phoenix's funeral pyre, around which the other birds have gathered, will eventually burst into flames, and its "harvest of fire" will only be reflected in their eyes.

The poem ends by challenging its audience.

> Then, drunk from its inner pain (*ranj-hā-yi darūnash*),
> [the Phoenix] throws itself on the awesome fire.
> A violent wind blows, and the bird is burned up.
> Ashes of its body it has collected up,[59]
> its chicks take flight from the heart of its ashes.

This image of the Phoenix in flames surrounded by the other onlooking birds indicates yet another shift in the perspective of the poem. While the Phoenix initially bore witness to the poetic past by composing its song from "a thousand different voices," the other birds now stop the flow of their passing lives to observe the Phoenix's end. By turning the other birds into witnesses in these final lines, the poem's conclusion suggests the possibility of their becoming conscious of the Phoenix's "inner pain" (*ranj-hā-yi darūnash*). We might then read the final line as indicating not the rebirth of the Phoenix but rather the transfer of the Phoenix's burdens to the birds in its audience. Again, by paralleling the story of Ḥallāj's matryrdom, "*Quqnūs*" sets itself up to function in the same way that Ḥallāj's willingness to die for his beliefs inspired the generations of followers who kept his story alive. Ḥallāj's well-known phrase summing up his total devotion to God had such a pronounced effect that it even inspired the French orientalist Louis Massignon to embark on his monumental and encyclopedic study of him.[60] The phrase likewise ended up in the title of Reuven Snir's book on ʿAbd al-Wahhāb al-Bayātī.[61] "*Rakʿatān fī al-ʿishq*," responded Ḥallāj when asked why he wiped blood on his face following the amputation of his hands, "*lā yaṣiḥḥ wuḍūʾuhumā illā bi-l-dam.*" ("Two series of prostrations suffice in love, but their ablution must be performed with blood.")[62] The Phoenix's unwavering stare out of the fire parallels Ḥallāj's lack of fear at the moment of his death due to his ultimate faith in his everlasting existence in the Divine.

Metapoetically, the last line might thereby be understood to be gesturing to the reader as witness to the poet's pain just like many of Ḥallāj's disciples witnessed his execution. The reader, then, is left to carry out the project the poem lays the foundation for: a radically open modernity that operates in dialogue with Persian cultural patrimony. Because of its radical openness, this modernity is untethered to any specific teleology of what modernity ought to be and directly opposed to the Pahlavi importation of Western modernity wholesale.

In the end the poet-phoenix's immeasurable pain erupts in his own destruction. "Drunk from its inner pain, / it throws itself on the awesome fire. / A violent wind blows, and the bird is burned up." But in the final two lines, Nīmā breaks away from ʿAṭṭār's version (and other familiar stories of the Phoenix), for usually only a single new Phoenix rises out of the ashes. Instead, in "*Quqnūs*," "[The Phoenix's] *chicks* (*jūjah-hā-sh*) take flight from the heart of its ashes." The difference with ʿAṭṭār's poem is striking, leaving the reader to draw particular conclusions about Nīmā's decision to use a plural. Considering that "*Quqnūs*" comes early in Nīmā's development of metrical form, the final line may represent his hope that other poets might continue the innovations he was making in Persian poetry. The metapoetic thrust of these final lines is primed by the immediately preceding image of the other passing birds turning their full attention to the Phoenix and reflecting its immolation in their eyes. Yet again, the poem collapses categories together in a blatant challenge to administrative modernity, transferring the revolutionary perspective of the Phoenix into the eyes of the other birds, which we might also understand the chicks in the final line to symbolically represent. Their challenge, then, is to succeed where the Phoenix fails: to break out of the cycle's teleological repetition and create something truly new.

As I suggested in the Introduction to this book, we cannot limit our engagement of modernist developments to the ones that led to the rise of modernism in the European literary scene in 1922. That same year was not only when we find Nīmā beginning to explore the possibilities of modernism in *Afsānah*, but it was also the thousand-year anniversary of Ḥallāj's execution. Ḥallāj's reemergence in Persian and Arabic modernist poetry corresponds with an increased interest in him from the West, best represented in the French Orientalist Louis Massignon's *The Passion of al-Hallāj: Mystic and Martyr of Islam*, which also came out in 1922. However, Arab and Iranian modernists like Bayātī, Adūnīs, ʿAbd al-Ṣabūr, and Nīmā used Ḥallāj's story to develop a locally specific modernist myth to their own ends.

Nīmā's Phoenix emerges at a significant node within a transnational network of exchange that retained elements of the Islamic past by sublating them, in stark contrast to the modernization project of the Pahlavi state. Ḥallāj's ghost haunts "The Phoenix" by way of the poem's immediate intertextual reference to ʿAṭṭār. Nīmā's retelling of the Phoenix myth and the bird's immolation on a pyre surrounded by acolytes at the end of the poem parallels ʿAṭṭār's account of Ḥallāj's execution, though Nīmā makes no explicit claim that he is here referencing Ḥallāj's story. Such subtle intertextual engagements of premodern figures like Ḥallāj also shaped the modernist movement in the Arab world and contributed to a network of transnational transaction that existed beyond the bounds of European modernism.

Nīmā's Modernist Poetic Craft as a Technique for Sublation

Nīmā's modernism is directly tied up with the idea of poetry as craft and thus allows us to explore how the modernist poets use the rhetorical and linguistic tools available to them. Because Nīmā frequently takes recourse in the language of building – *sākhtimān, banā, mīsāzam, bunyād,* and so on – we have considered the structural elements of his approach to composing modernist poetry, beginning with his formal basis in premodern Arabic metrics. Nīmā's use of premodern prosodic patterns and his ingenious reformulation of the elements making up the poetic line represent the first instance of transnational movement between the Arabic and Persian modernist traditions, as Persian prosody was (and is still, to a huge extent) anchored in the science of prosody al-Khalīl invented many centuries ago in Basra, Iraq. I turn to the technicalities of Nīmā's metrical innovations during the early years of his modernist experiments to lay the foundation for my later discussion of the persistence of premodern prosodic patterns in both Arabic and Persian modernist poetry. While Nīmā's use of symbolism represents a revolutionary moment in the history of Persian poetry, the changes he brought to prosody ought to be understood not in opposition to earlier verse forms but rather as a technique to sublate the premodern into the modern that parallels the Arab modernists' innovations on premodern Arabic metrics.

Likewise, as far as modernist themes in Nīmā's poetry go, the import of a poem like "The Phoenix" only begins to materialize when the reader attends to the interrelationship of form and content within it. Building on the dissonance of form and content found in the poem's first stanza, Nīmā goes on to present a metrical and symbolic model for modernist Persian poetry in the rest of the poem. Further developing the metapoetic perspective found in his earlier poem "The Swan," where the title swan stands in for the poet, Nīmā puts the Phoenix in place of the poet as well. In addition to the foundational elements of traditional prosody upon which "The Phoenix" relies, the poem's content remains closely linked to the premodern Persian poetic tradition through its intertextual connections to, most directly, ʿAṭṭār's *Conference of the Birds*. Nīmā's near-*muʿāraḍah* contrafaction of ʿAṭṭār's poem begins a series of associations with the mystical tradition of Islam, reaching all the way back to one of its most prominent figures, Ḥallāj, whose traces we find across Arabic and Persian modernist poetry. The movement backwards in time that Nīmā's approach to composing New Poetry suggests provides a solid traditional genealogy for a poetic process often considered to be the result of a complete and total break with the past. The way Nīmā engages with the Islamic and pre-Islamic Iranian past contrasts sharply with contemporaneous Pahlavi cultural projects, which the regime used to create the fabricated nationalist history it employed to fashion its strict concept of modern citizenship.

In conclusion, Nīmā's modernist poetry – which is open to the past and therefore attuned to the realities of history that came before it – is a continuation of a long tradition defined by prolonged interaction between Persian and Arab cultures. The transnational interconnection of Arabic poetry and Persian poetry manifests in Nīmā's continued reliance on the science of Arabic *'arūḍ* and its history of reception in Persian prosody. Nīmā's formal experiments would continue in the work of future poets like Shāmlū and Farrukhzād, whom we will come to in later chapters. Nīmā was willing to engage his poetic predecessors on their own terms and refused to allow his poetry to become subject to the realities of the Pahlavi national project. Rather than bowing to an externally constructed reality, Nīmā offers an alternative, self-reflexive attitude of modernity. Nīmā's engagement of received Arabic prosodic patterns constitutes a significant instance of transnational, lateral exchange taking place beyond the bounds of colonial interference and Western poetic influence. In the end, Nīmā's modernist innovations in Persian poetry retain many elements of a local cultural and poetic heritage that also shape Arabic modernist poetry as part of a significant modernist geography. I have so far situated these shared features of Arabic and Persian modernist poetry under the rubric of a shared transnational unconscious. In the second part of the book, I turn my focus from this transnational unconscious to the early development of a shared transnational consciousness linking the Arab and Iranian modernists together with the budding solidarity movements of the decolonial world.

PART II

Imagining New Worlds

CHAPTER 3

Aḥmad Shāmlū's Manifesto and Proto-Third World Literature

When we think of Persian literature on the world stage, several poets might come to mind: Ḥāfiẓ, Khayyām, perhaps Saʿdī or Firdawsī, and of course Rūmī. These doyens of poetry in the premodern period have been and continue to be translated and discussed across the planet. However, when we turn our attention to the modern era of globalization, we find among scholars of world literature a troubling lack of consideration for Iran's modern poets and what their poetry has to tell us about the planetary courses of modernism and modernity. As a result, premodern Persian literature often comes to stand in for the whole of Persian literary production for many readers. This academic and popular focus on premodern Persian literature in the West makes it difficult for those who may be interested in reading broadly to engage with the modern literature of Iran other than in extremely limited circumstances, such as the modicum of interest paid to the work of last chapter's subject, Nīmā Yūshīj. Of these few instances when Persian literature is even acknowledged, we might also note the handful of courses on modern and premodern Persian literature offered in Western universities or the frequently dubious popular translations of mystical Persian poetry into English available in bookstores and on the internet.

Working against this trend, this chapter introduces proto-Third Worldism as an ideological rubric we might use to carve out a place for modern Persian literature within world literature. Moving from unconscious transnational connections across modernist contexts (like Nīmā's modernist *khayāl* imagination) to conscious transnational and international political alignments, we now turn to the poetic and political development of the Iranian poet Aḥmad Shāmlū from Romanticism to Leftist political commitment early in his career. I take up Shāmlū's 1951 collection *Qaṭʿnāmah* (*The Manifesto*),[1] which has been for the most part ignored in Anglophone criticism, as an example of Persian literature as world literature. Shāmlū's poetry develops as part of what scholars have recently dubbed the "planetary" movement of literature. Although

I depend heavily on the term "transnational" throughout this book, I here again invoke the more open, less-overdetermined "planetary" as Friedman conceives of it. "[*T*]*ransnational* suggests the ongoing tension between nation-states and globalized postnational political formations" to Friedman. "Planetary," however, "echoes the spatial turn in cultural theory of the twenty-first century. It is cosmic and grounded at the same time, indicating a place and time that can be both expansive and local [. . .] . *Planetary* has an open-ended edge that *transnational* and *global* lack."[2] While Shāmlū's poetry has an undeniable planetary dimension in its openness to shared humanity, nature, and time, the political realities it negotiates cannot escape the transnational tensions of the mid-twentieth century.

The Manifesto announces Shāmlū's rebirth into political commitment (*taʿahhud*) following the roundly dismissed and derided juvenilia of his first collection, *Āhang-hā-yi farāmūsh shudah* (*Forgotten Songs*, 1947). *The Manifesto*'s poetic persona suddenly awakens from an earlier Iranian nationalism and, to have Shāmlū himself explain it, the Romanticism that accompanied it, to an acute realization of the poet's place in a nascent revolutionary Third World. The collection constitutes an early instance of transnational solidarity that predates the Afro-Asian Bandung Conference held in Indonesia in 1955 and the Non-Aligned Movement, which began in earnest in 1961.[3] Although Iran was a participant in both, Muḥammad Rizā Shāh's alignment with the neocolonial West contrasts sharply with Shāmlū's poetic vision of solidarity, which nonetheless draws heavily on Western literature – especially, in the case of *The Manifesto*, on the life and work of the Spanish poet Federico García Lorca (1898–1936). By approaching *The Manifesto* as an example of proto-Third World literature, I intend to create a category that can help us form those significant geographies that have remained largely unexplored within the broader category of world literature. This is all the more relevant because Shāmlū's *Manifesto* has until now remained outside the purview of world literature scholars, despite the collection's reflections on what it means to be of and in a globalized world stretching across the planet and bringing far-flung individuals together in an inescapable network of connections driven by capitalism.

What Is Proto-Third Worldism?

I propose the concept of proto-Third Worldism as a theoretical frame for bringing literatures Western academics often think of as minor (i.e. non-Western but also perhaps non-Anglophone literature) into our discussions of world literature.[4] The phrase "proto-Third Worldism" appears in a few places. Zeynep Çelik uses it when discussing Turkish modernist poet Nâzım Hikmet's (d. 1963) position vis-à-vis European imperialism.[5] Daniel Widener employs the term in his discussion of Black internationalism in the context of the Korean War.[6] Patrick Iber brings it up in his analysis of Jorge Amado's (d. 2001) brand of "Communist cultural criticism": "a combination of Latin American nationalism, indigenism, and a kind of Proto-Third Worldism."[7] Still, the concept has remained undertheorized as an analytical tool and an ideological space that writing might occupy. My goal here is to buttress proto-Third Worldism as a theoretical frame for use within the study of world literature through my reading of Shāmlū's *Manifesto*, to move our considerations of modern Persian literature beyond the realm of the national and into the transnational.

The roots of proto-Third Worldism reach down into a literary history existing on the margins of European metropoles. Connections across literary contexts and continents challenge us now in the Western academy, where it seems we cannot forget English (or French, or German, etc.) because the disciplinary boundaries of English departments, naturally, and Comparative Literature departments, unfortunately, and the gatekeeping functions that form them have largely proven too staid to allow for academic engagements of other literatures on their own terms.[8] In casting proto-Third Worldism as a politically conscious literary stance, I draw on Lionnet and Shih's concept of "transnationalism from below."[9] Again, they define "transnationalism from below" in opposition to "transnationalism from above," or "the transnationalism of the multinational corporate sector, of finance capital, of global media, and other elite-controlled macrostructural processes."[10] As I will also suggest in my discussion of Sayyāb's experience with the Iraqi and Iranian Communists in Chapter 4, we may need to tweak this definition of "transnationalism from above" in the case of Soviet Communist imperialism and its top-down approach to local Communist movements in the Third World. In Shāmlū's case, although he expresses his solidarity with Marxist revolutionaries across the planet, he neither toes a specifically Soviet line nor adopts wholesale Communist socialist realism in *The Manifesto*. I therefore look to the way he builds transnational solidarity in his poetry as an instance of "transnationalism from below."

In returning to the literary history of the twentieth century and thinking of poetry in Iran as it relates to an ongoing and interconnected process of social, political, and economic development, I am taking my cue from Aarthi Vadde, who, in *Chimeras of Form*, argues for the simultaneous considerations of internationalism and global consciousness, though these trends are generally associated with either end of the twentieth century. "Rather than assert that globally oriented analytical terms such as *transnationalism*, *cosmopolitanism*, *planetary*, and *world-system* supersede older terms such as *empire*, *anticolonialism*, and *internationalism*," she explains, "I contend that they sublate them – that is, absorb their lessons in the process of claiming to move past them."[11] My first goal in analyzing an example of Third World literature *avant la lettre*, then, is to begin, however modestly, writing a missing chapter in the history of world literature with a view toward the sublation of these earlier terms into new ones. My second, inspired by Karima Laachir, Sara Marzagora, and Francesca Orsini, is to establish modern Iranian literature within a significant modernist geography of decolonization in the Third World. That is, as one of "the wider conceptual, imaginative and real geographies that texts, authors and language communities inhabit, produce and reach out to."[12] So, our first question is how we might conceive of the coalescing Third World as a significant literary geography.

The Third World, the Non-Aligned Movement, the Global South.[13] The terms for "the rest"[14] of the world outside of the West have changed along with the prevailing world order. Following the outset of the Cold War, analysts split the world up into thirds: the First World of capitalism (the developed nations), the Second World of the Communist Bloc, and the Third World (non-aligned, undeveloped nations). As the Cold War heated up, Western powers and the Soviets alike sought to bring developing nations into their spheres of influence, thus providing the impetus for declarations of non-alignment from countries across the Asia, Africa, and South America, beginning in 1961 and continuing until the fall of the Berlin Wall. The terms we use to refer to "the rest" have an historical basis, one which reaches back to the era of colonial domination and yet further. But what possibilities could we open up should we attend to the various sublations of older terms into newer? Vadde suggests that we can better understand the recent past not through "the usual narratives of rupture around 1945 (the end of World War II and the beginning of decolonization) or 1989 (the end of the Cold War) [. . .] ." Rather, Vadde offers as an alternative the possibility of "reenergizing the relationship between early and late twentieth-century thought," which "furnishes contemporary 'globalization talk' with a richer understanding of its own world-making vocabularies."[15] With Vadde's words in mind, I propose creating a literary history that takes into consideration instances of proto-Third Worldism; "proto" not because authors writing in the Third World were unaware of their subordinate position to the Great Powers, but because the term "Third World" had not yet become an organizing principle prior to the Bandung Conference. Yet, as I will show in my readings of Shāmlū's poetry from the time, the poet was already actively engaged in imagining new futures for formerly colonized nations that emerged in the shadow of Cold War internationalism. Adom Getachew has recently addressed this type of activity as "worldmaking," that is, a "reinvented self-determination" that "reach[ed] beyond its association with the nation to insist that the achievement of this ideal required juridical, political, and economic institutions in the international realm that would secure non-domination." Shāmlū's poetic worldmaking, then, might bring us to a new understanding of what the "world" of world literature could be, a creation that, as Getachew puts it, could offer a "global anticolonial counterpoint that would undo the hierarchies that facilitated domination."[16] Finally, I retain the term "Third World" here not as a pejorative (though it certainly has been used as one), but instead to reclaim it as a term for collective solidarity across the Global South, a rubric with which we might imagine a revolutionary significant geography within world literature studies.

I use Shāmlū's work as an exemplary case because of the nascent Third World consciousness that transformed his poetry as the internationally turbulent 1940s rolled into the domestic unrest of the 1950s in Iran. This attitudinal shift occurs partly through an encounter Shāmlū stages between his poetic persona and Lorca's poetry and biography, offering us a remarkable case where a Spanish poet becomes a revolutionary icon in modern Persian poetry. Once Shāmlū's poetic persona learns about the circumstances of Lorca's execution, it gives up the centrality and individuality of the Romantic lyric "I" and devotes itself to a collective "you." I thus position Shāmlū's *Manifesto* within broader transnational trends in the Global South and Third World at the dawn of the Cold War and in the midst of American aggression in Korea (1950–1953). While I account for the indelible mark Lorca's poetry left on Shāmlū's work and acknowledge the relationship between Jean-Paul Sartre's *engagement* and Persian literary political commitment,[17] I also aim to provincialize traditional modernist centers – Paris and London positioned at the heart of empires and at the usual centers of modernist geographies – by reorienting our focus to lateral networks of literary exchange. These East-East or South-South networks often operated beneath the radar of Western metropoles as a Third World consciousness, drastically different from the transnational unconscious that initially generated Arabic and Persian modernist poetries, began to develop and carve out its own significant literary geography, a "*locally* produced" concept of what "world" might mean or be.[18]

Proto-Third Worldism in Aḥmad Shāmlū's *Manifesto*

Let us now turn to Shāmlū's *Manifesto* to see just how it presages the birth of Third Worldist solidarity in literature. The title of the first poem in the collection, "*Tā shikūfah-'i surkh-i yak pīrāhan*" ("Until a Shirt Blossoms Red"), metaphorically evokes the image of blood blossoming across the chest of a bullet victim and subtly alludes to transnational Communist commitment in its flowing red. It begins with a metapoetic reflection on the act of writing politically committed poetry.

Sang mīkasham bar dūsh,
sang-i alfāẓ
sang-i qavāfī rā.
Va az ʿaraqrīzān-i ghurūb, kih shab rā
dar gawd-i tārīkash
        mīkunad bīdār,
va qīrandūd mīshavad rang
dar nābīnāʾī-'i tābūt
va bī-nafas mīmānad āhang
az hirās-i infijār-i sukūt,
man kār mīkunam
        kār mīkunam
                kār
va az sang-i alfāẓ
        bar mīafrāzam
ustuvār
        dīvār
tā bām-i shiʿram rā bar ān naham
tā dar ān binshīnam
dar ān zindānī shavam...

I carry stones on my shoulders,
stones of words,
of rhyme
and from the sweating sunset that awakens
night
        in the pit of its darkness,
and becomes pitch black
in the blindness of a coffin
the song remains breathless
fearing an explosion of silence,
I work
        work
                and work
and from stones of words

I steadily
construct
a wall,
until I build the roof of my poetry over it
until I sit down inside it
and become a prisoner . . .[19]

The poem starts with the persona carrying stones of words and rhymes, the building blocks of a poem, on his shoulders. He not only constructs a poem with them but also the walls that will eventually surround and imprison him. Language becomes not a refuge for the poet, but a prison. By trapping meanings in written or spoken words, poets might even land themselves in a real prison when those words are written or spoken under the watch of an autocratic political regime. The above lines would eventually prove prophetic, as Shāmlū was arrested for his political poetry following the Shah's crackdown on leftists after the 1953 royalist coup d'état against Prime Minister Mosaddegh.

Alongside the revolutionary content of the above lines, Shāmlū extends Nīmā Yūshīj's formal poetic experiments. Where Nīmā changed the standard arrangement of premodern Persian poetic feet upon the page while maintaining their repeated patterns, Shāmlū goes yet further with his "poetic-prose style," in which "line breaks and punctuation are neither predictable nor determined by the accusing expectations of those readers who would dismiss them as non-poetic."[20] "Until a Shirt Blossoms Red" does indeed break with the regular predictability of Nīmā's metrics, instead depending more heavily on the devices of repetition and internal rhyme. *Sang* (rock) appears four times in these lines and rhymes with *rang* (literally meaning color, which I have combined into the word "darkness" in the translation) and *āhang* (song) at the ends of lines seven and nine. The shared rhyme, which appears clearly in the original Persian, spreads across the beginnings and ends of five lines and formally constructs a prison out of rhyming words. I have mirrored this formal feature in my translation with the consonance of "s's" concentrated in the initial lines that gradually fades out into only a few instances of the letter by the end of the section.

Moreover, Shāmlū continues Nīmā's effacement of the lyric "I," which was a significant departure from earlier Persian poetry, especially poetry from the premodern period, and signaled the genesis of modernist Persian poetry. In the foundational modernist poems that we addressed earlier, such as "The Swan" and "The Phoenix," Nīmā introduced the figures of the swan and the Phoenix as stand-ins for the poet's "I" and presented the poems in the third person. As the modernist movement grew and attracted younger poets like Shāmlū, Nīmā further contributed to the displacement of the "I" with 1952's "*Murgh-i amīn*" ("The Amen Bird"), which, as Karimi-Hakkak explains, "features a bird with no known identity in Persian poetry or mythology, either as a real animal or a mythical creature. True to his habit of placing himself in his poems, often through the figure of a bird, Nima may have made up the bird's name by inverting the letters of his own pen name, thus: Nima → Amin." Karimi-Hakkak goes on to add that Nīmā uses the figure of the bird to proclaim a new vision for a happy future to the people (*mardum*) and the masses (*khalq*),[21] highlighting the political stakes at play in poetry at the time in Iran.

While Shāmlū does not replace the lyric "I" with another figure in the poems of *The Manifesto*, he does subordinate it to his audience, a collective *shumā* (you) that parallels the *mardum* or *khalq* in both Nīmā's poem and Communist-inspired poems in other literary traditions.[22] Whereas Nīmā plays on the premodern literary device of the *takhalluṣ* (the incorporation of a pen name into the final lines of a poem) in "The Amen Bird" by rearranging the letters of his pen name, in this collection Shāmlū foregoes centering the "I," thereby signaling his newfound political commitment. We might even consider this shift away from an "I" focused on mystical union with the Divine (as we might find in, for instance, Rūmī's poetry) to one trained in the service of "the masses" as symbolic of an awakening Third-World consciousness. The eventual formation of the Third World inheres within a move toward solidarity across the Global South as but one instance of "how colonialism and de-colonization engendered new significant geographies both in the metropoles and the colonies."[23] In Shāmlū's poetics, as I will show below, the "I" makes space for an emergent collective "you": the toiling masses of what would become the Third World.

This function of the lyric "I" has significant consequences for the political import of Shāmlū's poems as heralds of the Third World's emergence as a category. In the second poem of *The Manifesto*, "Song of a Man Who Killed Himself" ("*Surūd-i mardī kih khudash rā kushtah ast*"), Shāmlū's new political commitment overflows in a violent renunciation of the Romanticism of 1947's *Forgotten Songs*. If we think of "Until a Shirt Blossoms Red" as Shāmlū's declaration of commitment to a collective *shumā* (you), then "Song of a Man Who Killed Himself" represents the poet's following through with his promise, his sacrifice of his first lyric "I" for its betrayals and dedication of his poetry to revolutionary change. This second poem begins,

Nah ābish dādam
nah du'ā'ī khᵛāndam
khanjar bih gulūyash nahādam
va dar iḥtiżārī-'i ṭūlānī
ū rā kushtam

bih ū guftam:
"*– bih zabān-i dushman sukhan mīgū'ī!*"
va ū rā
kushtam!

I gave him no water
I said no prayer
I put a knife to his throat
and in prolonged agony
I killed him.

I told him,
"You speak the enemy's language!"
And I
killed him.[24]

The unnamed "him" (*ū rā*) is the man (*mard*) from the poem's title. In the following stanza, it becomes obvious exactly who this mysterious man speaking the enemy's language is: the speaker from *Forgotten Songs*.

Nām-i marā dāsht
va hīch kas hamchanū bih man nazdīk nabūd,
va marā bīgānah kard
bā shumā
bā shumā kih ḥasrat-i nān
pā mīkūbad dar har rag-i bītābtān

va marā bīgānah kard
bā khᵛīshtanam

He had my name
no one was closer to me than him,
and he alienated me
from you
from you whose yearning for bread
beats in every one of your impatient veins.

He alienated me
from myself[25]

In these lines, the speaker declares his disillusionment with the Romantic lyric "I," which in *Forgotten Songs* alienated the experience of the individual

"I" from that of the collective "you" to whom the now-committed speaker intends to dedicate his life. The Romantic "I" attempts to subsume the experience of the collective within itself, but in doing so it discounts the heterogeneous voices that exist within the collective. The experience of the individual cannot stand in for everyone else's. Shāmlū has the lyric "I" of *Forgotten Songs* speak in "Song of a Man Who Killed Himself" so that the persona's "I" can respond to him.

Bih man guft ū: " – Larzishī bāshīm dar parcham,
parcham-i niẓāmī-hā-yi Urūmiyyah!"
Bidū guftam man: " – Nah!
khanjarī bāshīm
bar ḥanjarahshān!"

"We are but ripples in a flag," he told me,
"the Urmian soldiers' flag."
"No," I replied.
"We are a knife
in their throat!"[26]

The earlier lyric "I's" outburst in these lines could easily be understood as a delayed reaction to Shāmlū's experiences as a young man in Urmia, where he openly opposed the occupying Allied Forces (that is, the Soviets) during World War II.[27] The Romantic "I" takes refuge in the nationalist symbol of a flag waving in the wind, an image the now-committed poet rends to shreds. Shāmlū specifically references the Romantic nationalism found in many of the poems he wrote in *Forgotten Songs*. Two in particular from this first collection of Shāmlū stand out here: "The Anthem of the Parthian Spearmen" ("*Surūd-i nīzahdārān-i 'Pārt'*"), dedicated to the Riżā'ian Youth[28] and "Flag-bearer!" ("*Parchamdār!*"), written to a patriotic soldier led by Brigadier General Zanganah, who resisted the Allies in Urmia toward the end of the war. Consider how these lines from "Flag-bearer!" romanticize death for the nation:

Āhāy, parchamdār! Rafīq-i man! [. . .]
Iftikhār kun, iftikhār . . . tū yak tārīkh chand hazār sālah rā dar dast dārī.
Tū ḥāmil-i parchamī hastī kih mā barā-yi surkhī-'i ān khūn-hā rīkhtah-īm [. . .].[29]

Ahoy, Flag-bearer! My comrade! [. . .]
Be proud, proud . . . you have thousands of years of history in your hands.
You carry a flag whose red we spilled our blood for.[30]

In *The Manifesto*, however, Shāmlū responds to the blind nationalism found in his *Forgotten Songs* with a simple, direct language that calls its reader to social engagement and lashes out against the Romantic lyric "I" who ignores the collective in favor of individual experience and action. With "Song of a Man Who Killed Himself" Shāmlu goes so far as to murder the lyric poet from *Forgotten Songs*. Estranged from his earlier poetry and awakened by his newly found political commitment, Shāmlū rails against his earlier Romantic collection, calling it out by name to bury it in the past with a brutal scene of murder-suicide.

Āhangī-'i farāmūsh shudah rā tanbūshah-'i gulūyash qarqarah kard
va dar iḥtiżārī-'i ṭūlānī
shud sard
va khūnī az gulūyash chakīd
bih zamīn,
yak qaṭrah
hamīn!

Khūn-i āhang-hā-yi farāmūsh shudah
nah khūn-i "Nah!"

He cooed a forgotten song in his windpipe
and in prolonged agony
went cold
and blood dripped from his throat
to the ground,
one drop
and that was it!

The blood of forgotten songs
not the blood of "No!"[31]

Shāmlū, Lorca, and Proto-Third World Solidarity

Continuing on with "Song of a Man Who Killed Himself," the poem's speaker encourages Shāmlū's poetic and political awakening to a budding Third World solidarity movement through an encounter with the work of Lorca.[32] The poem retells the story of the Spanish poet's death at the hands of Franco's fascists at the beginning of the Spanish Civil War (1936–1939), which animated leftists across the planet. Shāmlū writes,

Frānkū rā nishānash dādam
va tābūt-i Lūrkā rā
va khūn-i tantūr-i ū rā bar zakhm-i maydān-i gāv bāzī.
Va ū bih ru'yā-yi khūd shudah būd

va bih āhangī mīkhᵛānad kih dīgar hīchgāh
bih khāṭirah-am bāz nayāmad.
Ān vaqt, nāgahān khāmūsh mānad
chirā kih az bīgānagī-'i ṣadā-yi khūd
kih ṭanīnash bih ṣadā-yi zanjīr-i bardagān mīmānast
bih shakk uftādah būd.
Va man dar sukūt
ū rā kushtam.
Ābish nadādah, du'ā'ī nakhᵛāndah
khanjarī bih gulūyash nahādam
va dar iḥtiżārī-'i ṭūlānī
ū rā kushtam
    – khūdam rā –
va dar āhang-i farāmūsh shudah-ash
kafanash kardam,
dar zīr zamīn-i khāṭirah-am
dafnash kardam.

I showed him Franco,
Lorca's grave,
and the blood of his iodine in the wound from the bullring
He went into his own dream
and sang a song that will no longer
come to my mind.
He went silent suddenly, since
he had fallen into doubt
from the alienation of his own voice
echoing the sounds of slaves' chains.
And I silently
killed him.
I gave no water, said no prayer
I put the knife to his throat
and in drawn out agony
I killed him
    – myself –
and I shrouded him in his forgotten song.
In the basement of my memory,
I buried him.[33]

The poetic persona forces the poet from Shāmlū's *Forgotten Songs* to face the grave consequences of the thinking that shaped his first collection of poems as they contemplate the blood in the bullring. The scene amounts to an admission that Shāmlū's earlier poems evoked nationalism, even jingoism, and bordered on propaganda. In fact, Shāmlū may have been worried that his earliest collection might be read as unabashed support of the Fascist ideology popular in Iran during the late 1940s.[34] In the above lines, Shāmlū has his poetic persona serve as teacher and mentor to his younger, misguided self by forcing him to witness Lorca's death at the hands of reactionary forces.

Lorca, therefore, plays an important part in the revolutionary development of Shāmlū's poetic persona. Shāmlū's engagement with Lorca's poetry has been well-documented, and he eventually produced several translations of Lorca's poetry and dramatic work into Persian – a significant instance of the place of Lorca's work in minor contexts.[35] As the critic Hamid Dabashi argues, Shāmlū's readings of Lorca had a profound impact on his verse as well as modern Persian poetry more broadly, and the transnational movement of Lorca's poetry following Shāmlū's reception of his work is evident in the lines quoted above.[36]

Shāmlū is not the only one who lionized Lorca as a martyr and remembered him as a paragon of the poetry of resistance. While a Westerner like Stephen Spender (d. 1995) could denounce (Western) Communist instrumentalization of Lorca's death as "crude" "atrocity propaganda" – which he did in his repudiation of Communism in *The God That Failed*[37] – poets in the Arab world looked to Lorca for political and poetic inspiration and developed his memory to mythic proportions. Elegies to Lorca appear among the poems of such Arab luminaries as Sayyāb, Bayātī, and Palestine's late poet laureate Maḥmūd Darwīsh (d. 2008).[38] Furthermore, sustained interest in Lorca and his poetry among these poets extends beyond the period during which Shāmlū composed *The Manifesto*. We can therefore follow later poetic invocations of Lorca in the East as but one of many threads connecting a nascent feeling of Third World cohesion extending from before Bandung all the way through official Third World solidarity movements like the Non-Aligned Movement.[39]

Additionally, we would be too hasty to tag Lorca's poetry as distinctly Western. Not only did Lorca draw on poetic influences coming from the margins of Spanish literary production, but he also hailed from a small town outside Granada, in what had been Andalusia. In his poetry, he often referenced the history of Andalusia, which had been a site of cultural exchange between Christians and Muslims for hundreds of years under Islamic rule. Modern Arab poets thus frequently see Lorca as a rebel, revolutionary, and martyr who "express[ed] his deep reverence for the Arabic civilisation which once flourished in Spain."[40] Lorca himself gestured to these connections with Spain's Islamic past in his poetry –

particularly in the Arab-Andalusian inspired *gacelas* (*ghazals*) and *casidas* (*qaṣīdahs*) of his *Tamarit Poems*.[41]

Moreover, Lorca's wide range of influences also extended beyond Granada's Arab past to the Harlem Renaissance in New York, where Lorca visited in 1929–1930, and to the Spanish-American *modernismo* movement of Nicaraguan poet Rubén Darío (d. 1916).[42] Lorca "acknowledged [his] debt to developments in Spanish America," where – like in the Arabic and Persian contexts and despite the rise of the novel as a global form – poetry remained "the dominant literary genre until the 1960s."[43] As for Darío's place in the development of modernism as a broad movement, Alberto Acereda and Rigoberta Guevara argue, "Within the Spanish and Spanish American literary atmosphere of the end of the [nineteenth] century, modernist poetry bloomed in an unmistaken way with the arrival of Darío in Spain. Without him the fullness of literary Modernism would have hardly been as global on both sides of the Atlantic." They go on to add that "in the early works of Federico García Lorca, and in some of his poems recently recovered, Darío's influence is palpable."[44] So it was that Lorca's range of influences, coming from the peripheries of European empire, drew the attention of poets across the Global South, including Aḥmad Shāmlū.

In the particular case of Shāmlū's "Song of a Man Who Killed Himself," the paraphrase of a line from Lorca's "*Llanto por la muerte de Ignacio Sánchez Mejías*" ("Lament for the Death of Ignacio Sánchez Mejías") shows Shāmlū to be attentive to the contemporary reception of Lorca's poetry. When Shāmlū writes, "the blood of his iodine in the wound from the bullring," he sends us back to Lorca's line, "*cuando la plaza se cubrió de yodo*" ("when iodine covered the ring").[45] The paraphrase is an early example of Shāmlū's participation in what Dabashi has recently termed a "transnational revolutionary public sphere" that shaped literature in Iran. "As is perhaps best exemplified by Lorca," Dabashi adds, " [. . .] a defiant combination of lyricism and politics informed the poetics of this global pantheon of iconoclastic poets. In his own Persian poetry, Ahmad Shamlou, the most widely celebrated poet of his time, evocatively represented the universal pantheon, achieving a poetic diction with a cosmic certainty."[46]

To now consider Shāmlū's invocation of Lorca in these lines, the Spanish poet's "Lament" emerged out of a real scene of violent death. Lorca wrote the poem in 1934 following the bloody demise of his friend in the bullring. Scholar of Spanish literature Allen Josephs reports that even before the fight started "Lorca knew intuitively that the matador would be killed. When it proved true he told a friend: 'Ignacio's death is like mine, the trial run for mine.' The matador, he commented, 'did everything he could to escape from his death, but everything he did only helped to tighten the strings of the net.'"[47] Not long after, in 1936, Fascist rebels would assassinate Lorca outside Granada.[48] Shāmlū brings Lorca's biography and poetry to bear on a foreign poetic tradition where he might otherwise have remained unknown. He creates a poetic parallel between Lorca's grief for the death of his friend and his own speaker's coming to terms with a new political commitment by "murdering" his past self.

The scene at Lorca's grave mirrors Shāmlū's real life encounter with Lorca's work and the transformation it caused in his poetry. A moment of reflection sends the poetic persona from *Forgotten Songs* "into his own dream," where he "sang a song that will no longer / come to my mind," that is, the *Forgotten Songs* themselves. After seeing Lorca's grave, Shāmlū's earlier poetic persona "went silent" and "fell into doubt." Unable to continue after being confronted with Lorca's poetry and biography, the old, alienating lyric "I" is killed, transformed, and reborn as the committed persona his readers know him as today.[49]

Shāmlū's intertextual reference to Lorca's poem uses the memory of the poet's death ("I showed him [...] / Lorca's grave") to reveal the folly of *Forgotten Songs*. It is as if Shāmlū calls on his old "I" to admit its complicity in its author's political naïveté to weaken and eventually kill it in favor of a new, politically committed poetic self. The poem of this new "I" thus exposes the violence inherent in Fascism and the *Forgotten Songs*' complicity with said violence due to its nationalist fervor. The poem then brings together Lorca's "Lament" for his friend with his premonition of his own death. Shāmlū's poem does not mention the original's Ignacio Sánchez Mejías, and the reader is therefore left with an image of Lorca being the one who is wounded in the bullring instead of the matador. By describing the wounded poet as well as his grave, Shāmlū's poem gestures also to the ultimate sacrifice its lyric "I" is willing to make in realizing his new political commitment, its readiness to offer itself up to achieve a political goal. Shāmlū's new lyric "I" plays with the intentional fallacy to cast its predecessor as the embodiment of the younger Shāmlū's misguided intentions, a blemish that the now-committed "I" must remove to fully come into its own. We might consider Shāmlū's repudiation of his past lyric "I" here also as his relinquishment of authorial intent and dependence instead on the poem itself as the creator of meaning.[50]

Third World Commitments in *The Manifesto*

Having moved through the transitional moment of self-realization that followed his reception of Lorca's poetry and the circumstances of his death, the speaker in Shāmlū's "Song of a Man Who Killed Himself" admits for the first time that the man he has murdered is an earlier version of himself. "I killed him / – myself – " ("*ū rā kushtam / – khᵛūdam rā*"). With his past self now dead and buried, the speaker announces his rebirth into a new political commitment that extends beyond Iran into what would become the Third World, as I will show later in this section.

Ū murd
murd
murd . . .
Va aknūn
īn manam
parastandah-'i shumā
ay khudāvandān-i asāṭīr-i man!

He is dead
dead
dead . . .
And now
this is me
your worshiper
O Gods of my myths![51]

The speaker turns to the collective "you" (*shumā*), declaring himself to be the "worshiper" (*parastandah*) of *shumā*, whom he further describes as the "Gods of my myths" (*khudāvandān-i asāṭīr-i man*). Instead of declaring allegiance to God, country, or self – a declaration we find in the *Forgotten Songs* and some but not all other Romantic poetry[52] – Shāmlū's lyric "I" now links itself with the collective, the masses to whom it will now attempt to give voice. Sloughing off the dead weight of national myths and Romantic nationalism, the lyric "I" is reborn through and in its newfound political commitment to the subjugated and forgotten.

A refrain rings out in the second half of "Song of a Man Who Killed Himself," "*aknūn īn manam*!" ("Now this is me!"). Nine times the speaker declares his new existence as a committed poet after metaphorically burying Shāmlū's Romantic past and announcing the old poet's death.

Aknūn īn manam
bā gūrī dar zīrzamīn-i khāṭiram
kih ajnabī-'i khᵛīshtanam rā dar ān bih khāk sipurdah-am

dar tābūt-i āhang-hā-yi farāmūsh shudah-ash . . .
ajnabī-'i khᵛīshtanī kih
man khanjar bih gulūyash nahādah-am
va ū rā kushtah-am dar iḥtiżārī-'i ṭūlānī,
va dar ān hangām
nah ābish dādah-am
nah du'ā'ī khᵛāndah-am!

Aknūn
īn
manam!

Now this is me
with a grave of the basement of my memory
Whose foreign self I have buried in the earth there
in the coffin of forgotten songs . . .
A foreign self whose
neck I have put a knife to
and have killed in drawn out agony,
and at the same time
I have given him no water
and I have said no prayer!

Now
this
is me![53]

In the final section of the poem, the verb tense used in the initial stanza changes to represent the speaker's rebirth. When the poem opens, the verbs are in the simple past: "*nah ābish* dādam" ("I *gave* him no water"), but now as the poem ends the speaker uses the *māżī-'i naqlī* (relational past), which roughly corresponds to the English present perfect. However, the relational past in Persian has a number of uses not found in the present perfect. For example, "[w]hen historical truths are felt to be of *special relevance* to the present, or to *transcend the past*, they are couched in this tense."[54] Reborn in commitment to *shumā* (you) rather than *khᵛīshtan* (the self), the speaker employs the relational past to indicate the continued relevance of killing his own poetic past along with his previously uncommitted poetic self in the present moment, from which point he will devote himself to others. Although the translation of these verbs into the present perfect tense makes for clumsy English, there is no other way to indicate how, for instance, the relational past tense of "*nahādah-am*" ("I *have put*") chronologically extends the import of the speaker's murder-suicide. "I *have put* a knife," "I *have killed*,"

"I *have given* no water," and "I *have said* no prayer" convert the simple past tense of the earlier verses into a past that still resonates in the present.

Moreover, the words repeated throughout the poem, "now this is me," flank the final stanza, affirming the speaker's newfound identity. The speaker declares his rebirth, "Now this is me / in the grave of the basement of my memory / Whose foreign self I have buried in the earth there / in the coffin of forgotten songs . . . ." The speaker looks back on his past in Shāmlū's Romantic collection of *Forgotten Songs* and remembers in vivid detail how he "killed" his previous poetic identity.

In the process of burying his old poetic self along with the *Forgotten Songs*, Shāmlū metapoetically recreates himself in the pages of *The Manifesto* as an engaged revolutionary poet ready to sacrifice himself to obtain justice for a collective "You." His paratextual comments on *The Manifesto* provide yet more evidence to help us understand his view of the collection's place in relation to his earlier poetry. He writes that its first two poems, "Until a Shirt Blossoms Red" and "Song of a Man Who Killed Himself," are the "direct result of the regret and spiritual pain I felt after the childish mistake I made publishing a handful of weak poems and worthless fragments in a book called *Forgotten Songs*."[55] By killing off his previous poetic persona and burying him along with the *Forgotten Songs*, Shāmlū is born again in *The Manifesto* as the politically committed poet his readers are familiar with. Indeed, Shāmlū's awakening in this collection would continue throughout his poetic career, during which he often "underlined his continued loyalty to the perception of poetry as a tool for political activism and social reform."[56]

While the first two poems of *The Manifesto* announce the poetic persona's devotion to social justice for his own people, the third poem, "*Surūd-i buzurg*" ("The Grand Anthem"), contains the most explicit example of proto-Third Worldism in the collection, reaching beyond the borders of Iran to address a soldier in Korea. Shāmlū dedicates the poem to one Shen-Cho, "an unknown Korean comrade."[57] Written on July 6, 1951, the poem addresses Shen-Cho as the speaker's *barādarak* (little brother) who is fighting against the United States and United Kingdom in the Korean War. Although calling his addressee "little brother" may at first seem patronizing, it quickly becomes clear that the poetic persona only intends affection. In fact, although the poem begins by immediately calling out to Shen-Cho, the speaker (that is, the lyric "I") waits to introduce itself until the eighth line, and then only as an enclitic pronoun: "*am*":

Shin-chū!
Kujāst jang?
Dar khānah-'i tū
dar Kurah
dar Āsiyā-yi dūr?
Ammā tū
Shin
barādarak-i zardpūstam![58]
Hargiz judā madān
zān kulbah-'i ḥaṣīr-i sifālīn-i bām
bām u sarā-yi man.
Paydāst
Shin
kih dushman-i tū dushman-i man ast
vān ajnabī kih khūrdan-i khūn-i tū rāst mast
az khūn-i tīrah-'i pisarān-i man
bārī
bih mayl-i khᵛīsh
nashūyad dast!

Shen-Cho!
Where's the war?
Is it in your house
in Korea
in far-off Asia?
As for you
Shen
my little Asian brother!
Don't ever think that
your clay-roofed straw hut is different from
my own roof and palace.
It's clear
Shen
that your enemy is my enemy,
and that foreigner who gets drunk from drinking your blood
will never
let go of
my sons' dark blood
on his own![59]

The poem begins with a direct address to Shen-Cho, followed by a series of questions and commands. The lyric "I" may be speaking here, but all we find are lines directed at Shen-Cho, "you." Here, Shen-Cho's individual "you" (*tū*) replaces the collective *shumā* of the previous poems, yet this singular "you" continues to serve a similar function. The lyric "I" praises

Shen-Cho's "you" for fighting imperialism in Korea, and even suggests that it is there with him in "your clay-roofed straw hut" resisting the same enemy. As the poem progresses, the speaker continues exhorting Shen-Cho to fight imperialism. In the final stanza, the speaker encourages him to sing an anthem for the victims of Fascism, connecting Nazi atrocities with the contemporary experience of war in Korea.

Shin-chū
bi-khᵛān!
Bi-khᵛān!
Āvāz-i ān buzurg dilīrān
āvāz-i kār-hā-yi marbūṭ bā bashar, makhṣūṣ bā bashar
āvāz-i ṣulḥ rā
āvāz-i dūstān-i farāvān-i gumshudah
āvāz-hā-yi fāji'ah-'i Bilzin va Dakhāū
āvāz-hā-yi fāji'ah-'i Vīyūn
āvāz-hā-yi fāji'ah-'i Mūn Vālih-rayīn
āvāz-i maghz-hā kih Ādūlf Hītlir
bar mār-hā-yi shānah-'i fāshīsm mī-nahād,
āvāz-i nīrū-yi bashar-i pāsdār-i sūlḥ
kaz maghz-hā-yi sar-kash-i Dāwnīng Istrīt
ḥalvā-yi marg-i bardah-furūshān-i qarn-i mā
āmādah mī-kunand
āvāz-i ḥarf-i ākhir rā
nādīdah dūstam
Shin-Chū
bi-khᵛān
barādarak-i zardpūstam!

Shen-Cho
sing!
Sing!
The song of those heroes
the song of weighty deeds
the song of deeds connected to mankind, particular to mankind
the song of peace
the song of all those friends lost
the songs of the Belsen tragedy, and Dachau[60]
the songs of the Haute-Vienne tragedy[61]
the songs of the Mont-Valérian tragedy[62]
the song of the brains that Adolf Hitler
gave to the snakes of Fascism's shoulders
the song of the peacekeeping force of humanity
who are serving
the rebellious brains of Downing Street

as sweets at a funeral for the slave-traders of our century
the song of the last word
                my unseen friend
Shen-Cho
        sing
                my Asian brother![63]

As the poem comes to its end, the speaker employs an extended anaphora with the repetition of "song" or "songs" at the beginning of eleven lines, within which he makes three references to Nazi ethnic cleansing and violence in Europe. In a nod to ancient Iranian mythology, the poem also uses the story of Żaḥḥāk as a corollary for Hitler's murderous policies.[64] Żaḥḥāk, a notorious villain in Zoroastrian literature whom we also find in Firdawsī's *Shāhnāmah* (*The Book of Kings*, completed in 1010), was cursed with two snakes growing out of his shoulders. He had to feed the snakes human brains daily, otherwise they would feast upon his own.[65] The poem not only makes these references to reflect upon the terrible events of World War II but also draws a connection between the brutality and carnage of Hitler's Germany and the war that had recently begun in Korea. There, the British (represented in the poem by Downing Street) joined the United States, Canada, Australia, and several other countries against North Korea, China, and the Soviets. The final lines imagine a North Korean victory against this US-led coalition, whom the speaker derides as "the slave-traders of our century."

Continuing the collection's focus on Communist resistance against imperialism, the fourth and final poem, "*Qaṣīdah barā-yi insān-i māh-i Bahman*" ("Ode for the Man of the Month of Bahman"), celebrates the memory of Taqī Arānī (d. 1940), a member of the group of fifty-three Communists arrested by Reza Shah Pahlavi's government in 1937.[66] The government murdered Arānī in prison, and Shāmlū's poem presents his bodily sacrifice as a revolutionary gate for future freedom fighters to pass through.

Va sūrākh-i har gulūlah bar har paykar
darvāzah'īst kih sih nafar ṣad nafar hazār nafar
                kih sīṣad hazār nafar
az ān mīguẕarand
rū bih burj-i zumurrud-i fardā

And each bullet hole in each body
is a gate which three people, a hundred people, a thousand people
                which three hundred thousand people
pass through
going to the emerald tower of tomorrow.[67]

In this fourth poem, the lyric "I" again recedes into the background as it praises Arānī's heroism, appearing only once throughout the entire poem. The poem links the holes in Arānī's body to the people his sacrifice will eventually free through the repeated rhyme of *paykar* (body) and *nafar* (literally a "person" or an "individual"), which appears four times in ever-growing number: "three people, a hundred people, a thousand people / [. . .] three hundred thousand people."

Shāmlū's *Manifesto*, Proto-Third Worldism, and World Literature

In sum, *The Manifesto* marks a distinct moment both in Shāmlū's poetic career and in the history of modernist Persian poetry. Having encountered the scene of Lorca's execution and witnessing the continued depredations and deprivations of formerly colonized and decolonizing countries throughout what would soon become the Third World, Shāmlū transformed his poetic persona. He directed both toward the realization of social justice in lieu of what he himself called the "mistake" of his Romanticism in *Forgotten Songs*. Shāmlū wrote poetry for the rest of his life following *The Manifesto*, finally devoting himself to a multi-volume investigation of the Persian language as used among the masses, *Kitāb-i kūchah* (*The Book of the Alley*).[68] While his magnum opus may reflect a redirection of focus inward to Iranian society, Shāmlū kept working to bring foreign voices into modern Persian literature following his political awakening. Other than Lorca, Shāmlū also translated into Persian Mikhail Sholokhov's (d. 1984) *And Quiet Flows the Don* (working from the French translation)[69] as well as a selection of many poems by Langston Hughes (d. 1967),[70] along with many others.[71]

Many of these translation choices show Shāmlū's motivation to bring the work of figures central to anti-imperial resistance to Iranian readers, despite the waning of his explicit Communist affiliation after he was thrown in prison following the 1953 coup.[72] By that point, too, international politics were shifting in the aftermath of the Korean War as it became apparent that the United States and the Soviets were each prepared to militarily intervene to both defend and extend their respective spheres of influence. Not long after, the Bandung Conference brought together the nations of the Third World, which sought to find their own way within the geopolitics of the Cold War.

The features of proto-Third World literature – notions of transnational solidarity, nascent political commitment, and a focus on current events taking place across the globe – carried over into the literature of the Third

World, and indeed we can trace these through to Fredric Jameson's thoughts on national allegory and Third World literature.[73] However, as I have made a point to avoid doing throughout this chapter, we should not anachronistically declare writers as representatives of Third World literature when discussing an historical period during which the category did not yet exist. Hence, my suggestion of *proto*-Third Worldism as a rubric for literary works expressing a will toward transnational solidarity among colonized and decolonizing nations prior to the coining of the term "Third World" and before the self-organizing of many of these same nations at Bandung.

Shāmlū's *Manifesto* came out only a few years before Bandung, but the poet was already at pains to present his readers with a robust Third World solidarity pitted against the neo-imperialism of the Cold War. The collection is a prime example of political commitment in literature, announcing as much in its title, which might remind us of Marx and Engels's 1848 *Manifesto of the Communist Party*. Yet however much the poetic persona of *The Manifesto* might stress his support for Communist revolutionaries, the poems themselves resist the strictures of socialist realism.[74] Instead, Shāmlū's verses tell the story of the poet's own political awakening through a rich combination of Persian modernist style (irregular rhymes and metrical patterns) and intertextual references to both foreign and Iranian literature: Firdawsī's *Shāhnāmah*, Lorca's "Lament for the Death of Ignacio Sánchez Mejías," and Shāmlū's own first collection *Forgotten Songs*. In announcing his political rebirth in *The Manifesto*, Shāmlū puts his lyric "I" in the service of his audience, whom he invites to consider the growing forces united against Western imperialism inside Iran and across the globe, and in Korea in particular.

In Chapter 4, we will continue mapping out the various networks that shaped modernist poetry during the middle of the twentieth century. Turning to the famed Iraqi poet Badr Shākir al-Sayyāb, we will compare his conversion from Communism to Western Liberalism in the aftermath of the 1953 coup, which he saw with his own eyes in Iran. The Iranian Left never recovered from the shock of the coup against Mosaddegh, but Shāmlū remained committed to a progressive, transnational platform focused on achieving social justice through his career. Sayyāb's opposite trajectory set him at odds with committed Leftists in Iraq and abroad and aligned him with Western Communist turncoats like Stephen Spender and Ignazio Silone (d. 1978). While Shāmlū's individual political convictions may have been shaken by the coup, they did not break. Still, the coup marks a watershed moment in Iranian political life. Furthermore, the same year also saw the spread of disillusionment among Communists and fellow travelers all over the world following revelations about the realities of Stalin's totalitarian rule after his death on March 5, 1953. These events contributed to an urgent need for the alternative political alliances that coalesced in the Bandung Conference and the subsequent establishment of the Non-Aligned Movement.

To conclude our analysis of Shāmlū's place within the modernist geographies we have been imagining so far, his works and others by writers and translators from what would later become the Third World present us with a different type of world literature, one driven not by canon, prestige, or economic power but rather by a will for solidarity and resistance against the military and industrial might of the West. This literature emerges from a significant Third World literary geography that challenges both the actual world order during the twentieth century as well as the concept of world literature itself. Thus, formulating the category of proto-Third World literature pushes us to recognize a more capacious world literature, one that engages works openly antagonistic to its current composition: the untranslated, uncanonized, parochial, or provincial literature that looks outside the West for its readers and critiques the development of global capital from their perspective. By recognizing literary networks that operate outside those driven by the Western imagination we can create new ways to conceive of what a yet worldlier literature might be.

CHAPTER 4

Badr Shākir al-Sayyāb between Communism and World Literature

Peace to the whole wide world
        Peace to the Ganges, overflowing with blessings

Peace to China, the farmers,
        And tanned fishermen,
The blood of revolutionaries planted in the ground,
        Shining from the red flag

Peace to the whole wide world
        To East and West alike,
Peace to Avon, which filled the veins
        Of Shakespeare, the flowers, and the waterwheel

Peace to the Paris of Robespierre,
        Éluard and the dreaming forest.

To Tunisia, where a shadow circles a burning flame,
        And around bloodied Rabat, there is a roar.

Glory is yours, O Asia!
        Peace to Venice and the Carnival.[1]

In the early 1950s, the Iraqi poet Badr Shākir al-Sayyāb found himself torn between his commitment to internationalist Communism and his growing devotion to Pan-Arabism and Iraqi nationalism. The turbulent politics of a decolonizing region and the 1953 coup d'état to return the Shah to power in Iran forced Sayyāb to grapple with a political consciousness suspending him between membership in the Iraqi Communist Party (ICP) and a developing Iraqi patriotism. We find a point of rupture in Sayyāb's poetry during this period. In this chapter, I take up the divergent roles of the local and the global in Sayyāb's 1954 long poem "*al-Asliḥah wa-l-aṭfāl*" ("Weapons and Children"). This poem marks a transitional point between Sayyāb's involvement with the Communists and their local Iraqi affiliate organization, the *Anṣār al-salām* (The Peace Partisans). The Partisans were a transnational pacifist group connected to the Soviet-backed "Ban the

Bomb" movement that began in March 1950 with the Stockholm Appeal to ban nuclear weapons, and the local branch of the Partisans played a significant role in Iraqi politics throughout the 1950s. As a young Communist, Sayyāb wrote poetry in support of the Partisans' global pacifist agenda, and the above lines from "Weapons and Children" evince his poetics of worldwide pacifism.[2] Their calls for peace in areas as geographically and historically dispersed as Shakespeare's Avon, Robespierre's Paris, Tunisia, Venice, and China render the global imaginary of Communist internationalism in meter and rhyme.

Yet the above lines only show us the global side of "Weapons and Children." In my reading of the poem, I reveal how its setting in the Iraqi countryside produces an internal tension with its broad vision for an international, Communist, peaceful future. The poem's reliance on Iraqi-specific language, imagery, and symbolism – the waterwheel (*nāʿūrah*), the marsh Arabs' *muḍīf* dwellings made of *qaṣab* reeds, and ancient Mesopotamian mythology – celebrates the local as much as it glorifies the global, the national as much as the international, with its glocality. This tension between local and global betrays inklings of the exclusionary, Arab-chauvinist *qawmī* (i.e., pan-Arab) nationalism that Sayyāb would come to outwardly support later in his career after aligning himself with a politics informed by Western Liberalism.[3] Below, I investigate the relationship of these two opposing positions in "Weapons and Children" as well as in a 1959 series of articles titled *Kuntu shuyūʿiyyan* (*I Was a Communist*) that Sayyāb wrote for the Iraqi newspaper *al-Ḥurriyyah* (*Freedom*) and an infamous 1961 speech on literary commitment that he gave at a conference on contemporary Arabic literature in Rome.

Furthermore, I address how Sayyāb's experience with the Communists of Iran's Tudeh Party in the lead up to the 1953 coup caused him to lose faith in the movement and eventually become a virulent Iraqi nationalist. The Soviets' tepid response to the coup in Iran – a blatant ploy engineered by neoimperial Western powers to retain their sphere of influence – amounted to a betrayal of their anti-colonial rhetoric in support of national liberation. The Iranian Tudeh's failure to respond offers an important case from which to further develop current modes of transnational analysis. We might at this point recall *Minor Transnationalism*, where Lionnet and Shih address two opposed modes of transnationalism: "from above" and "from below." "Transnationalism from above" occurs when, for instance, global finance capital moves across national borders to reconstruct localities in accordance with the needs of the market. "Transnationalism from below," on the other hand, emerges from the actions of "nonelites" who "refuse assimilation to one given nation-state."[4] While Sayyāb's experience of Communism as a youth in Iraq fits squarely within the category of transnationalism from below (because local Iraqi Communism traced its own courses outside the direct influence of the Soviet Union), the Communism he saw at work in Tehran during the coup would be better understood as an alternative type of transnationalism from above, with local interests ignored in deference to the larger project of Soviet-centered leadership within the global Communist movement.

This chapter addresses the tension between these different transnational formations to understand Sayyāb's changing views of literary commitment from his time as a young Party member in Iraq until his ultimate break with the Communists after the coup in Iran. "Weapons and Children," which Sayyāb wrote in 1953 and published in 1954, will help us in our examination of the poet's struggle to reconcile his Communist commitment with the clear influence Western literature had on his poetry. We will also see how his comrades' rejection of his abiding interest in Western authors like William Shakespeare, T. S. Eliot, and D. H. Lawrence contributed to his disillusionment with the Party. In my treatment of the 1953 coup, I show how Sayyāb's turn away from Communism only accelerated after he witnessed what he saw as the Tudeh's betrayal of local Iranian interests in deference to the needs of the Soviet Union. In the end, we will see how a Soviet version of transnationalism from above caused Sayyāb to abandon Communism in favor of an uncompromising Iraqi nationalism.

Sayyāb and the Communists

Sayyāb started on the path to Communism while growing up in Jaykūr, a small village in southern Iraq. Jaykūr lies on the banks of Buwayb, a tributary of the Shaṭṭ al-ʿArab river which divides Iraq and Iran. The closest Iraqi city to Jaykūr, roughly twenty miles to the northwest, is Basra, and the Iranian city Khurramshahr (al-Muḥammarah in Arabic) lies to the east. Sayyāb first learned about Communism in Jaykūr, where Communist activity ranged from holding small weekly gatherings to using Sayyāb's hometown and other small villages in the area of Abū al-Khaṣīb to the east of Basra as staging grounds for cross-border missions to Iran.[5] The porous border between Iraq and Iran near his hometown would later play an important part in his decision to return there when his political activism brought him to the attention of the Iraqi authorities.

Sayyāb officially joined the ICP while he was a student at the Baghdad Teachers College in 1945.[6] He later took part in many popular demonstrations that brought together his Communist and Iraqi nationalist sympathies, including January 1948's *Wathbah* ("the Leap"; a revolt against continued British influence in Iraq after the signing of the Portsmouth Treaty on January 15, 1948) and the *Intifāḍah* (the "shaking off" of British influence in Iraqi politics) that stretched across the latter half of 1952 and came to a head with widespread demonstrations in Baghdad on November 22–23 of the same year. For his participation in the *Wathbah* and his affiliation with the ICP, Sayyāb lost his first teaching job in al-Ramādī.[7] He worked there only four months (September 1948–January 1949) before the government imprisoned him until April 1949.[8] These were only the first in a series of indignities Sayyāb would suffer due to his Communist beliefs as he continually struggled to find gainful employment throughout his life after being blacklisted by the Iraqi government.

Yet even when Sayyāb was a card-carrying member of the Party, he refused to bow to the demands of Communist literary critics. In *I Was a Communist*, Sayyāb derides the Communists' dismissal of the poets who so profoundly influenced his own work, including Eliot, Shakespeare, and even the Arab poet al-Mutanabbī (d. 965 CE) as "feudal," "reactionary," and "bourgeois."[9] He gives a particularly absurd example of an Iraqi Communist's ahistorical reading of Mutanabbī in the speech he made at the 1961 Rome Conference on Modern Arabic Literature.[10] This conference, attended by the Western ex-Communists Stephen Spender and Ignazio Silone as well as quite a few luminaries of modern Arabic literature like Jabrā Ibrāhīm Jabrā (d. 1994), Adūnīs, Salmā al-Khaḍrā' al-Jayyūsī, 'Ā'ishah 'Abd al-Raḥmān (Bint al-Shāṭi'; d. 1998), and Maḥmūd al-Masʿadī, among others, was organized by the Congress for Cultural Freedom (CCF), an anti-Communist organization surreptitiously funded by the United States Central Intelligence Agency and meant to promote the tenets of Western Liberalism.[11] Here is what Sayyāb had to say about the Communists in Rome:

> One Iraqi Communist wrote an article on Mutanabbī and his poem about Bawwān Valley [near Shiraz in Iran], using the following line as a starting point:
>
> In Bawwān Valley my horse asked,
> "Shall we leave this life of ease for battle?"
>
> He concluded from this that Mutanabbī was in favor of war while his horse supported peace. Despite the fact that I was a Communist at the time, I commented on his article, saying that Mutanabbī's horse must have signed the Stockholm Appeal with its hoof.[12]

Sayyāb was further incensed by another Iraqi Communist who "described Shakespeare as a 'reactionary, feudalist poet' who only talked about kings, princes, and pimps and never workers and peasants." Sayyāb responded by asking how Shakespeare had the option to be a Communist since Marx had not even been born yet. He then wonders to himself, "Why should we blame this Iraqi Communist for such a position when *The Daily Worker* – the newspaper of the British Communist Party – has taken the same position on Shakespeare, attacking him because he did not express the interests and hopes of the proletariat?"[13]

Sayyāb's literary tastes were not limited to the socialist realism the Iraqi Communists championed. In his Rome talk, he argues,

> I would not be going too far if I were to say that modern European civilization has faced no deeper or more violent ridicule than that of T. S. Eliot in his poem *The Waste Land*, not in everything Communist writers and poets have written against capitalism's role in said civilization. [. . .] Everything the Communist poets have said against capitalism pales in comparison to *The Waste Land*, despite how much hate and revulsion they have expressed about capitalism.[14]

Even while Sayyāb was an avowed Communist he appreciated Western poets like Shakespeare and Eliot from an historical perspective based more on aesthetics than politics. However, the rural, local, communal models of Communism toward which he was inclined as a youth gradually came into conflict with the internationalist Communism he confronted later in life. Likewise, the more familiarity he gained with the foundational works of Western modernism, the less capable he felt of adhering to the Party's strict, at times dismissive and ahistorical, aesthetic line.

We must remember that Sayyāb wrote the articles included in *I Was a Communist* after his turn away from Communism, but it is nonetheless worth considering how the Party is intimately bound up with his recollections of childhood and adolescence in Jaykūr. As Sayyāb explains, his hometown's impoverished and marginalized socio-economic situation as a forgotten backwater played an important part in his early profession of Communist beliefs. While his family was not nearly as well off as those of his later intellectual coterie in Baghdad, their small landholdings provided his grandfather with the resources to hire laborers. One of the anecdotes in Sayyāb's memoir that takes place at his grandfather's house dramatizes his early Communist-inspired idealism.

> My grandfather had one peasant named Maḥmūd Ṭayyārah who had been living on his plot of land for only a few months, and when he left, he took

> the shovels, sieves, and other tools with him. Anyone would recognize it as theft and robbery. My grandfather found out about it and sent someone to bring Maḥmūd Ṭayyārah to him. At the time, I had been suspended from the Baghdad Teachers College.[15] It being around sunset on a winter night, I was sitting by the fireplace in the reception room reading *The Mother* by Maxim Gorky, and the novel had stirred up my feelings. When my grandfather confronted Maḥmūd, he asked him about the shovels, sieves, and the rest of the tools. "They are not your shovels and sieves," the peasant audaciously replied, "they are mine, the peasant's!"
>
> My grandfather, who was a strong man, launched at the peasant, flung him down on a wooden bed, and started beating him with a cane. Do you know what I did? I intervened and separated the two of them. I was able to get the cane away from my grandfather, so I put it in the peasant's hand. Then I took his hand in mine, and – since he would never dare to do it himself – I started beating my grandfather over the head with the cane.

I thought what I had done was the most heroic thing ever, a victory for the toiling peasant over the hateful feudal lord – even if the peasant was a thief! In sum, these are what Communist morals are like wherever they may be, not just in Iraq.[16]

While Sayyāb's break with Communism colors his presentation of this recollection, it still gives us a clear instance of his acknowledgement of the role foreign literature – not doctrinaire Marxist texts – played in his political development. Rossen Djagalov points out the important place of literature such as Gorky's *The Mother* in Soviet socialist internationalism during the middle of the twentieth century.[17] In Iraq, *The Mother* (which was serialized in English translation in 1906 and in Russian in 1907) was popular among the Communists, and Sayyāb elsewhere mentions that it was even read in Arabic translation (undertaken in 1934) at local Communist meetings.[18] In his own case, the book so "stirred" him that he was driven to violently break his filiative ties with his grandfather and physically align himself with the peasant, hand in hand united against "the hateful feudal lord."

The late 1940s and early 1950s were a busy time not only for Sayyāb's development as a Communist, but also for his poetry writing. After his pioneering reconfigurations of premodern Arabic poetic forms in the late 1940s, when he first started experimenting with forms based on the poetic foot rather than the line in shorter poems, he began exploring the possibilities such a formal approach offered for long poems. One of these, the 422-line "Weapons and Children," he wrote as his political interests began to shift from global, international Communist calls for peace to local Iraqi nationalism.

"Weapons and Children" between Local Form and World Literature

Representative of a transitional period in Sayyāb's poetic career, "Weapons and Children" combines elements of purely Communist commitment with nuanced poetic imagery that challenges the poem's explicit political stance. Sayyāb draws on the work of Western poets throughout the poem, defying categorization within the Communist-backed literary mode of socialist realism and suspending the poem between local Arab and Iraqi forms and themes and globally circulating world literature such as the plays of Shakespeare and story of Sindbad from *The Arabian Nights*. As we will see, the poem reaches out to and resists a number of significant geographies in its engagement of the Western literary tradition, continued reliance on local Arabic poetic form, and ambivalence about the internationalist Soviet project and the rise of Iraqi nationalism.

"Weapons and Children" was initially published in a chapbook (*kurrās mustaqill*) in 1954, but Sayyāb wrote it in 1953. At first blush, the poem seems to fit the standard for committed poetry, which had taken off in the Arab world following the 1948 disaster in Palestine. However, the poem struggles to balance its speaker's conflicting commitments to the transnational pacifist movement on the one hand with his Iraqi nationalism on the other. The speaker of the poem oscillates between a transnationally inflected Communist perspective on the world, where the Soviet Union and postcolonial nations are pitted against an aggressive, capitalist West, and a local, rural, and Iraqi frame of reference, focused on a nameless village on the Shaṭṭ al-ʿArab. The main target of the poem – whether we read it as an example of Communist commitment or Iraqi nationalism – is a merchant who stands in for both global capitalism and Western colonial regimes.

The poem narrates a few interwoven stories, each of them punctuated with the merchant's incessant calls for *ḥadīd* (iron) and *raṣāṣ* (lead or bullets), which he buys up to resell to the warmongers of the world. The merchant's cry structures the shape of the poem as these two words match the constituent foot of its meter, the *mutaqārib* (tripping). In its perfect form, the *mutaqārib* consists of eight repetitions of the poetic foot *faʿūlun* (˘ ¯ ¯), four to each hemistich.[19] In keeping with Arabic modernist techniques, Sayyāb varies the number of feet per line in this poem from one to four. The merchant's cries for *ḥadīd* and *raṣāṣ* both have a metrical value that exactly matches the basic foot of the poem's meter, a short followed by two longs.[20] The repetition of these words ties the poem together formally and thematically. The metrical link between the words in the merchant's cry and the poem's meter sonically represents how capitalism's omnipresence forms the rhythm of modern life.

Thematically, "Weapons and Children" deftly incorporates ouroboric Mesopotamian myths of death and rebirth. These same myths laid the groundwork of earlier Western modernist poems, like Eliot's *The Waste Land*, which in turn inspired Sayyāb's own integration of mythic themes into his poetry. I say inspired rather than influenced here because Sayyāb was careful about how he used references to Western literature in his poetry. In fact, when discussing his reading of Eliot's essay "Tradition and the Individual Talent" in a letter to Yūsuf al-Khāl (d. 1987), editor of the Lebanese poetry magazine *Shiʿr*, Sayyāb argues that Arabic poetry "must not be some kind of Western monstrosity in Arab or semi-Arab garb. We must make use of the best there is in our poetic heritage at the same time we make use of what the Westerners have perfected – especially by those who speak English – in the world of poetry."[21] Sayyāb's knowledge of Western modernist poetry developed over a period of many years, and he worked diligently to create a new poetics through his engagements of both Western poetry and the Arabic tradition.[22] Sayyāb came to myths of death and rebirth through his readings of Eliot, and his understanding of these myths was mediated by *The Waste Land* until at least 1954, when he read Jabrā Ibrāhīm Jabrā's translation of James Frazer's *The Golden Bough*.[23]

Frazer's work also inspired Eliot, who cited *The Golden Bough*'s influence on *The Waste Land*.[24] Poets from across the Arab world such as Adūnīs, Ṣalāḥ ʿAbd al-Ṣabūr, Yūsuf al-Khāl, Khalīl Ḥāwī, and many others who took inspiration from the same myths of death and rebirth were called the Tammūzī poets after Tammūz, an ancient Mesopotamian deity who died each year and came back to life. The ancients worshipped Tammūz, also known as Adonis or Osiris, in a variety of ways throughout broader Mesopotamia and North Africa, but the central elements of the vegetation and fertility ceremonies honoring him are similar.[25] The Tammūzī poets drew on Eliot's poem and used the figure of the continually reborn deity as a multifaceted symbol representing the potential for the rebirth of the Arab nation after colonialism, a revolutionary model for spiritual renaissance, or sometimes a tragic figure, continually stuck in an endless cycle, doomed to live and die again forever. All these versions of Tammūz appear in Sayyāb's poetry. However, his poetry's ambivalent relationship to its political context requires that we consider it with this final, tragic Tammūz in mind.[26]

The first section of "Weapons and Children" immediately takes us into myth with a reference to the Iraqi sailor and adventurer hailing from Basra, Sindbad (*al-Sindibād*) – his only appearance in all of the poem's 422 lines.

Birds? Or children laughing,
A glint of tomorrow sparkling at them?
Their bare feet
Are seashells clinking on a waterwheel (*sāqiyah*)
The hems of their robes are the north wind,
Blowing over a field of wheat,
The hiss of bread baking on a holiday,
Or a mother gurgling her newborn's name
Sweetly whispering to him on his first day.
It is as if I hear the sails flapping
As Sindbad storms out to sea.
He saw a vast treasure between his ribs,
Chose no other treasure, and returned.[27]

Terri DeYoung discusses how these first lines set up an idyllic scene – like many others found throughout Sayyāb's body of work that describe country vistas around his hometown of Jaykūr.[28] Sindbad is the ideal hero who always returns after his adventures at sea. The idea of return along with the repeating pattern of stories telling about Sindbad's seven journeys sets up the overall sequence of the poem. DeYoung further points out that since this is the only mention of Sindbad, these lines – filled with hope, new life, and productive nature – contrast sharply with later sections defined by the coming of capitalism (which the merchant symbolizes), war, and death.[29] Additionally, Sindbad's presence here at the beginning of the poem suggests the start of a journey following a usual sequence, which indicates the poem's primary organizational feature: the general pattern of death and rebirth myths.[30] Sayyāb's integration of the Sindbad cycle into these lines continues the Sindbad myth, adding an eighth journey into the unknown. By mentioning Sindbad in these initial lines, "Weapons and Children" introduces the reader to the cyclical theme that structures the poem. Finally, because Sindbad's journeys always begin in Basra, the poem's first lines are squarely situated in a local southern Iraqi setting.

Furthermore, if we tease out the didactic threads that hold the poem together after its initial Sindbad allusion, its explicit Communist-inspired commitment soon unravels to reveal a modernist patchwork that challenges any one overarching narrative. By combining citations of Western drama with descriptions of the Iraqi countryside, the poem invites us to explore the tension between the local and the global within it as well as the more obvious socio-political reading that invited the Iraqi Communists' praise upon its publication.[31]

The poem's first section ends by using children to symbolize hope, optimism, innocence, and new beginning in defiance of death and its agents, represented up to this point only by natural phenomena: winter and old age.

> On long winter nights, [children] are
> A spring of warmth and good health,
> From which the elderly collect roses
> Gazing once again on childhood
> Dancing among the hills
> And rocking in a cradle of imagination
> With a virgin on a moonlit night
> In the shadow of an apple blossom
> Where birds sleep.
> In the morning, they
> Are the sound of steps on the ladder
> Hands on sleepy faces
> Playfully tickling them awake.
> They are one of those songs of the road,
> One of those old tunes
> One of those rushing voices.
> They are beside Mother when she wakes up,
> When the fire is lit on the hearth
> Like a line you can see tomorrow begin on.

In the world of the poem, children are the only ones who can defeat death. The above lines begin by describing children as a spring season (*rabīʿ*) during winter and go on to associate them once more with an idyllic scene that reminds the elderly of their childhood. The early morning dawning over the final lines of the section combines with the symbolism of the children to represent a new beginning in the fire on the hearth (signifying home, health, and protection) that is "like a line (*khayṭ*) you can see tomorrow begin on." By suggesting that tomorrow "begins" on a *khayṭ*, the poem references the well-known method for determining when dawn has broken and the Ramaḍān fast must begin found in Qurʾān 2:187: "[E]at and drink until ye can discern a white thread [*al-khayṭ al-abyaḍ*] from a black thread [*al-khayṭ al-aswad*] by the daybreak [*al-fajr*]."[32] The poem thus both harks back to Sayyāb's 1950 pacifist poem "*Fajr al-salām*" ("The Dawn of Peace") with its suggestion of a new day's dawn at the same time it alludes to the privation and restraint of the fast during Ramaḍān.

In its second section, the poem shifts its intertextuality from Mesopotamian myth and the Qurʾān to the Western literary tradition. Apart from the poem's implicit and explicit Communist commitment (in its criticism of the merchant and capitalism more broadly), it directly references poets as canonical to the Western tradition as Shakespeare. These intertextual references are integral to the poem's meaning, though Sayyāb's willingness to engage with Western poetry falls foul of ICP hardliners' requirements for committed literature. Consider Romeo and Juliet's dialog in these lines, which come at the beginning of the poem's second section following the extended description of the idyllic rural scene populated with children, flowers, butterflies, and birds:

> Birds? Or children laughing
> Or water, ripened by stone,
> So the grass becomes moist and the flowers dewy
> Flowers and light
> A lark singing,
> And an apple blossom.
> The flap of bird wings has
> An echo of a mother's kiss on her baby's cheek
> "Wilt thou be gone? That was not the lark!
> Believe me, [love,] it was the nightingale,
> Yon light is not daylight."[33]
> Are those the ships that lost course
> On the way to a harbor lamented by the winds?
> Soldiers' hands beckoning there
> To a thousand Juliets on the dock,
> "Goodbye, goodbye to those who don't return."
> For a mother, all alone during fall
> Behind the darkness, a tree stripped of her leaves
> Whose songbirds have fled!

In the first line, the speaker asks whether it is birds singing or children laughing that he hears. The confusion between the two began in the first section, where the persona likens birds leaving their nest to children leaving home. The poem continues playing on this mixture between the two, connecting child, mother, and bird wings in a single moment, "The flap of bird wings has / An echo of a mother's kiss on her baby's cheek." Suddenly, the innocent scene between child and mother collapses with Juliet's question to Romeo at the end of their first (and only) night together, "Wilt thou be gone? That was not the lark (*al-qubbarah*)! / Believe me, [love,] it was the nightingale (*al-bulbul*), / Yon light is not daylight." Although Juliet attempts to deny the coming of daybreak by claiming she hears a nightingale instead of the lark, the sunrise indicates that the time has come for Romeo to leave her bed before being discovered as he is wanted for the murder of Juliet's cousin Tybalt and faces a death penalty in Verona. In "Weapons and Children," these lines represent the impossibility of holding on to childhood innocence, which passes away with time. Shakespeare's lines reverse the motif of dawn as rebirth to reveal it instead as the herald of ever-approaching death. The lines thus upend the idyllic imagery from the first section of the poem and signal the coming of the inevitable: the children grow up to become soldiers, cast out on the seas like Romeo on the road to Mantua. Now adults of fighting age, they long for their idyllic past. "Soldiers' hands beckoning there / To a thousand Juliets on the dock," while the mother whose kisses fluttered on her children's cheeks like bird wings is left alone, "a tree stripped of her leaves / Whose songbirds have fled!"

Just as Juliet's wishful thinking cannot halt the progress of time or stop the break of day, so too the children's transformation into adults makes them targets for the merchants of death. Shakespeare's lines indicate the untenability and end of the idyll, a finality further compounded by autumn's approach (the mother who loses her children like a tree stripped of leaves) and the flight of the songbirds. These lines make way for the terror, disease, and death to come, and only after the idyllic scene is firmly situated in the past following Juliet's question does the merchant's cry first appear in the poem.

By quoting lines from *Romeo and Juliet*, Sayyāb adds a new aesthetic dimension to "Weapons and Children," creating a transitional space between the initial descriptions of the idyll and the scenes of war that follow them. Romeo and Juliet's only night together ends, and they must give in to the reality of their situation and the impossibility of their love as a new day dawns. Likewise, the rural, communal, and local Communist idyll of the poem's first half (and indeed, we might say, of Sayyāb's childhood in Jaykūr suggested by the subtle reference to the Qur'ān at the end of section one) must give way to the global, internationalist visions of the Party that structure the second half of the poem. Furthermore, because Sayyāb ensures that his Arabic translation of Shakespeare's dialogue remains faithful to the meter of the poem, we might also understand these lines as an example of *taḍmīn*, an Arabic intertextual rhetorical technique of "poetic quoting" that we will explore further in Chapter 5.

After Romeo leaves Juliet, death and destruction take over the poem as the merchant's cry for iron and bullets resounds throughout its lines. Although the first line repeats again, the reader knows the sounds are no longer birds – which fled in the previous verse – but instead children's laughter or rippling water, soon to be drowned out in the clash of war:

Birds? Or children laughing
Or water, ripened by stone,
Running over a bloodied corpse (*juththatin dāmiyah*)?
And a lark singing
For a dilapidated ruin (*khirbatin bāliyah*)?
Birds?!
No, children singing,
Their lives in a tyrant's hands (*fī yadi'ṭ-ṭāghiyah*),
And rising over their sweet, pure songs
A far-off call,
"Old iron
          Bullets
                    Iron."
And like the shadow of a hawk in open country –
When he strikes, like a passing blade,
Birds will sing out over the hills –
Thrown at the feet of innocent children,
A call I smell blood in,
"Old iron
          Old iron!
Bullets." As if the air
Were bullets, and as if the road
Were old iron.
Scattered about, like pickaxes,
The terrifying sound of the merchant's steps.
Woe unto him! What does he want?
"Old iron
          Bullets
                    Iron!"
Woe unto you ill-omened merchant (*la-ka 'l-waylu min tājirin ashʾam*),
Who plunges into a stream of blood (*wa-min khāʾiḍin fī masīli 'd-dam*)
Who has no idea that what he's buying (*wa-min jāhilin anna mā yashtarīh*)
To stave off hunger and want from his own children
Are the very graves they'll be buried in!
"Old iron
          Bullets
                    Iron"
Old iron for a new death!

With Juliet now left alone and Romeo on his fateful trip to Mantua, the promise of their love recedes into the past, just as the mother-as-tree's protection of her children-as-birds faded away with time in the earlier lines. The lark, who heralded Juliet's dreaded dawn, sings a requiem for lost memories of the past. The end-rhymes of the lines link together death and destruction; "*juththatin dāmiyah*" ("a bloodied corpse") rhymes with "*khirbatin bāliyah*" ("a dilapidated ruin") as well as "*fī yadi 'ṭ-ṭāghiyah*" ("in a tyrant's hands"), to which the children are now entrusted. (The phrases' shared metrical weight, ¯ / ˘ ¯ ¯ / ˘ ¯ [¯], creates what the Arab rhetoricians call *tarṣī'*, a rough equivalent to isocolon, and adds to their interconnection.) As the children's innocence fades away, the merchant's cry rises above their songs in a refrain that will repeat throughout the rest of the poem.

When the speaker of the poem hears the call, "Old iron / Bullets / Iron," he takes on a prophetic tone of admonishment, "Woe unto you ill-omened merchant." The parallel grammatical and metrical structure of "*tājir,*" "*khā'iḍ*," and "*jāhil*" (three active nouns all in the *fā'il* form literally meaning "one who trades," "one who plunges," and "one who is ignorant of") further accentuates the irony of the merchant's trade by linking all three words together with the same active participle form. Although the merchant "plunges into a stream of blood" to complete his business transactions, he "has no idea that what he is buying / To stave off hunger and want from his own children / Are the very graves they'll be buried in!"

A surface reading of the poem's critique of capitalism and militarism fits a universal model of mainstream Communist ideology. However, we can also locate undercurrents of a more local brand of commitment, focused not on advancing a Communist agenda but rather on the Arab and Iraqi nationalism that would occupy the poem's author during the final years of his life. Moving to section three, the merchant's cry rings out in the first line: "Iron," and the speaker asks,

> Who is all this iron for?
> For a chain twisting around a wrist
> A blade held to breast or vein
> A key to the prison door for those that are not slaves
> A noria that scoops blood.
> "Bullets"
> Who are all these bullets for?
> For miserable Korean children
> Hungry workers in Marseille
> The people of Baghdad and the rest.

By moving between the local and the global, the poem links the individual experiences of oppression witnessed by its narrator in Iraq with those of other downtrodden people across the globe: children suffering during the Korean War (1950–1953), the working class in southern France, and the immiserated subjects of neocolonialism and monarchy in Baghdad. The merchant's iron will turn into shackles for prisoners, weapons for tormentors, and keys to lock up anyone who cannot be controlled otherwise. In these lines, the poem's explicit Communist inspiration emerges in an alternative mode of transnationalism from above – one driven and controlled by Communism's reliance on a flattening of human experience based solely in class consciousness that collapses together all groups bearing the burden of capitalism. The poem challenges this global view of class struggle by including imagery specific to local Iraqi life such as the noria, a type of waterwheel that has irrigated the fields of Iraq for thousands of years. For instance, the "noria that scoops blood" ("*nāʿūratun l-ightirāfi 'd-dam*") appears again in line 234, while "the norias whisper" in line 207. In a continuation of its overall theme, the poem here transforms the life-giving symbol of the noria into an implement of death and in so doing ties daily life in southern Iraq to the global conflict between Communism and capitalism.

However, in the middle sections of the poem, optimism for the future remains grounded in the local. The speaker describes how the daily realities of war and war readiness have become commonplace.

> My mind has gotten used to – like far off thunder –
> The din of footsteps, the crash of stones,
> And the flicker of lamps in the mine,
> What oozes out of naked backs,
> And tasting blood in a cough!
> Our tongues are filled with iron dust,
> Silence rings out where church-bells did...

Out of this apocalyptic scene, a glimmer of hope flashes in the southern Iraqi countryside.

> The norias whisper, and the farmers too.
> In every field – like life beating on –
> Plows swing to and fro in the heart of the soil.
> The villages build
> Villages – their mud made from the tyrant's rotted corpse –
> They make mortar from the tiniest pebbles,
> And even the desert wastes give rise to
> A city,
> Another, and another, on and on!

While the majority of the imagery here could be used to describe most agrarian communities, the presence of the noria specifically calls to mind Sayyāb's birthplace along the banks of the Shaṭṭ al-ʿArab. The villages constructed with "mud made from the tyrant's rotted corpse" suggest the dwellings the southern Iraqi marsh Arabs have built out of mud and reeds for centuries. The imagery of desert wastes giving rise to city after city extends beyond southern Iraq but remains an idealist vision of the development of Arab civilization against great odds. By locating hope for the future in a quintessentially local Iraqi scene, these lines complicate the poem's overarching narrative of international Communist commitment.

Once we get to the eighth and final section, the poem's perspective returns to the universal, in line with what we would expect in mainstream committed literature. The final lines are:

> Every holiday, the waterwheels (*wa-inna 'd-dawālība fi kulli ʿīd*)
> Are spurred on by the wind. Spirits lift up,
> We overcome the dark ages,
> Arriving at a world bathed in light
> (Bullets, bullets, bullets, bullets
> Old iron) . . .
> For a new existence!

Indicating the poem's return to a more global view, the waterwheels here are no longer the norias found in the earlier descriptions of local Iraqi imagery but *dawālīb* – another Arabic term for waterwheels, but one Sayyāb uses only rarely.[34] The poet reserves the word noria (*nāʿūrah*) to indicate a specifically Iraqi scene both in this poem and elsewhere. The juxtaposition of the spinning waterwheels with the Arabic word for holiday (*ʿīd*), the root letters of which have to do with "return," reminds us once again of the mythic cycle of death and rebirth.

The last line recapitulates the death-rebirth cycle, formally representing the whole of the poem again by laying bare how life replaces death and death life. All the elements of the poem are metrically tied together, and the poem shows how all of its contents are interchangeable through its regular rhythm. It accomplishes this through a combination of rhetorical elements: *ṭibāq* (antithesis)[35] and *jinās* (or *tajnīs*; paronomasia).[36] To demonstrate, the final three lines are transcribed "(*raṣāṣun raṣāṣun raṣāṣun raṣāṣ / ḥadīdun ʿatīq*) / *li-kawnin jadīd*." The quick repetition of the merchant's cry for bullets in the antepenultimate line continues into the penultimate one, "(Bullets bullets bullets bullets / Old iron)." These two lines are offset by parentheses from the last line of the poem, which includes the speaker's concluding optimistic hope for a future when all the destruction wrought by bullets and iron will eventually lead to a new existence. "Iron" and "new" are linked by their metrical equivalence (each is ˘ ¯ ¯), as well as their paronomasia. The only difference between the two words is the lack of a dot on the *ḥāʾ* of *ḥadīd* (ح) and the presence of a dot indicating the *jīm* of *jadīd* (ج).[37] The final word of the poem, *jadīd* (new), opposes *ʿatīq* (old) in the previous line, and again the words share the same metrical pattern – a result of Sayyāb's continued reliance on the prosodic rhythms described in the premodern Khalīlian system. The *ṭibāq* antithesis of dark and light, old and new rhetorically symbolizes the final victory of the "world bathed in light" over the calls of the merchant by creating "a new existence" out of the ashes of the past.

Although "Weapons and Children" ends with lines directly addressing themselves to the global pacifist ideology of the Iraqi Peace Partisans and the Communists, the poem's mythical foundations and inclusion of Iraqi imagery betray an internal tension between Sayyāb's Communist political commitment and developing feelings of Iraqi nationalism. Having presented how this tension emerges with Sayyāb's reference to Shakespeare in the poem, I now consider its publication history with regard to Sayyāb's biography.

Sayyāb's Transnational Turn

The modernist aesthetics of "Weapons and Children" implicitly work against the poem's explicit narrative of commitment. Sayyāb had a troubled relationship with Communism when he wrote and published "Weapons and Children." The poem contains elements of Communist commitment, but its references to Western literature challenge the literary mode of socialist realism the ICP championed. Looking to Sayyāb's memories of his political involvement during the early 1950s, we can further explore how his proclivity for the avant-garde in Arabic and appreciation of Western literature troubled his Communist commitment.

During the 1952 *Intifāḍah* in Iraq, Sayyāb first witnessed the violent tactics he would later vilify the ICP for using, and his experiences during the uprising would ultimately transform his poetic vision and complicate his Communist beliefs. His disgust with what happened during the protests influenced his recollections about the Party. According to his own account, on November 23, at the height of the *Intifāḍah*, protestors carried him through the streets as he recited poetry urging them on. His group marched west from the banks of the Tigris into the Bāb al-Shaykh neighborhood of Baghdad, coming under fire as they reached the ʿAbd al-Qādir al-Gīlānī Mosque. As a couple of participants tried to load the wounded into vehicles bound for the hospital, the rest of the protestors took off down an alley behind the mosque. One of them shouted that they should take the local police station by cutting across the mosque's graveyard, which they did. In

Sayyāb's recounting, they lost their mettle when gunfire "from only one or two rifles" rang out from the station as they approached. Enraged at not being able to continue, the crowd

> seized a poor, unfortunate fellow – one of their own countrymen – who was wearing a *kūfiyyah* dyed blue to indicate that he was a descendant of the Prophet. He also had two blue tattoos on his temples,[38] but when one of the comrades caught sight of him, he shouted "He's with the Secret Police!"

As punches and kicks rained down upon him he cried out for help.

"By God, I swear I'm not police!" he screamed. "I'm just a poor man!"[39]

Sayyāb never forgot what happened next. The crowd ended up killing the man, regaining its courage, and making for the police station once more. There, three or four men overcame one of the officers, killed him as well, and set fire to the building. A second officer made his escape, hiding in an abandoned house in the neighborhood. The protestors fanned out, searching every corner until they found him, at which point they stabbed him numerous times until he succumbed and, in a fit of rage, kept on stabbing him even after he was dead. Finally, they threw his body in the street, poured gasoline on it, and lit it ablaze.[40]

In his account of the events, Sayyāb expresses his sympathy for the victims of the crowd and his horror at what the protest devolved into, excoriating the Communists for their use of violence and blaming them for the actions of the protestors. It is impossible to know what role, if any, Sayyāb really had in stirring up the protesters' emotions or even in the taking of the police station, for the only source we have about what the poet did in Bāb al-Shaykh is his own memoir. Whatever happened that day, November 23, 1952 represents the beginning of the end of Sayyāb's affiliation with the Iraqi Communists. Although he was appalled by the murderous actions of the crowd (at least when he wrote about it later on), his mere presence at the protest made him a target for the government in the aftermath. He had to flee the country.

Facing a possible death sentence for his involvement in the *Intifāḍah*, Sayyāb disguised himself as a Bedouin and took the train to Basra. In Abū al-Khaṣīb, a group of relatives handed him over to some Iraqi smugglers they had hired to sneak him into Iran. The first traces of Sayyāb's Arab chauvinism appear in his recollection of the escape years later. "It was dawn on a cold winter day," Sayyāb remembers, "when one of the smugglers woke me up in their house. I walked behind him until we reached a rivulet separating Iraq and Iran, which in actuality only separates two parts of a single Arab land that resemble each other in every way."[41]

Sayyāb's first sojourn in Iran extended from late November 1952 until January 1953, and he seems to have spent the whole time in Khurramshahr, roughly ten miles east of Jaykūr. Out of money but unable to return to Iraq, he eventually ended up in Kuwait. Life in Kuwait was difficult for him. He took up residence with a group of comrades, some of whom were suffering from tuberculosis, which meant many of the daily chores like washing dishes, making tea, and going on errands fell to him. While he had felt solidarity with the lower classes during his time at the Teachers College because of his humble beginnings in southern Iraq, when hiding out in Kuwait his affectations marked him as a member of the upwardly mobile *effendi* class, and his housemates considered him a *petit bourgeois*.

In the narrative he tells about his eventual break with Communism, his account of the conflicts that emerged in the Kuwaiti safe house clarifies his later opinions about the Communist position on literary commitment. He writes:

> There was a continual battle between me and them about what I read. If you wanted to read a story, then it had to be one by Maxim Gorky, Chekhov, or Ilya Ehrenburg, or maybe those of the Communists in Syria and Lebanon like [Muḥammad] Dakrūb, Ḥannā Mīnah, etc. If you wanted to read poetry, then you had to read Nâzım Hikmet, Pablo Neruda, and so on – Communist poets. The newspaper you were supposed to read was the Communist Lebanese paper *al-Thaqāfah al-waṭaniyyah* (*National Culture*), and our journal was *al-Ṭarīq* (*The Way*) – also Communist.

Once, he brought home a copy of D. H. Lawrence's *Lady Chatterley's Lover*, and "upon seeing it, the comrades forbade me from reading it and took it away from me." The radio stayed tuned to Moscow.[42]

That Sayyāb's broad literary interests went beyond Communist orthodoxy to include Western writers like D. H. Lawrence brought him into direct conflict with "the comrades" in Kuwait who required a Communist political alignment in the writing they consumed. Not only did their politics determine what they read, it also led to the dogmatic Communist literary criticism we saw earlier. At the Communist safe house in Kuwait, Sayyāb's taste for Western literature only exacerbated his feelings of estrangement from his homeland and his people.

Fed up with life in Kuwait, he returned to Iraq in May 1953 but found that conditions had not improved: There was still a warrant for his arrest, and the police had come to his father's house looking for him. Considering his situation, he decided to flee to Iran once again. Although his Communist affiliation had been shaken again during his time in

Kuwait, he remained an active member of the party and sent the ICP a letter requesting support for his trip. The local branch of the ICP in Abū al-Khaṣīb gave him a letter of introduction to present to the Tudeh, and he returned to Khurramshahr. There, he turned the letter over to a member of the Tudeh who contacted the Party Headquarters in Tehran for him.[43]

Soon, Sayyāb was in Tehran. While he was hiding out with the Tudeh there, the American and British spy agencies removed from power Mohammad Mosaddegh, the Iranian Prime Minister elected in 1951 amid a wave of popular support. The coup happened on August 19, 1953. Sayyāb witnessed its aftermath while making his way back to Tehran from the summer vacation destination Shamirān with members of the Tudeh Party on August 20 or 21. He found the streets filled with trucks carrying soldiers, whom he would later discover were supporters of the coup and not of Mosaddegh as he first believed. The next day, he woke to find a small group of fifty or sixty reactionaries taking control of the streets around where he was staying. Their number hardly compared to the crowds that had gone out in support of the Prime Minister only days before, and he wondered where their opposition was. The Party did not seem to be organizing any response at all. Perplexed, he asked his Tudeh companions why they were not trying to reverse the coup and calling for mass protests in the streets. One responded,

> "Listen, Arab comrade. We're on the border of *Ittiḥād-i shūravī*" – that's what they called the Soviet Union.
>
> "Sure," I replied, "I know that."
>
> Then my interlocutor started talking again.
>
> "So, if we take control of the government – us, the Communists – do you think the Americans will stay silent about it? Of course not! They'll intervene, and once they do, it will cause problems for the Soviet Union.'
>
> My blood boiled in my veins, and I screamed back at him, my voice charged with emotion, "But you all are Iranians, not Soviets! Your job is to defend the interests of your own people, the Iranian people, not the Soviet Union and its people. Comrade, the Soviet Union is capable of defending itself!"[44]

This conversation represents why Sayyāb ultimately turned from Communism to Iraqi nationalism. After he witnessed the Tudeh defer to Soviet interests following the coup, his already fragile faith in Communist ideals was shattered. Ironically, after the Tudeh contacted "their Kaaba" – as he refers to Moscow in his retelling of the story – the Soviets said they would support the Tudeh in a move against the Shah's new government in Iran, which had by that point regained full control of the country. Sayyāb ruminates on why he initially became a Communist after witnessing what happened in Iran, asking himself,

> Did I become a Communist because I wanted to defend the interests of a foreign nation and its people? No, I became a Communist out of love for my own people: my neighbors, those I know. I used to think that Communism was the best solution – no, the only solution to our problems [. . .] . But now Communism seemed very different to me.[45]

Although Sayyāb's nationalism only reached fever pitch years later, his experience of the Tudeh Party's betrayal of the Iranian people after the coup against Mosaddegh marks a pivotal moment in his political development. Returning to his memories of that period in his life, he quotes Mutanabbī's poem about Persia and describes his thoughts and feelings when he first arrived in Iran.

> The abodes of [Bawwān] Valley are
> as pleasant as springtime,
> But an Arab man there is
> strange of face, hand, and tongue

> Yes, I was strange of face, hand, and tongue in this Arab land [that is, across the Iran-Iraq border in Iran]. Long lost feelings of nationalism and Arabism rose up in my soul. I exulted in my Arabness. I swore to myself that I would never abandon or betray it just because a cold-hearted, dirty Jew who claimed to have embraced Christianity during the nineteenth century wrote a book called *Das Kapital* – motivated by his hatred, jealousy, Jewish fanaticism, and what he read in the Torah. And after him came another Jew, from Russia, who revolted against the revolution of the bourgeoisie and established a rule in which man is but a tool: he neither thinks nor feels anything that is not in line with what the system forces upon him.[46]

While these sentiments are not an aberration in light of the rest of his memoir, their blatant racism and anti-Communism are almost surely a distortion of reality, the memory tainted by his renunciation of Communism later in life.

As Iraq's fortunes changed following the withdrawal of direct British influence and the end of the monarchy in 1958, Sayyāb became an unapologetic Iraqi nationalist and Arab chauvinist, eschewing the earlier streams of nationalist and Communist ideologies he had shifted between. Notwithstanding his turn from Communism after the "bitter Iranian experience,"[47] the poetry he published upon his return to Iraq in 1954 marked a transitional phase between his period of outright commitment and that of his more ambivalent later verse. He was well aware of the discernible vein of Communist commitment in line with Soviet transnationalism from above in "Weapons and Children," and consequently tried to change how later readers would understand the poem by stripping away its explicitly Communist references and criticisms when including it in his 1960 *dīwān*.

Iḥsān ʿAbbās had a copy of the first printing of the poem from 1954 and includes some of the original lines in his biography about Sayyāb. The first edition of the poem refers to the "lords of Wall Street" ("*arbābu wūli stirīt*") as "merciless" ("*al-qusāh*").[48] For the 1960 version, Sayyāb excised the entire line.[49] He also removed an extended description of the lives of African Americans in Mississippi, which ʿAbbās quotes for us, "And neither did fire lay low the neighborhood of the blacks / Nor did the pavement spit out blood there / Nor did criminal toughs sweep through it / With the heavy ropes they drag / And what they fetter men's necks with."[50] Sayyāb likewise took the following, from the poem's last section, out of the later version: "For the daybreak of the slaves' release has dawned / And we have raised the banner of peace / We have raised it up, so let darkness be driven away!" Finally, he changed the line "Peace to the Don" (a river south of Moscow) to "Peace to the Ganges,"[51] clearly showing his desire to disconnect the poem from any perceived sympathy for the USSR. By taking out his commentary on racial tension in the United States and stripping the poem of its direct references to Communism and the Soviets, Sayyāb marked his disillusionment with what he saw to be the empty promise of Soviet anti-imperialism. At the local level, these later emendations were made for solely political reasons after his total split with the ICP, which had taken up ʿAbd al-Wahhāb al-Bayātī as its champion during Sayyāb's absence in 1953.[52]

Sayyāb makes an explicit break with the transnational networks he had been affiliated with in the edits he introduced to *Weapons and Children*. With these changes, he openly aligns himself with the West in opposition to the Eastern Bloc, even going so far as to claim that the danger facing Iraq from Communism is no less than the danger posed by colonialism. "We are in a war of ideas (*ḥarb ʿaqāʾidiyyah*) with the Communists," he declares in his 1959 memoir. "We were certainly able," he posits,

> to deal with colonialism and its traitorous spies and agents, like Nūrī al-Saʿīd[53] and his gang, along with his treaties, such as the Baghdad Pact. We

> must escape the Communist nightmare and Communist control that plagues us. We are in a struggle (*jihād*) through which we defend our nationalism (*qawmiyyatanā*), our religion (*dīnanā*), our traditions (*taqālīdanā*), and our cultural heritage (*turāthanā*), through which we defend our independence and our being. O enemies of Communism, unite and join together, every group, every religion, and every nationality![54]

Sayyāb's experience of the Soviet Union's failure to support local nationalist movements against neocolonial regimes exposed Communist anti-imperialism as an empty promise. Yet instead of continuing to espouse his deeply held beliefs in global pacifism following his transnational turn, he became increasingly nationalist. In the above passage, he even employs the language of Muslim religious struggle ("*jihād*") in a reactionary diatribe about the Iraqi nationalist fight against Communism. By the end of his life, Sayyāb was a clear enemy of the Communists, both in Iraq and abroad.

After Sayyāb's Turn

We must reformulate the model of transnationalism from above found in earlier studies of non-Western literature if we want to understand where a poem like "Weapons and Children" fits in Sayyāb's poetic development and that of Arabic modernist poetry more generally. In his case, the demands of Communist socialist realism were just as aesthetically limiting and ideologically imbricated in foreign interests as those of capitalism and global trade. By taking a page from Sayyāb's own interpretive book and considering his poetry with regard to its dynamic symbolic meaning, divorced from his unpleasant and at times hateful attacks against non-Arabs and Jews, we can counter the static, nationalist reading he attempted to situate his *œuvre* within at the end of his career. Although he was a Communist for many years, his political affiliations changed drastically after witnessing the inaction of the Iranian Tudeh party in the wake of Mosaddegh's ouster. Overall, his transnational experiences encouraged him to further incorporate ancient mythic themes into his poetry in opposition to explicit Communist political commitment, but they also led him to advocate for an unsavory political ideology later on. We cannot ignore the problem of his eventual political positions. However, by looking to his poetry in terms of its mythic foundations and as part of a significant modernist geography, we can keep it out of the quagmire of nationalism he hoped to leave it in.

In closing, the convergence of networks in Sayyāb's poetry calls us to trace new lines of interest and influence moving not just from West to East, but also tying Arabic modernist poetry to other, non-Western parts of the planet as well as local literary heritage. Lateral transactions shaped modernist poetry in significant ways that we can trace within the poetic forms and content shared across the Arabic and Persian poetic traditions. Furthermore, when we look to the literary production of someone like Sayyāb who wrote at the margins of empire, we see just how the discipline of world literature now in vogue fails to account for the multiplicity of competing demands placed upon non-Western literatures. Sayyāb negotiates between the local and the global, pan-Arab sentiments and international Communist sympathies, and the continued relevance of premodern Arabic poetic form and the innovations made possible by the modernist movement. His poetry thus opens up to us a significant modernist geography that has heretofore remained outside of broader academic understandings of modernism as a global or planetary phenomenon. In the following chapter, we will continue mapping this shared modernist geography in Iraq during the 1950s and 1960s with the work of Sayyāb's contemporary, the staunch Leftist ʿAbd al-Wahhāb al-Bayātī.

PART III

Aftermath

Modernist Ends in Arabic and Persian Poetry

CHAPTER 5

Honoring Commitments
ʿAbd al-Wahhāb al-Bayātī's Existential Trials

بُحتُ بكلمتين للسلطانْ
قُلتُ له : جبان

عبد الوهاب البياتي، "المحاكمة" من "عذاب الحلاج" (١٩٦٤)

With two words I let the Sultan know the secret
"Coward!" I said to him

—ʿAbd al-Wahhāb al-Bayātī, "The Trial" from
"The Passion of Ḥallāj" (1964)

In the previous chapter, we saw how Sayyāb went about taking out and replacing certain words in "Weapons and Children" to obscure the poem's (and the poet's) earlier Communist commitments following his turn to Western Liberalism. This chapter, which covers the work of Sayyāb's compatriot and poetic rival, ʿAbd al-Wahhāb al-Bayātī, likewise revolves around the absence and presence of words that help us map out those geographies significant to the development of modernist poetry in the Arab world and Iran. To do this transnational mapping of literary networks, we now turn our attention to *taḍmīn* quoting, having already explored the function of a comparable Arabic rhetorical device in Nīmā Yūshīj's poetry with *muʿāraḍah* contrafaction. While *muʿāraḍah* intertexts connect a poem to an earlier one by copying meter and rhyme, *taḍmīn*s do so with "the incorporation in a poem of a line, or part of a line, by another poet by way of quotation [...]."[1] Like we saw with Nīmā's playful use of *muʿāraḍah* to bring ʿAṭṭār's *Conference of the Birds* to bear on modernist Persian poetry, here we will consider how Bayātī incorporates premodern poetic and mythic traditions into a modernist Arabic poetry that imagines significant geographies extending outside the borders of modern Iraq. In his poetry from the 1960s, Bayātī focuses on establishing universal justice while also dealing with the existential crises that had begun to plague Arab intellectuals as local politics started to shift back to despotism after brief moments of hope following decolonization.

You may have noticed something missing from the lines of poetry quoted in the epigraph above, which comes from Bayātī's 1965 collection *Sifr al-faqr wa-l-thawrah* (*The Book of Poverty and Revolution*) – the quoted poem, "*ʿAdhāb al-Ḥallāj*" ("The Passion of Ḥallāj") was written in 1964, the year Sayyāb died. Instead of the poetic persona saying "two words" to the Sultan as he divulges his secret, he instead says just one, "Coward!" The dissonance produced by our expectation to find two words but being given only one constitutes yet another key moment for our analysis of Arabic and Persian modernist poetry. This chapter treats the absence of these "two words" and the presence of the word "Coward!" to address the role of literary commitment (*iltizām*) in the poetry and a dramatic piece of a steadfast Leftist who worked to create broad geographical networks of solidarity across the literatures of the Global South even after the failures of Arab socialism and the replacement of Soviet internationalism with stark authoritarianism.

We will return to this poem and find out what the missing "two words" might be later on. However, in order to fully understand Bayātī's rhetorical trick in these lines, we first need some background information about the poet, his philosophical influences and development, and his relationship with premodern Arabic and Persian poetic and mythic traditions. Therefore, this chapter will proceed first through a short discussion of Bayātī's biography, with special attention paid to his engagements with Persian literary heritage. Next, we will cover Bayātī's philosophical grounding and his syncretic understanding of philosophy and religion that moves across geographic and chronological borders to imagine a more just future for humanity. We then move into the core of the chapter, an extended analysis of Bayātī's use of *taḍmīn* quoting in his poetry. We will consider *taḍmīn* as yet another tool for the poetic sublation of the premodern into the modern that shapes modernist poetry across the Arab and Iranian contexts. Finally, I address how Bayātī deploys the life stories of Ḥallāj and Khayyām– the famous yet mysterious scientist and reputed author of the *rubāʿiyyāt* quatrains – to elaborate his concept of existential revolt. Overall, I argue that Bayātī's modernist poetic technique constitutes a method for honoring not just modern political literary commitments but also the legacy of a shared cultural heritage unbounded by the borders of nation states.

Bayātī the Transnational Poet

Before we get to the central role *taḍmīn* plays in Bayātī's poetry and expand my reading of *taḍmīn* to his incorporations of Ḥallāj and

Khayyām into his poetry, it is worth pointing out that Bayātī is the most obvious candidate among the modern Arab poets for the type of transnational analysis we have been engaging in this book. After the publication of his breakthrough collection *Abārīq muhashshamah* (*Broken Pitchers*) in 1954, he was forced to leave Iraq in 1955 because of his involvement with the Iraqi Communist Party.[2] For much of his life after that, he traveled and lived abroad, moving among the continents of Africa, Asia, and Europe and taking up residence in Cairo, Moscow, and Madrid. His itinerant life prompted a flurry of academic interest in his work.[3] He counted among his friends and acquaintances not only other Arab writers and poets – including but not limited to Sayyāb (who became a decidedly vicious enemy of his later on), Louis Awad, Ṣāliḥ Jawdat (d. 1976), Tawfīq al-Ḥakīm (d. 1987), Yaḥyā Ḥaqqī (d. 1992), Khalīl Ḥāwī, and even Najīb Maḥfūẓ – but also non-Arabs, such as Rafael Alberti (d. 1999), Robert Lowell (d. 1977), Gabriel Garcia Marquez (d. 2014), and Nâzım Hikmet, whose funeral he attended as a pallbearer.[4] After the end of the Iraqi monarchy in 1958, he was appointed as a cultural attaché and spent much of his time in Moscow from 1959 to 1964 before moving to Cairo, where he lived from 1964 to 1971. Years later, he would move to Madrid, which was his base from 1979 to 1989. In the last year of his life, he finally visited the country whose culture had so inspired his poetry throughout his career, traveling to Iran only a few months before his 1999 death in Damascus, Syria.[5]

He may have become enthralled with Iranian culture and literature through his early readings of Khayyām, Nūr al-Dīn ʿAbd al-Raḥmān Jāmī (d. 1492), Jalāl al-Dīn Muḥammad Rūmī (d. 1273), and ʿAṭṭār, as he relates in one of his autobiographies.[6] Or perhaps it was a youthful infatuation with one of his classmates (the daughter of the Iranian cultural attaché in Baghdad) at the Baghdad Teachers College that led him to engage, for the entire length of his poetic career, with Iran in his poetry.[7] Several Iranian scholars have taken particular notice of his references to historical and literary figures from Iran and studied them.[8] As you flip through his collected poems, you sense a distinct Persian presence both in the masks the poet puts on and the cities he sets many of his poems in. Khayyām first appears as a character in 1957s *Ashʿār fī al-manfā* (*Poems in Exile*) in the poem "*al-Rajul alladhī kāna yughannī*" ("The Man Who Was Singing"); 1965's *Book of Poverty and Revolution* includes "The Passion of Ḥallāj," which we will address in some detail.[9] Later poems with Persian-influenced themes or persons include "*al-Majūsī*" ("The Magus")[10] and "*Hakādhā qāl Zarādusht*" ("Thus Spake Zarathustra")[11] from *al-Kitābah*

ʿalā al-ṭīn (*Writing on Clay*, 1970); the collection titled *Qamar Shīrāz* (*Shiraz's Moon*, 1975), which includes a poem by the same name;[12] "*Maqāṭiʿ min ʿadhābāt Farīd al-Dīn al-ʿAṭṭār*" ("Selections from the Passions of Farīd al-Dīn al-ʿAṭṭār") in *Mamlakat al-sunbulah* (*Kingdom of Grain*, 1979);[13] and one of his final poems, "*Bukāʾiyyah ilā Ḥāfiẓ al-Shīrāzī*" ("A Lament for Hāfiẓ al-Shīrāzī," 1998), which we will also examine briefly in the conclusion to this chapter. Persian cities other than Shīrāz also appear in his poetry: Iṣfahān, Nīshāpūr, and Tehran.[14] Bayātī drew much poetic inspiration from the Persian tradition, though his journeys did not physically take him to Iran until the very end of his life. His interest in Iran came instead from his long study of Persian culture through books, particularly Persian philosophy and poetry translated into Arabic.

Bayātī's Existential Commitment

Turning to Bayātī's political and philosophical development, the poet's philosophy of commitment depends on the existential tradition's recognition of death as the shaper of life, an old idea that plays the primary organizing role in Martin Heidegger's (d. 1976) *Sein und Zeit* (*Being and Time*). Bayātī's understanding of revolutionary death follows from the work of the Egyptian philosopher ʿAbd al-Raḥmān Badawī (d. 2002), whose own engagement with existentialism began during his studies with the Russian philosopher Alexandre Koyré (d. 1964). Koyré, in turn, had worked with Edmund Husserl (d. 1938) – Heidegger's advisor and mentor – and the esteemed French orientalist Henry Corbin (d. 1978), who was the first to translate parts of Heidegger's *Being and Time* into French as *L'Etre et le temps* in 1938 and conducted extensive research on Persian mystic and philosopher al-Suhrawardī's (d. 1191) Neoplatonic Philosophy of Illumination.[15] Therefore, Badawī's existentialism emerged from, on the one hand, his prolonged engagement with European existential thought and, on the other, his ultimate goal to combine Sufism and existential philosophy.[16] We can accordingly locate a poetic analogue to Badawī's philosophical project in Bayātī's work as each represents an attempt to bring together Sufism and twentieth-century thought, though the latter added elements of political commitment we do not find in the former's work.

In order to understand Bayātī's philosophical *Bildung*, therefore, we must return to Heidegger through Badawī. In *Being and Time*, Heidegger outlines how a person can only live an authentic life by orienting their life in full knowledge of the certainty of death, a concept he calls "being-toward-death." To live authentically, a person must admit the inescapability of their *own* death and anticipate it. As Heidegger puts it, "this anticipation includes the possibility of taking the *whole* of Dasein in advance in an existentiell way, that is, the possibility of existing as a *whole potentiality-of-being*."[17] Heidegger uses the term "existentiell" to address the empirical existence of *Dasein* ("being there," or simply human existence) from an ontic rather than an ontological perspective – that is, from the perspective not of the study of being, but of being itself. This distinction provided a starting point for Badawī, who brought Heidegger's thought to the Arab world. As Yoav Di-Capua tells us, "Badawi subscribed to two of the main themes of existentialism: first, *existence precedes essence* (i.e., who a human being is [his or her essence] is the result of his or her choices [existence]); and second, *time is of the essence* (i.e., human beings are time-bound, and the lived time that they experience is different from measured clock time)."[18] Building on this notion of lived time, Heidegger tells us, "Being-toward-death is essentially anxiety,"[19] a philosophical attitude – and we have been interested in attitudes throughout this book – that provides the foundation of the French existential tradition.[20] Bayātī's existentialism, though founded in his understanding of the French existentialists, harkens to Heidegger's notions of authentic life through the recognition of death's inevitability, an anxiety with an added strain of political commitment that extends beyond the individual being or existence (*Dasein*, roughly) to concerns with others (an area where Heidegger's philosophy fails miserably).

Di-Capua argues that Badawī's reception of the European existentialists offered him "a new philosophical frame of reference" through which they "fostered the rise of Arab phenomenology and taught Badawi that death is not simply an event that happens at the end of one's life, but rather an experience that shapes one's entire way of being and, especially, illuminates the condition of authenticity upon the eventual encounter with death itself."[21] Although Bayātī's notions of authenticity come from the same tradition, they do not exactly align with Badawī's. As Di-Capua further explains, "Badawi's existentialism was indeed apolitical, as it was a pledge to one's authentic way of being," in the vein of Heidegger's philosophy.[22] Bayātī's introduction to existentialism occurred during the late 1940s and 1950s, and he therefore came to the philosophical movement after it had filtered through Ṭāhā Ḥusayn's comments on Sartre's *What Is Literature?* in the journal *The Egyptian Writer*.[23] Existentialism in the Arab world had by that point moved away from philosophy and into commitment (*iltizām*) and committed literature in particular. Badawī's initial project represented a direct encounter with Heideggerian thought and "sought to update the medieval Sufi doctrine of the 'Perfect Man' (*al-Insān al-Kāmil*)." That is, man as "an 'isthmus (*barzakh*) between necessity (*wujūb*) and possibility (*imkān*), the mirror which combines the attributes of eternity and its laws with the attributes of the generation of being (*ḥidthān*).'"[24] Bayātī's existentialism came out of its reception in French and then Arab thought, and "al-Bayati, who counted himself as an existentialist and a Camusian Third World poet, quoted [Che] Guevara's conviction that 'what we must create is the man of the twenty-first century.'"[25] Of interest to us, however, Bayātī goes about "creat[ing] the man of the twenty-first century" by returning to men of the tenth and eleventh centuries (and others) and bringing their voices into a European-inspired existentialist poetry in new and creative ways through the Arabic rhetorical technique of *taḍmīn* quoting.

The Function of Taḍmīn (Poetic Quoting) in Bayātī's Poetry

In Chapter 2, we saw how Nīmā Yūshīj indirectly alludes to Ḥallāj's martyrdom in his poem "The Phoenix." In the same way Nīmā intertextually references ʿAṭṭār's poetry and prose, Bayātī uses *taḍmīn* to sublate elements of premodern poetic and religious tradition into a poetry dealing directly with the contemporary moment. While Khayyām, the purported author of the Persian *rubāʿīyyāt*, provides Bayātī with the poetic mask of an existentialist hero, as we will see later on, the Iraqi poet puts on a Ḥallāj mask when engaging in mystical contemplation. It is worth comparing Bayātī's engagements with these two figures to elaborate how he goes about sublating the past into his modernist poems.

Although Bayātī's literary scope encompassed a broad swath of cultural and linguistic traditions, his primary source of poetic inspiration was Arabic literature. He continually returns to his own tradition to imbue his verse with resonances from deep within Arab cultural history. Before we turn to Bayātī's innovative method for bringing Ḥallāj's and Khayyām's voices into modernist poetry, I offer two examples of *taḍmīn* quoting from elsewhere in Bayātī's *œuvre* to set the stage for how these sorts of intertexts work and as a direct parallel to Nīmā's modernist technique in "The Phoenix." As we have already seen with Nīmā, Shāmlū, and Sayyāb (and as we will further explore with Farrukhzād in Chapter 6), Bayātī relies on myths of death and rebirth in his poetry. In his 1968 collection *al-Mawt fī al-ḥayāh* (*Death in Life*), the second poem is titled "*al-ʿAnqā*'" ("The

Phoenix"). Bayātī here employs a *taḍmīn* from the Arab poet and skeptic Abū al-ʿAlāʾ al-Maʿarrī (d. 1057), including – word for word – part of one of his verses at the end of the poem. "And [Abū al-ʿAlāʾ] told me, 'Take heed, for the Phoenix / is too big to hunt / So go back to the graves, / the yellowed books, and the inkwells / Keep moving from one country to another.'"[26] By borrowing from Maʿarrī's line, "I understand that the Phoenix is too big to hunt, / so be headstrong in taking on what you can,"[27] the poem spurs its speaker onward to keep him writing despite the impossibility of sparking the Marxist revolution he hopes for, a challenge it equates to hunting the elusive Phoenix. Similar to what we saw with Nīmā's *muʿāraḍah* of ʿAṭṭār's *Conference of the Birds* in the Persian context, Bayātī's use of *taḍmin* sublates a premodern poetic and mythic past into Arabic modernist poetry.

In a second example, from Bayātī's breakthrough collection *Abārīq muhashshamah* (*Broken Pitchers*, 1954), the poet plays with the formal limits of Arabic free verse by including a *taḍmīn* from the poet Mutanabbī (d. 965). In the collection's title poem, Bayātī fully integrates the quoted line, which is from a poem in a different meter. He pushes the boundaries of *taḍmīn* quoting yet further by splitting one of the poetic feet across two lines in his new poem, in the fourth and fifth lines here:

Allāhu, wa-l-ufqu[28] *'l-munawwaru, wa-l-ʿabīd*
yataḥassasūna quyūdahum:
ʿshayyid madāʾinaka'l-ghadāh
bi-l-qurbi min burkāni Fīzūfin, wa-lā taqnaʿ
bi-mā dūna'n-nujūm
wa-li-yuḍrama'l-ḥubbu'l-ʿanīf
fi qalbika'n-nīrāna wa-l-faraḥa'l-ʿamīq'[29]

Though it is difficult to reflect the use of *taḍmīn* and the innovative enjambment of the foot between lines 4 and 5, I offer this translation to show how the quoted line fits seamlessly into the poem's meaning:

God, the glowing horizon, and the slaves
feel the weight of their chains:
"Build your cities in the morning
beside the volcano, Vesuvius, and do not be content
with anything less than the stars.
Let violent love light
fires and boundless joy in your heart."

Bayātī uses a novel method of enjambment in these lines. In the following, the "/" indicates separations between poetic feet. The poem is in the *kāmil* (perfect) meter, a favorite of Bayātī and the other pioneers of Arabic modernist poetry.[30] It generally consists of four repetitions of the foot *mutafāʿilun* (˘ ˘ ¯ ˘ ¯) or a variant *mutfāʿilun* (¯ ¯ ˘ ¯). Bayātī includes both in this poem, like so:

— — ˘ — / — — ˘ — / ˘ ˘ — ˘ —

˘ ˘ — ˘ — / ˘ ˘ — ˘ —

— — ˘ — / ˘ ˘ — ˘ —

— — ˘ — / — — ˘ — / — — ˘ — / — —

˘ — / — — ˘ —

— — ˘ — / — — ˘ —

— — ˘ — / — — ˘ — / ˘ ˘ — ˘ —[31]

He splits the first two syllables of the fourth foot of line 4 from the second two, which begin line 5, thus calling the reader's attention to the lines. (Someone listening to the poem would neither experience the lines in the same way nor would they notice the splitting of the foot, so we also have a clear indication of the written textuality of Arabic modernism here.) Even if one were not familiar with the reference to Mutanabbī, the enjambment of the poetic foot signals that something noteworthy is happening in these lines. The line quoted from here is "*idhā ghāmarta fī sharafin marūm / fa-lā taqnaʿ bi-mā dūna'n-nujūm,*" which translates, "Should you go to great lengths in search of a desired honor / do not be content with anything less than the stars."[32] Surprisingly, Mutanabbī's poem is not in the *kāmil*, but rather in the *wāfir* (exuberant) meter.[33] The *wāfir* has a variant as well (either ˘ ¯ ¯ ¯ or ˘ ¯ ˘ ˘ ¯), but its feet do not ever exactly match either of the variants found in the *kāmil* (¯ ¯ ˘ ¯ or ˘ ˘ ¯ ˘ ¯). Mutanabbī's line scans: ˘ ¯ ¯ ¯ / ˘ ¯ ˘ ˘ ¯ / ˘ ¯ ¯ // ˘ ¯ ¯ ¯ / ˘ ¯ ¯ ¯ / ˘ ¯ ¯. In splitting the first foot of the second half of Mutanabbī's line, Bayātī's ingenious *taḍmīn* allows him to incorporate the quotation without breaking from the meter of the new poem. Invoking Mutanabbī's line about striving for one's goals and never giving up even in the face of great odds strengthens the wish of the persona in "Broken Pitchers" with the force of Mutanabbī's original imperative. Moreover, the quotation marks denoting another speaker internal to the poem do not demarcate the *taḍmīn* but instead surround a longer demand – from whom we cannot be sure. The poet takes on Mutanabbī's voice and adds the speaker's to it, following the traditional requirements of *taḍmīn* while also bringing premodern Arabic poetry into the avant-garde of the new modernist poetic movement.

Ḥallāj on Trial in Bayātī's Poetry

Although Bayātī frequently draws on the Arabic poetic past, his use of the premodern tradition extends beyond Arabic to include poets and thinkers from the Persian-speaking world. He wrote poems about ʿAṭṭār, Suhrawardī, and Ḥāfiẓ, among many other luminaries of the Persian philosophical and poetic past. He also carried out an extended poetic and dramatic engagement with the works and biography of Khayyām, which I have addressed at length elsewhere and which we will turn to briefly following our discussion of Ḥallāj.[34] In this section, I bring our attention to Bayātī's engagement of Ḥallāj's story as a key instance of modernist themes shared across Arabic and Persian, though there are many other examples we might turn to, such as the centrality of the Phoenix in modernist poetry that we have already seen.[35]

When we consider Ḥallāj's role in Bayātī's poetry, we ought to first note that Bayātī conceives of Ḥallāj as an antiauthoritarian figure opposed to the cooptation of mysticism by the state. As a reminder, Ḥallāj's Sufism was distinctly non-hierarchical and at odds with more orthodox Sufi practice during the Abbasid era. We might here recall that Ḥallāj venerated Satan as the purest monotheist due to his refusal to bow down to Adam instead of God.[36] Furthermore, Ḥallāj built his own Kaaba in his house in Baghdad and performed the pilgrimage there. And, most famously, Ḥallāj is said to have proclaimed "*Anā al-ḥaqq*" ("I am the Truth") in public and therefore divulged the secret of Sufi mystical union with the Divine.[37] No matter the reasons Ḥallāj had for stepping outside the accepted bounds of Sufism, his actions took on a political meaning that only grew in influence after the Abbasids executed him.[38]

Remembering this brutal instance of state repression, Bayātī puts on the Ḥallāj mask both to speak out against authoritarianism and speak up for the downtrodden and dispossessed, whom Ḥallāj supported in his mission. Snir explains further in *Rakʿatān fī al-ʿishq* (*Two Prostrations in Love*) that

> the old sources discuss how Ḥallāj was a deviant among the Sufis of his age because he combined the spiritual stages of development he reached with an interest in the issues of society. Not only did he have a clear affinity for the miserable and untouchable and give money to the poor, he encouraged his followers to give up going on the pilgrimage, invite orphans to eat, and clothe them instead. Ḥallāj also called for a just distribution of the tax burden, and his concern with the social situation put the [political] authority on guard about the danger of undermining the foundations of society and rule of law.[39]

Bayātī's Ḥallāj mask allows the poet to participate in a revolutionary Sufism devoted to achieving social justice. In his engagements with Ḥallāj's ministry and martyrdom, Bayātī investigates the possibilities for an individual's existential revolt against orthodoxy, whether political, religious, or even mystical.

Ḥallāj's Sufi contemporaries chafed at his unorthodox interest in issues of social justice just like the Abbasid state did because it challenged the concept of a mystical path oriented only toward knowledge of the Divine. Reading Ḥallāj's ministry this way, we might say that by connecting mystical development with ongoing concerns about the mundane world, he made the mystical path political. Bayātī's understanding of the Sufi path follows from this mode of politically committed Sufism. "My Sufism, if I can call it that," Bayātī explains,

> is a part of my poetic vision and the being I burn with. It is my vision at this or that poetic stage (*marḥalah*). As I have mentioned many times, I am not seeking the Kingdom of God in another world. I seek the Kingdom of God and of Man in this world (*hādhihi al-dunyā*). For me, Sufism doesn't mean Sufi clothing, being a dervish, or going to *dhikr* chanting circles but rather the renunciation of egotism, selfishness, jealousy, and all types of harm and evil, and unification with the spirit of this world and the music of the universe [. . .].[40]

Ḥallāj provides Bayātī with a model for a revolutionary Sufi while also offering an example of someone whose political engagement with society led him to take real action in this world, which he refers to as the "*dunyā*" in the above passage.

Bayātī inverts the local phenomenon of Sufism through his universalist ideal of bringing the "Kingdom of God and of Man" to *this world*, the lowly, base, material *dunyā*. To place Bayātī's vision of Sufism within the frame of world literature as something made up of significant geographies, as Laachir, Marzagora, and Orsini suggest, then, Bayātī is here asking "the question 'for whom?' that puts 'people' back into the 'world,' unsettling the static idea of the world as a disembodied abstraction."[41] Precisely because of his focus on the individual's existence within the material world, Bayātī's *dunyā* transforms into a realm of Divine possibility.[42] His existential heroes are therefore good examples of the intersubjective, transnational figures Laura Doyle examines in her analysis of "existential phenomenology's account of the person-in-the-world," to which Laachir, Marzagora, and Orsini point us in a footnote. "There is much talk," Doyle argues, "of resistance and counterproduction but, with some exceptions (most often in feminist theory), in the main there is still a dearth of theory about the radical, *involuntary* interconnectedness of subjects who live in history and together shape, suffer, enjoy, and resist its forces."[43] This "involuntary interconnectedness" is yet another instance of the transnational unconscious that lies at the generative core of the modernist networks we have been exploring. I take Bayātī's existentialist heroes, like Ḥallāj and Khayyām, to be representations of this interconnectedness across the modernist movements of the Global South and beyond. They are fundamentally transnational figures that nevertheless populate a particular geography significant to Bayātī's poetry and to Bayātī himself – the Middle East, for lack of a better term.[44]

Ḥallāj features prominently as the title character of Bayātī's 1964 "*'Adhāb al-Ḥallāj*" ("The Passion of Ḥallāj").[45] In it, Bayātī's poetic persona puts on a Ḥallāj mask as he poetically reconstructs ʿAṭṭār's narrative of Ḥallāj's ministry and execution. In so doing, Bayātī also extends the possibilities of *taḍmīn* quoting to their furthest ends in inverting the poetic device by not quoting at all. Instead, he obliquely refers to Ḥallāj's notorious statement, "*anā al-ḥaqq*." As with Nīmā's "The Phoenix," a mythic past haunts and thereby generates Bayātī's poem, calling us to look at it in a different light.

To briefly address the poem's content, it moves through six sections mirroring Ḥallāj's biography. It starts with "*al-Murīd*" ("The Novice"), then "*Riḥlah ḥawla al-kalimāt*" ("A Journey through Words"), "*Fusayfisā'*" ("A Mosaic"), "*al-Muhākamah*" ("The Trial"), "*al-Ṣalb*" ("The Crucifixion"), and finally "*Ramād fī al-rīḥ*" ("Ashes in the Wind"). Of most interest to us is the fourth section, "The Trial," which begins with the two lines at the start of this chapter and a novel inversion of the *taḍmīn* device.

Bayātī's Ḥallāj persona starts the section by railing against a political leader. "*Buḥtu bi-kalimatayn li's-sulṭān / qultu lahu: jabān*" ("With two words I let the Sultan know the secret / 'Coward!' I said to him").[46] Instead of quoting Ḥallāj's famed two-word proclamation, "*anā al-ḥaqq*," Bayātī puts a single new word in Ḥallāj's mouth, "*jabān*," or coward. Other than the fact that *jabān* rhymes with *sulṭān*, there are at least two more possible interpretations of Bayātī's choice to not quote Ḥallāj here. First, we could read Bayātī's replacement of the "two words" he alludes to in the first line with "coward" as a specifically political choice that transforms Ḥallāj from a Sufi seeker into a political revolutionary whose socially just religious practices set him at odds with the state. In this interpretation, by not including the *taḍmīn* the poem takes on an explicit political function when its persona calls out the (unnamed) Sultan for his cowardice. Second, however, we might regard the missing "*anā al-ḥaqq*" as a sign of Bayātī's reticence to repeat Ḥallāj's ultimate sin once more, whether we want to consider it in relation to the poetic persona or perhaps even the poet himself. This second interpretation would then cast a pall of political ambivalence over the poem, as the poet's neglect to actually say Ḥallāj's phrase might be read as a subtle indication of his will to distance himself from its revolutionary power, *anā al-ḥaqq*'s direct disavowal of worldly political authority. This reading would suggest instead a general disillusionment with the limited range of political possibilities available in the 1960s following the establishment of nation states and entrenchment of new, local political and economic elites.

In either case, "The Trial" section of the poem only makes sense when understood in relation to the traditional Ḥallāj myth. By having his Ḥallāj declare the Sultan a "coward" instead of using a *taḍmīn* of "*anā al-ḥaqq*," Bayātī challenges the reader's expectations and draws our attention to the interplay between Ḥallāj's myth and the present moment. Even though we do not find the expected quotation of Ḥallāj's dictum, a reader familiar with the Ḥallāj legend would recall it anyway. Here, Bayātī's mere suggestion of a *taḍmīn* (but lack of any real quoting) cleverly sublates the content of the Ḥallāj myth into the present moment. This example takes us to the very limits of modernist experimentation in the Arabic context, techniques that draw not just on Western modernist developments but rather depend on a poetic, historical, and religious tradition shared between the Arabic and Persian speaking worlds. The fourth section of the poem ends,

> In the wastes of the city, the poor,
> my brothers, raised a tumult
> crying, and terrified I awoke to the footsteps of time
> to find nothing but people bearing false witness and the Sultan
> circling around me, dancing at Satan's banquet
> among the wolves, here I am naked
> You killed me
> You abandoned me
> You forgot me
> You committed me to death a thousand years ago,
> and here I am sleeping,
> awaiting the dawn of my salvation, the hour of execution.[47]

Bayāti connects the historical event of Ḥallāj's execution with his revolutionary memory, which lay asleep for a thousand years to reawaken in the twentieth century. Here too, we find a powerful antithesis in the final line with "salvation" (*khalāṣ*) and "execution" (*i'dām*), linking the two together in such a way that we think not only of Ḥallāj's Passion but also that of Jesus. The final two sections of the poem, "The Crucifixion" and "Ashes in the Wind," imagine the torture and eventual burning of Ḥallāj's body and revolve around the death and rebirth cycle. They thereby link the popular story of Ḥallāj's life and death with the broader modernist movement.

Bayātī's existentialist view of death and life was fully formed by the time he published the first volume of his autobiography *Tajribatī al-shiʿriyyah* (*My Poetic Experience*) in 1968. When discussing the poetry he wrote during the late 1950s and 1960s, he relates death (*al-mawt*) to freedom (*al-ḥurriyyah*) in a way that reminds us again of Ḥallāj's willingness to die for what he believed in:

> In *Glory for Children and Olives* [1956], *Poems in Exile* [1957], *Twenty Odes from Berlin* [1959], and *Words Don't Die* [1960], death was for the sake of freedom. That is, death became the price for freedom and freedom the price for death. Meaningless death (*al-mawt bi-l-majjān*) never has any value since it strips the condemned man of all value such that the life he leaves behind has no meaning at all. However, dying for the sake of freedom, the noble martyrdom that is the death of those who fight back, is never separate from human death because those fighting back are not transformed into saints or miracle workers. They are instead pure, simple, good people [. . .] . Their deaths are capable of opening people's eyes, for they themselves choose it; it is a duty, not fate or a gift they present to others. Still, in the eyes of others, they transform into heroes since their deaths exemplify the path to freedom, and they become a mythical symbol of sacrifice (*ramzan usṭūriyyan li-l-fidāʾ*). They represent all the virtues of society, embody all of its hopes, and become exemplary heroes. This depiction of death shows up in *Fire and Words* [1964], *The Book of Poverty and Revolution* [1965], and *He Who Comes and Does Not Come* [1966] by way of introspection, journeying into the depths of those heroes' and martyrs' souls, and conjuring forth their exemplary characters.[48]

Bayātī's revolution against meaningless death (*al-mawt bi-l-majjān*) encapsulates the existentialist side of his project, which he combines with a heroic and radical Sufi opposition to orthodoxy, both political and religious.

The "revolt against meaningless death" first appears as a theme in a poem Bayātī wrote in 1962, six years before he outlined in retrospect the existentialist background to his notion of death in *My Poetic Experience*. The first instance I am aware of occurs in the 1962 poem "*al-Ghurāb*" ("The Raven"). This poem is found in one of Bayātī's most explicitly committed collections, 1964's *Fire and Words*, and it ends with a succinct and simple distillation of the motivations behind his philosophy of commitment: "*anā lā akhāfu'l-mawta / lākinnī akhāfu'l-mawta bi-l-majjān / b-ismi ghurābihim hādhā'l-la'īn*" ("I do not fear death / but I do fear meaningless death / in the name of this damned raven of theirs").[49] Bayātī's *ghurāb* conjures up for us the raven God sent to Cain (Qābīl) to show him how to bury the body of his brother Abel (Hābīl) after he killed him (see Qur'ān 5:26–31). The presence of the raven in the final line thus reminds us of the scene of fratricide in the Qur'ān, underscoring the uselessness of a meaningless death perpetrated not out of necessity but jealousy.

Bayātī's combination of existential themes with political commitment in his "revolt against meaningless death" emerges from a philosophical and literary approach that was, according to Di-Capua, particular to Iraqi intellectuals in the Arab world, and existentialism's popularity continued to grow in Iraq alongside the political upheavals of the 1960s.[50] Bayātī's struggle against meaningless death comes directly from of his understanding of existentialism, which was in line with the broader Arab intellectual view of the movement. In fact, prior to the disaster of 1967, "existentialist themes such as alienation, anticipation of death, absurdity, angst, estrangement, and revolt became dominant in much of the poetry, prose, and theater of the era."[51] While the Ḥallāj mask allows Bayātī to explore the interrelationship of premodern Sufi themes and modern existentialism, that of the Persian poet Khayyām provides him with a character through which he fully elaborates his vision for the ideal existentialist hero. In the next section, therefore, we move beyond *taḍmīn* quoting to the reimagination of a premodern figure's entire life story to address a progressive message to the modern world.

Khayyām on Trial in Bayātī's Dramatic Work

Bayātī made a conscious attempt to reach beyond uniquely Arab models for existentialism in his engagements with Khayyām. Because Bayātī's uses of Khayyām as a mask are numerous, we will here limit our discussion to Bayātī's 1962 play about Khayyām, *A Trial in Nishapur*. In it, Bayātī imagines Khayyām on trial in his hometown as he shapes him into a model existentialist hero. I read Bayātī's Khayyām against the grain of other Arabist understandings of the character, whom scholars have generally regarded as yet another Sufi figure in Bayātī's poetry.[52] On the contrary, I think that Bayātī's understanding of Khayyām shares much in kind with the opinion of the famed Iranian modernist prose writer Ṣādiq Hidāyat (d. 1951). Hidāyat refers to Khayyām as "a materialist philosopher" (*yak faylasūf-i māddī*), who was "from the days of his youth until the moment of material death a pessimist and a skeptic (or at least appeared to be so in his *Rubāʿiyyāt* quatrains)."[53] Bayātī also draws heavily on the American Harold Lamb's (d. 1962) narration of Khayyām's story in *Omar Khayyam: A Life*, particularly Lamb's imagining of a childhood friendship among Khayyām, the future Saljuq statesman Niẓām al-Mulk (d. 1092), and the founder of the Assassins, al-Ḥasan al-Ṣabbāḥ (d. 1124).[54] Lamb, in turn, came to Khayyām after his reputation as a rebel and free thinker had already been established in the West following Edward FitzGerald's (d. 1883) English translations of his quatrains, which appeared during the latter half of the nineteenth century. For both Hidāyat and Lamb, Khayyām was far from a Sufi mystic but was instead a rationalist philosopher and an atheist. Read this way, Bayātī's Khayyām is both the product of his readings of Persian literature and a result of his engagement with Western recensions of Khayyām. In any case, Bayātī's Khayyām is not the Sufi of Arab popular imagination.

Bayātī plays on Khayyām's mythical status in *A Trial in Nishapur* to offer a critique of political authority, tradition, and ungenerous readers of literature. The Nishapur of the Saljuq Dynasty (fl. eleventh and twelfth centuries), which marked the ascension of Sunnism in the Islamic world, sets the stage for Bayātī's existential ruminations with his Khayyām character. The play centers on Khayyām's experience at court, where members of Nishapur's ruling class consider whether the poet is guilty of committing *kufr*, that is, of blaspheming God. During the trial, a University Professor (*ustādh jāmiʿah*) brings a *kufr* claim against our hero. The Professor cites a "quatrain" as evidence of Khayyām's crime. "O You for whom we call out / we seek pardon / Tell me, where can You find pardon?"[55] He prefaces this quotation of the poem by telling the court,

> Khayyām has, every now and then, written quatrains collected in no single book but recited everywhere. The Sufis, in particular, know them and sinners repeat them, challenging the Qur'ān and the teachings of Islam. In my position as a humble servant of knowledge, I have collected many of these quatrains, written in different scripts across Persia but all composed by Khayyām.[56]

The Professor's testimony brings up a number of questions about the provenance of the quatrains, for they appear to already be a part of popular culture in the fictional world of the play. The Professor, not Khayyām, claims that the poet is involved with the Sufis. (Elsewhere, the play describes him as a man of science but not as a Sufi.) The Professor's admission that the verses he has collected are "written in different scripts" across the entire Persian-speaking land does less to support his claim that they are "all composed by Khayyām" than it does to refute it.[57] That is, the Professor has confused the broader cultural reception and textual recension of the quatrains with whatever philosophical positions Khayyām may actually have had. In the end, once his accuser recites the lines, Khayyām "looks at the University Professor in astonishment and opens his mouth for the first time: 'I didn't write this quatrain.'"[58] Bayātī toys with Khayyām's mythical status throughout the play, using a mythos that formed over time in Iran, was "discovered" again in Europe, and made its way back to the Arab world following FitzGerald's translations.

The above scene at court portrays Khayyām as an intellectual rebel forced into conflict with a state-sponsored view of Islam enforced by the local leaders of Nishapur. Beyond the University Professor, these also include the Chief Judge (*kabīr al-quḍāh*), the Head of the Religious Community (*rajul al-millah*), and even the theologian Abū Ḥāmid Muḥammad ibn Muḥammad al-Ghazālī (d. 1111), who admonishes Khayyām, "I have heard how you have gone outside the teachings of Niẓām al-Mulk – may God rest his soul – and how you practiced magic in Isfahan the way unbelievers do."[59]

Forced out of Nishapur by political and religious hardliners in the play, Khayyām joins a caravan heading for Aleppo in the employ of a Merchant, just as we find in Lamb's version of the story. Along the way, the spirit of the founder of the Assassins (*al-Ḥashshāshīn*) – the group of Ismāʿīli (i.e. Shia) rebels who opposed the Sunni Saljuqs – al-Ḥasan al-Ṣabbāḥ, appears to Khayyām and asks him to join the Assassins in their sectarian rebellion.[60] Ṣabbāḥ declares, "I have granted you the opportunity to be born again and here you are refusing it!"[61]

Khayyām declines to join the Assassins, despite their rebellion against the Sunni elites who forced him into exile from Nishapur, because his ideal revolution is total, unrelated to sectarian division and, more importantly, founded in the refusal of violence. He compares Ṣabbāḥ's feeding hashish to his men to steel them for their assassination missions to the Chief Judge's use of something yet more dangerous: endless talk of Paradise and Hell to pacify the people of Nishapur.[62] Khayyām then explains his own stance on revolution. "We must wait. The revolutionary doesn't risk his own head or others' for nothing. Revolution requires preparation, mobilization, and biding one's time – waiting for the critical moment to strike. If I were to be born again, I would give myself over to it."[63]

Ṣabbāḥ protests that if the circumstances are not right for revolt, one ought to draw first blood to spur on change, to which Khayyām replies, "The starlight of true revolution shines behind a thousand doors of long anticipation, but it will one day appear. People will mention how Khayyām died a soldier in a losing battle during the first fights for freedom [and] for the sake of humanity's victory in its final campaign." Immediately after saying this, Khayyām collapses from exhaustion, dead. His companions mention how he had been delusional, speaking to himself, before the Merchant proclaims to them all, "God forgive us our sins! I didn't pay him his due. When I reach Aleppo, I'll give what he was owed to the poor."[64]

At the end of the play, we find a clear example of the existentialist philosophical framework Bayātī elaborates through the Khayyām persona as well as elements of the poet's Marxist commitment to social justice. Although Khayyām dies poor and broken, "a soldier in a losing battle," he gives in neither to the prescribed orthodoxy of the elite class in Nishapur nor to the anarchic bloodshed Ṣabbāḥ invites him to join in. Instead, he keeps faith in his vision of a coming revolution, notwithstanding the fact that he knows he will not participate in it himself. On the road to Aleppo, he is like Sisyphus pushing his stone, and it is up to the audience to imagine him happy in the knowledge that he never compromised on his beliefs as he dies in the dirt.[65]

Bayātī's Khayyām reflects the existential dilemmas the poet introduced in his early work. He uses Khayyām to explore the existential anxieties his speakers face while attempting to come to terms with the contradictions of modernity. He deals with the changes to premodern poetry that came in the wake of the modernist movement alongside the conflicting projects of Iraqi nationalism on the cusp of its total transformation into Baathism (in 1968) and Communism, which he found himself struggling to negotiate due to his multiple exiles from Iraq, sometime residency in Moscow, and the growing disillusionment with Communism among intellectuals in the Global South that took off in the 1950s. It is thus my assertion here that the existentialism of Bayātī's poetry is best served by a reading that goes beyond the bounds of the national and into the transnational movements of ideas and political affiliations he participated in.

Bayātī Honors Past Commitments

Bayātī brought together existentialist philosophy and the premodern Arabic and Islamic mystical and philosophical traditions through his use of poetic masks. Like Shāmlū and Sayyāb, Bayātī was caught between the new political alignments of the Cold War and local nationalist developments in Iraq, which caused him to become more ambivalent about explicit Communist commitment as his career went on. After the early 1960s, Bayātī's poetic influences became increasingly transnational as his poetic vistas widened to include not only figures from the Arab past but also the gods of ancient Mesopotamia, Western writers, and Persian poets and philosophers. Of all of these, his sustained engagement with Iran stands out because of the overall number of poems and entire collections he devoted to Persians such as Khayyām, Ḥallāj, Suhrawardī, Rūmī, ʿAṭṭār, and others.

Bayātī's last collection, *Nuṣūṣ sharqiyyah* (*Eastern Texts*), published the year he died, offers a final example of how the poet's transnational commitment worked with regard to the poetic inspiration he drew from the Persian tradition. Among other poems dedicated to al-Maʿarrī, Damascus, and Baghdad, the collection includes the long poem "A Lament to Ḥāfiẓ al-Shīrāzī" as well as the title poem, "Eastern Texts." In it, the old poet's memories of the past bubble up in fifty short vignettes he completed at the end of November 1998.

The collection offers us yet another glimpse of the 1953 coup in Iran, which had a profound effect on Bayātī's life and work. In the vignettes of "Eastern Texts," Bayātī's persona reminisces about the aftermath of the coup. "The day the mob killed Fāṭimī in Tehran / I was playing chess with Sayyid Makkāwī," the poetic persona recalls.[66] Like with Sayyāb and Shāmlū's poetic trajectories, the coup looms large in Bayātī's memory as a transitional point in history, both political and personal. For instance, elsewhere in the series the persona remembers, "The Shah, / following the coup against Mosaddegh, / returned to Tehran with an Iraqi air escort / and the agents of imperialism. / As for me, / I went home / after giving / the barman my last dime."[67] The lines amount to an admission of a poet's inability to put up any real resistance against the coup; instead, we find a searing indictment of writers and intellectuals' failure to counter the rise of authoritarianism and nearly immediate decay of socialism in postcolonial Iraq and Iran under the Shah. Here, Bayātī's persona spends his "last dime" at a bar while the Shah returns to power with the support of the Iraqi monarchy's Air Force, a detail the poet includes to highlight the mutually supportive reactionary networks that led to the decline of Arab socialism and end of Mosaddegh's populism in Iran. Unlike the revolutionary heroes of Bayātī's other poems we saw earlier, the persona here bows out and goes home drunk instead of resisting.[68] We might read these lines from 1998 as a melancholic reflection on the continued failures the Arab Left suffered over the course of the twentieth century.

Khayyām appears in these late poems as well. In one, Khayyām "apologized for meeting me / at the Observatory, / in fear of the informers, / for he had been indicted for his religion, / and I / for kidnapping the Sultan's daughter, / being crazy for wine, / and dancing naked under the starlight."[69] During a later scene, the poetic persona spends two nights at Khayyām's Observatory, after which a servant girl gives him "three roses / and a piece of silver / The price of my trip / to Khurāsān."[70] Along with its nostalgic ruminations, then, *Eastern Texts* offers yet another example of Bayātī's continual references to Iran throughout his life and acknowledges the debt he owes to Khayyām as an exemplary revolutionary figure.

Throughout his career, Bayātī populated his poetry with themes and figures from the Iranian tradition, transnationally linking his modernist poetic content with the Persian literary past. Although there is no evidence that he was aware of the parallels between his poetry and that of the Iranian modernists like Nīmā, Shāmlū, or Farrukhzād, his poetic sensibilities led him to draw on the same mixture of European and premodern Arabic and Persian poetic influences that theirs emerged from. This again is the product of a shared transnational unconscious that developed and took hold among Arab and Iranian modernists during the twentieth century. Furthermore, by bringing in Persian poets and locales, Bayātī's Arabic poetry allows us to imagine an interconnected modernist poetic network spanning the Arab world and Iran.

Turning now to conscious poetic techniques and political motivations, Bayātī was, like Nīmā and Sayyāb, at the forefront of the formal development of Arabic metrics in the poetic line. In this chapter, we considered Bayātī's use of the *taḍmīn* poetic quoting technique. He employed this device to both bring the premodern Arabic poetic tradition into his verse through direct quotes and also to add a modern worldview by redeploying classical motifs, interrogating them, and offering a response informed by his view of existentialism, social justice, and the duty of the poet in the modern world. Through his use of poetic masks, Bayātī engaged the memory of premodern heroes, saints, and mythical figures in his contemporary struggle to reject meaningless death. Although he often questioned the utility of the death and rebirth motifs upon which modernist poetry is founded, he continually fought the inherent pessimism of eternal rebirths and the endless circle of repetition. His poetics of myth and his transnational commitment to creating a better world here in the material *dunyā* rather than waiting for justice to be done in the hereafter retain elements of the tradition that preceded him by paying attention to the shared cultural past of premodern Mesopotamian societies. Bayātī's mythic commitments thereby transcend artificial national borders to give form to a significant modernist geography that crosses Iran and the Arab world during the twentieth century.

In the next and final chapter, we will look to Iranian poet Furūgh Farrukhzād, who strikes a balance between the obvious influence European modernism had on her poetry and her continued reliance on Arabic metrical forms and the work of her modernist forebears in the Persian tradition. As we saw with Bayātī's inversion of the *taḍmīn* quoting device in "The Passion of Ḥallāj," we will likewise see how Farrukhzād takes premodern Arabic metrics to their utmost limits, almost to their breaking point, while she remains in direct conversation with the poetry of other Iranian modernists like Nīmā and Shāmlū.

CHAPTER 6

Winter in the Modernist Garden

Furūgh Farrukhzād's Posthumous Poetry and the Death of Modernism

اکنون
این
منم!

احمد شاملو، *قطعنامه*

Now
this
is me!

—Aḥmad Shāmlū, *The Manifesto* (1951)[1]

و این منم
زنی تنها

فروغ فرخزاد، « ایمان بیاوریم به آغاز فصل سرد»

And this is me
a woman alone

—Furūgh Farrukhzād, "Let Us Believe in the Beginning of the Cold Season" (1974 [1965])[2]

Furūgh Farrukhzād is one of the most well-known poets of modern Iran. No study of modernist Persian poetry would be complete without addressing the pivotal role she played (and continues to play) in its development, both within Iran and abroad. I have decided to end our study with a chapter focused for the most part on Farrukhzād's posthumously published poem "*Īmān biyāvarīm bih āghāz-i faṣl-i sard*" ("Let Us Believe in the Beginning of the Cold Season"), which brings us to the death of modernism. By this, I first mean that Farrukhzād's metrical experiments in this poem take Persian modernism (and premodern Arabic metrics) to their farthest limits. Her metrical expertise has remained for the most part unaddressed – other than in a few studies available in Persian – as scholars and fans have generally remained more interested in the content of her poetry and the new feminine perspective she introduced to the twentieth-century Persian literary milieu. Second, Farrukhzād's tragic February 13,

1967 death in a car accident marks for us a convenient end point on our modernist timeline. While modernist poetry obviously continued on in the Arab world and Iran after 1967, Farrukhzād's death and the Six-Day War between the Arabs and Israel were significant enough for later poetry that we can safely stop there and leave an investigation of post-1967 poetic exchanges between Arabic and Persian for another time.[3]

We begin this chapter with a line from Farrukhzād's final poem, published in full several years after her death, that responds to Shāmlū's refrain, "Now this is me!" in "Song of a Man Who Killed Himself." "*Va īn manam*" ("And this is me"), Farrukhzād begins her final poem. The "and" in this line continues a poetic conversation Shāmlū began years earlier, in 1951, which Farrukhzād traces back through the tradition of Persian modernist poetry even as she creates a new poetic world for herself, moving away from Shāmlū's committed poetry and the political realm into the existential, which we also explored in Chapter 5 through our readings of Bayātī's work. Farrukhzād's new poetic world thus brings together the wider courses of modernism with local formal poetic innovations and heralds the coming of winter to Persian modernism.

In the Persian critical tradition, Shāmlū and Farrukhzād are often considered to be the two most important modernist poets to follow Nīmā for their pioneering styles, overall popularity, and fresh poetic sensibilities. For example, the *engagé* critic Reza Baraheni writes, "In the 1950s, a decade during which Iran suffered following the CIA coup, two poets had a fundamental importance. Despite the fact that Nīmā was still alive, despite the fact that [Mahdī] Akhavān S̱āliṡ [d. 1990] composed several of his best poems during the same period, the first of the two is Shāmlū and the other is Farrukhzād."[4] Both position death at the center of their poetics, and each remains indebted to the new mythic themes Nīmā introduced to Persian poetry along with his early innovations on modernist poetic form. Shāmlū's poetics of death, as we have already seen, are – like Bayātī's – defined by his belief in death as a transformative step along a bloody path of revolution. Farrukhzād's approach to death instead connotes an ambiguous and ambivalent relationship between death and politics, private and public. While Shāmlū provides his readers with a symbolic code to unlock the meaning of his poetry from the get-go, Farrukhzād more often writes poetry that operates with a carefully crafted ambivalence about politics. As we found with Bayātī's meditations on death in Chapter 5, for Farrukhzād death serves an existential function as an indeterminate end that nevertheless defines life as it continuously approaches.

My focus here is on Farrukhzād's later verse because, as she herself admitted and as her biographer Michael Hillman and others have agreed, it was only in the latter portion of her career that she started to believe that she had truly begun to write fully modernist verse. For example, Hillman cites a radio interview Farrukhzād gave in 1964, where – answering a question about the relationship of her life to her poetry – she responds, "[I]f the point to this question is the explanation of a handful of circumstances and issues relating to one's life work, which in my case is poetry, then I have to say that the time for such a review has not yet arrived, because I have *just recently begun dealing with poetry in a serious way*."[5] Dominic Brookshaw and Nasrin Rahimieh, for their part, add that Farrukhzād's "own remarks in this interview point us away from a reductive reading of her poetry as a simple reflection of her life."[6] And although we must also recognize that Farrukhzād's earlier poetry has yet to receive a fair appraisal, Farzaneh Milani likewise admits, "It is true that Forugh reached the height of her poetic achievement in the later poems."[7] In light of all this and since we are here focusing on specifically modernist verse, I will only be dealing with a small selection of Farrukhzād's *œuvre*, notwithstanding the shortcomings inherent to such an approach. If I ignore the broad range of Farrukhzād's entire body of work, it is because her later poetry offers both an extremely personal reflection on the relationship between her life and her art as well as an acerbic commentary on what it means to be modern, a question central to our investigations in this book.

I begin our engagement with Farrukhzād's poetry by positioning her lyric "I" as an Iranian *flâneuse*, a modern female counterpart to the *flâneur* we are so familiar with from the French modernist tradition. After this investigation of Farrukhzād's lyric "I" as a witness to the modern age, we move into an analysis of her deft use of the metrical innovations that Nīmā pioneered. In this section, I explain how Farrukhzād takes the metrical sciences of Persian (and therefore also Arabic) poetry to their very ends without fully breaking away from them. Next, we turn to Farrukhzād's engagements of the traditional garden scene from premodern Persian poetry. Farrukhzād transforms the garden into a graveyard, and we will take up this transformation as yet another instance of a modernist imagining her own significant geographies within her poetry. By transmuting the garden into a graveyard, she also links her late poetry with the broader movement of modernism. As we reach the end of the chapter, I bring our attention to the profound links between Farrukhzād's "Let Us Believe" and T. S. Eliot's *The Waste Land*. We will thus come full circle, reconnecting the interlocked Arabic and Persian modernist movements once more with European modernism, which I have attempted to sideline throughout this study.

Farrukhzād's Lyric "I" as a Modern Iranian *Flâneuse*

The title of the last collection Farrukhzād published while she was alive, *Tavalludī dīgar* (*Another Birth*, 1963), announces the poet's engagement with the theme of death and rebirth that links together all the poems we have read in this book. Farrukhzād depends on a wide range of intertextual references to both Persian and Arabic poetic and mythic traditions, while she is also informed by the European modernists' preoccupation with degraded modern urban existence and their apotheosis of an unsullied past. She brings modernist Persian poetry to its apex in her late poetry, which includes both *Another Birth* and the posthumously published collection *Let Us Believe in the Beginning of the Cold Season*. In the poems of these collections, Farrukhzād's lyric "I" takes on the position of both observer of and participant in modern life, the Iranian female equivalent to Baudelaire's *flâneur*.

"And this is me / a woman alone /," Farrukhzād's lyric "I" declares in her last poem, "at the threshold of a cold season / at the beginning of understanding / the polluted existence of the earth / and the simple, sad pessimism of the sky."[8] In perfect harmony with her modernist forebears, from the Western tradition's T. S. Eliot to Iran's Nīmā, she integrates an undercurrent of pessimism about the cycle of life and death throughout the poem. Here at the opening of "Let Us Believe," Farrukhzād's lyric "I" positions itself at the "threshold of a cold season," that is, in the liminal position of a witness looking out on modern life like Baudelaire's *flâneur*.

I therefore argue that Farrukhzād's poetic persona is a *flâneuse* who traverses the boundary between public and private and "seeks refuge in the crowd" to bear witness to the modern condition.[9] To understand Farrukhzād's lyric "I" as a *flâneuse* we must do two things. First, we need to establish that the lyric "I" figures itself as feminine. While Persian is a non-gendered language that uses the same pronoun (*ū*) for "he," "she," and "it," and although we ought to avoid thinking Farrukhzād's lyric "I" to be co-terminal with herself and therefore necessarily feminine, at many points in her late poetry the lyric "I" addresses itself as female.[10] We have already seen "And this is me / a woman alone" from "Let Us Believe," where the speaker also mentions "that man who was my mate had returned within my seed / [. . .] and I became the bride of acacia blossoms" and asks, "Will

I once again comb / my hair in the wind?"[11] Second, I return to Walter Benjamin's comments on Baudelaire's *flâneur*, whose liminality, between past and present, public and private, we will trace through to Farrukhzād's lyric "I" as *flâneuse*. "The flâneur still stands on the threshold – of the metropolis as of the middle class," Walter Benjamin tells us about the *flâneur* in his essay "Paris, The Capital of the Nineteenth Century." "Neither has him in its power yet," he continues. "In neither is he at home. He seeks refuge in the crowd."[12] We might productively read Farrukhzād's poetic persona as a *flâneuse* in light of her lyric "I's" novel perspective on Iranian modernity by dint of not only its identification as female but also its oscillations between the public sphere of the street and the private one of the home.

Consider Farrukhzād's poetic persona as a *flâneuse* in 1963's *Another Birth* in light of the figure's erotic, voyeuristic underpinnings. In his discussion of Baudelaire's poem "*À une passante*,"[13] in "The Paris of the Second Empire in Baudelaire," Benjamin further explains, "Far from eluding the eroticist in the crowd, the apparition which fascinates him is brought to him by this very crowd. The delight of the city-dweller is not so much love at first sight as *love at last sight*."[14] Here is Farrukhzād's *flâneuse* looking out on the street in her collection's title poem in just this way.

Zindagī shāyad
yak khiyābān-i dirāzast kih har rūz zanī bā zaṃbīlī az ān mīguẕarad
zindagī shāyad
rīsmānīst kih mardī bā ān khūd rā az shākhah mīāvīzad
zindagī shāyad ṭiflīst kih az madrasah bar mīgardad

zindagī shāyad afrūkhtan-i sīgārī bāshad, dar fāṣilah-'i rikhvatnāk-i dū hamāghūshī
yā 'ubūr-i gīj-i rahguẕarī bāshad
kih kulāh az sar bar mīdārad
va bih yak rahguẕar-i dīgar bā labkhandī bīma'nī mīgūyad 'ṣubḥ bikhayr'

Perhaps life
is a long street on which a woman with a basket passes every day.
Perhaps life
is a rope with which a man hangs himself from a branch.
Perhaps life is a child returning from school.

Perhaps life is lighting a cigarette in the languid repose between two embraces
or the mindless transit of a passer-by
who tips his hat
and with a meaningless smile says 'good morning' to another passer-by.[15]

In what follows, I hope to separate Farrukhzād's lyric "I" as *flâneuse* in these lines from the figure of Farrukhzād herself, who has frequently been understood in erotic terms merely due to her active participation in the masculine sphere of Persian poetry in the 1950s and 1960s.[16] I too read Farrukhzād's *flâneuse* as an erotic figure, but on the basis of aesthetics instead of biography. "Farrokhzād's life," Jasmin Darznik summarizes for us, "offered a narrative whose dramatic flourishes – divorce, sexual independence, artistic self-invention – scandalized the Iran of her day."[17] Farrukhzād was and remains so well-known, both in Iran and elsewhere, because she was a woman writing poetry with openly erotic themes. However, we should be cautious about limiting the range of her poetry to a mere contemplation of personal identity. Rahimieh reminds us, "[A]s [Farrukhzād] pointed out in interviews, her poetry was *not concerned exclusively with the predicament of women* but rather called for a change in attitudes which create and reinforce *all manner of stereotypes*."[18] Still, the critical tradition, whether in Iran or elsewhere, has often reduced Farrukhzād's poetry to an expression of her identity. "During her own lifetime," Darznik continues, "critics tended to conflate Farrokhzad's personality with the poetic persona of her verses, and when Forough Farrokhzad is remembered today, it is still most often as a confessional poet, one who drew directly from her life to her art or, more pointedly, from her sex life to her erotic verses."[19] Therefore, while I suggest that we read Farrukhzād's *flâneuse* in an erotic mode here and later on, we should avoid conflating the persona and the person – particularly in light of the reductive, misogynist, and sexist reception of Farrukhzād's work at home and abroad.

Looking at the above lines solely from an aesthetic perspective, then, we find four repetitions of "*zindagī shāyad*" ("perhaps life is"), an anaphora that highlights the poetic persona's continual attempts to find meaning in the fleeting experiences of the passers-by she witnesses. The *flâneuse* crosses beyond the boundary of the private sphere by looking out into the street at the modern city and its residents in the hopes of making some sense of life's purpose. She then returns from her foray into the public sphere to remember the quiet moment of lighting cigarettes after having sex. But as soon as she grasps these brief moments of daily life in words, they slip away in meaningless repetition. Experience, not metaphysical philosophizing, holds the only meaning in these lines, but experience is ephemeral. Farrukhzād's *flâneuse* persona reminds us of this by also repeating the word root for "passing by" ("*guzar*") in "*mīguzarad*" ("passes") and "*rahguzarī*" (passer-by), which bring to mind Baudelaire's pivotal reflections on modern life as well as those of other modernists across traditions. As a witness integral to her own poetic scene, the *flâneuse* attempts to record the short-lived moments that make up modern life in a continuation of a theme we can trace all the way back in Iranian modernist poetry to Nīmā's "The Phoenix," where "at far off points / people pass by" (*v-andar nuqāṭ-i dūr / khalq-and dar ʿubūr*),[20] and in the European tradition to both Baudelaire's flashes of insight on the streets of Paris and Eliot's Unreal City in *The Waste Land*. There, we might recall how Eliot's lyric "I" observes the street in the morning, looking on at the walking dead as they go to work. "And each man fixed his eyes before his feet. / Flowed up the hill and down King William Street, / To where Saint Mary Woolnoth kept the hours / With a dead sound on the final stroke of nine."[21] Farrukhzād echoes these lines throughout her late poetry, which lyrically represents for us the reorganization and regimentation of modern life into specific blocks of time.

Farrukhzād's *flâneuse* is a uniquely individual being in her experience of the modern city. Discussing her furthest modernist development in "Let Us Believe," which "avoid[s] the pitfalls of more mainstream modernist commitment to social and political *engagement* in verse," Hillman explains, "[Farrukhzād's] poetry of life may occasionally suffer because of its subjectivity, but at least life's vitality shows through, whereas in poetry of social commitment, sometimes only ideology is communicated, often lacking both verisimilitude and the subjective truth of personal experience."[22] If we follow Hillman's approach, we can further open "Let Us Believe" up to an interpretation that goes beyond any "subjectivity" critics might recognize in it and instead accounts for, on the one hand, Farrukhzād's masterful incorporation of and reflections on modernism as a global movement and, on the other hand, a process of local poetic exchange. In the next two sections, we will address, first, Farrukhzād's development of metrical sciences in Persian beyond Nīmā's prosodic innovations. Second, we will return to the garden of premodern Persian poetry and consider how Farrukhzād transforms this garden into a graveyard as she reimagines the geographies significant to her formulation of Persian modernism.

The End of Modernist Metrics in Iran

Farrukhzād's understanding of Persian poetic form starts with Nīmā. "Nima for me was a beginning," she tells us when discussing her poetic education.

> You know, Nima was a poet in whom I saw, for the first time, an intellectual atmosphere and a kind of human perfection, like Hafez. I as a reader felt I was dealing with a man, not just a bunch of superficial sentiments and trite, commonplace words – a factor in explaining and analyzing the problems, a vision and sensibility that rose above ordinary conditions and petty needs. His simplicity always astounded me, especially when behind this simplicity I would suddenly recognize all the complexities and dark questions of life, like a star that directs a person's face to the sky. In his simplicity, I discovered my own simplicity .... But the greatest impact Nima left on me was in terms of the language and forms of his poetry. I can't say how and in what way I am or am not under Nima's influence.[23]

With these comments in mind, we will in this section elucidate at least one way that Nīmā's metrical innovations influenced Farrukhzād's own, which in the end went on to surpass Nīmā's while remaining grounded in the same prosodic tradition going all the way back to al-Khalīl's science of Arabic prosody in eighth century Basra and the corpus of Arabic poetry he worked with.

Contra Shāmlū's *shiʿr-i sipīd* (blank verse, roughly, in that there is no rhyme but also no regular meter; the literal translation is "white poetry"), Farrukhzād continues to incorporate premodern poetic feet into her poetry. However, because she took their various combinations to new extremes and used different meters in a single poem, it is admittedly exceedingly difficult to discover the Arabic prosodic structures that underlie her later poetry. In her final two collections, she stretches the premodern poetic feet of *ʿarūḍ* prosody to their greatest limits, yet her poetry still finds its formal ground in their rhythms.[24] In "Let Us Believe," Farrukhzād goes beyond the formal innovations Nīmā pioneered in the 1930s by introducing new and irregular combinations of poetic feet from different meters into the same poem.[25]

In the following analysis of Farrukhzād's use of metrics in "Let Us Believe," I am thus guided by her own comments on meter, which she sent to fellow poet Aḥmad Riżā Aḥmadī (b. 1940). I quote her at length to highlight the importance she placed on metrics.

> My dear Ahmad Reza – don't forget the "meter." Listen to me, and never forget it.
>
> [...]
>
> Everything which comes into existence and lives follows a line of distinct forms and arrangements and grows within them. Poetry is also like this, and if you say it is not, and if others say it is not, then they are in my opinion

> mistaken. If you do not harness force within a form, you have not utilized that force, you have wasted it. It's a shame for your sensitivity to come to naught and for your beautiful and lively words to not find their artistic form.[26]

Farrukhzād emphasizes the indispensable role that meter plays in poetic composition. "Don't forget the meter," she implores her poetic colleague, going on to suggest that all the "sensitivity" and the "beautiful and lively words" that go into a poem should be wasted if a poet does not "harness [their] force within a form." In another interview, conducted in 1964, she answered the question "When you began (writing poetry), did you turn to Western literature?" by saying, "No. I looked at its content. That's natural. But at the meter, no – it is different. The Persian language has its own music, and it is this music that creates and directs the meter of Persian poetry."[27] While Farrukhzād's comments on meter have guided my approach to poetic form throughout this book, we will now turn to her poetry with them in mind to see exactly how she goes about retaining "this music that creates and directs the meter of Persian poetry" in her modernist poems.

I focus on "Let Us Believe" because it represents the epitome of Persian modernist poetry due to its dual connections to both modernism as a global movement and the formal tradition of premodern Persian (and therefore also Arabic) prosodic science. Furthermore, a striking feature of this poem that has remained completely ignored in English scholarship is Farrukhzād's innovative use of premodern metrical patterns. Just as Eliot ironically employs traditional English meters such as iambic pentameter in blank verse in *The Waste Land*, Farrukhzād uses a unique combination of premodern metrical feet throughout "Let Us Believe."[28] While the majority of the lines follow a pattern based on a standard *mużāriʿ* (similar) meter, Farrukhzād sometimes uses an irregular version of the *mużāriʿ* (which could scan as another meter entirely: the *mujtas̱s̱* ["docked" or "amputated"])[29] to distinguish certain lines from others and to bring our attention to the central theme of the poem: a meditation on the approach of death and the ultimate meaning of life.

Take, for example, the use of metrics in the following lines, which come toward the beginning of the poem after a long set of lines with fairly regular metrical progressions.

Dar āsitānah-ʾi faṣlī sard
dar maḥfil-i ʿazā-yi āyinah-hā
va ijtimāʿ-i sūgvār-i tajribah-hā-yi parīdah rang

va īn ghurūb bārvar shudah az dānish-i sukūt
chigūnah mīshavad bih ānkasī kih mīravad īnsān
ṣabūr,
sangīn,
sargardān.
Farmān-i īst dād.
Chigūnah mīshavad bih mard guft kih ū zandah nīst, ū hīchvaqt zandah nabūdahst.

On the threshold of a cold season,
In the mournful assembly of mirrors
in the dirgeful gathering of pale experiences
in this sunset impregnated with the knowledge of silence
how can one tell a person who goes along
patiently,
seriously,
lost
to stop?
How can you tell a man he's not alive, that he's never been alive?[30]

Notice the near breakdown of the poetic feet in the following as the poem posits, "how can one tell a person who goes along / patiently, / seriously, / lost / to stop?" and then rushes to ask, "How can you tell a man he's not alive, that he's never been alive?" The feet of the entire section are as follows, using the Arabic method of representation.

Mafāʿilun faʿilātun faʿ
mustafʿilun mafāʿilun faʿilun
mafāʿilun mafāʿilun mustafʿilun mafā
mafāʿilun mafāʿilun faʿilātun mafāʿilun
mafāʿilun mafāʿilun mafāʿilun mafāʿīlun
mafā
mustaf
mafʿūlun
mustafʿilun mafā
mafāʿilun mafāʿilun mafāʿilun mustafʿilun faʿūlun mafāʿilun fāʿilātun

Or, in Western-style longs and shorts, with " /" separating the feet:

⏑ – ⏑ – / ⏑ ⏑ – – / –
– – ⏑ – / ⏑ – ⏑ – / ⏑ ⏑ –
⏑ – ⏑ – / ⏑ – ⏑ – / – – ⏑ – / ⏑ –
⏑ – ⏑ – / ⏑ – ⏑ – / ⏑ ⏑ – – / ⏑ – ⏑ –
⏑ – ⏑ – / ⏑ – ⏑ – / ⏑ – ⏑ – / ⏑ – – –
⏑ –
– –

¯ ¯ ¯
¯ ¯ ˘ ¯ / ˘ ¯
˘ ¯ ˘ ¯ / ˘ ¯ ˘ ¯ / ˘ ¯ ˘ ¯ / ¯ ¯ ˘ ¯ / ˘ ¯ ¯ / ˘ ¯ ˘ ¯ / ¯ ˘ ¯ ¯

While the metrics of the first five lines do not match, they do, as Iranian critic Sīrūs Shamīsā explains, consist of feet from either the *mużāriʿ* or the *mujtass* meters.[31] Farrukhzād's innovation in this and other posthumously published poems – which even go beyond her own metrical experiments in *Another Birth* and signal the culmination of Nīmā's pioneering metrical techniques – is to repeat one foot out of a metrical pair as many times as she needs, such as we find in the fifth line above: *mafāʿilun* repeats four times (with an additional long syllable in the fourth: *mafāʿīlun*).[32] The usual pattern of the meter's feet (*mafāʿilun faʿilātun mafāʿilun faʿilun*) never completes. The lines remain unfinished, for their metrics lose their way as the poetic persona contemplates death. We might understand the unraveling metrical form of these lines to be a refusal to give in to the end, to the inevitability of death. However, if this is the case, we would then be faced with a life that unravels and falls apart with the meter as death approaches, a reversal of the existential commitment to revolt against "meaningless death" that we found in Bayātī's poems in Chapter 5.

The metrical games Farrukhzād plays here allow her to slow down and speed up the poem at certain points while the persona struggles to keep the meter together. As the imagined person the speaker considers telling "that he's not alive" "goes along / patiently, / seriously, / lost," the meter itself is almost lost, switching between disconnected parts of broken feet, searching for itself: "*mafā / mustaf / mafʿūlun*" (˘ ¯ / ¯ ¯ / ¯ ¯ ¯). This slog of long syllables comes to a halt with a complete poetic foot followed by another fragment in the *mujtass* meter: *mustafʿilun mafā* (¯ ¯ ˘ ¯ / ˘ ¯),[33] when the speaker says, "*Farmān-i īst dād*" ("tell [. . .] to stop"). Finally, the words burst forth from the speaker in the poem's longest line, which initially repeats a single foot three times (*mafāʿilun mafāʿilun mafāʿilun*) and follows that with four more complete feet.[34] The quick succession of feet, punctuated by eleven short syllables at irregular intervals (of twenty-seven, compared to the three short syllables of thirteen total in the previous four lines), formally manifests the speaker's gasps for breath as she tries to ask the poem's central question: "How can you tell a man he's not alive, that he's never been alive?"

Farrukhzād's metrical expertise, plainly displayed in these lines, and her willingness to go beyond the bounds of Nīmā's metrical innovations while not leaving premodern metrics completely behind brings Persian modernist poetry to its furthest formal limits. Farrukhzād is, therefore, not only Nīmā's poetic heir but also an indispensable figure in the wider development of premodern Arabic prosodic science precisely because of her retention of certain elements of the Arabic *ʿarūḍ* as an essential part of her poetry. As I have already mentioned, the parallels between Farrukhzād's use of metrics and that of Eliot in *The Waste Land* are many. Farrukhzād's use of metrical feet that might be understood to come from two separate meters as well as her frequent inclusion of alternative poetic feet not found in Persian prosody but available in Arabic complicate any sense of overall unity we might hope to find in the poem.[35] This lack of unity reflects the general uncertainty about modern existence that lies at the heart of the poem and functions in parallel with Eliot's alternation between metered and unmetered lines to reflect the same idea in *The Waste Land*.[36]

Having addressed Farrukhzād's revolutionary employment of premodern metrics in "Let Us Believe," we now move into a discussion of her thematic engagements of both premodern Persian poetry and modernism as a broader, global phenomenon.

Winter in Farrukhzād's Modernist Garden

Just as Nīmā formed his modernist project out of the dual influences of modern French poetry and the premodern Persian tradition, Farrukhzād also looked both to earlier Persian poetry as well as the West, finding new sources of inspiration Nīmā did not, including, most saliently, the poetry of T. S. Eliot. While Nīmā came to the modernist tropes of death and rebirth through his readings of the French modernists alongside writers from the Persian literary heritage, like ʿAṭṭār and Ḥāfiẓ, Farrukhzād's fascination with Eliot's English poetry – *The Waste Land* and "The Hollow Men" in particular – brought her to fruitful poetic ground.[37] I here connect how Farrukhzād pushes premodern metrics to their breaking point with her inversion of premodern Persian poetic themes associated with the garden. In her late poetry, Farrukhzād transforms the garden from premodern Persian poetry into a graveyard to reflect the deadening effects of modernity. By tarrying in Farrukhzād's reimagination of garden as graveyard, we can better explore the significance of the garden as a poetic space, from premodern to modernist Persian poetry as well as within the wider modernist movement. As we will see, the garden for Farrukhzād – like Iran for Bayātī, Korea for Shāmlū in *The Manifesto*,

Jaykūr's Buwayb rivulet for Sayyāb, or the shores of the Caspian Sea for Nīmā – becomes the locus for her persona's reflections on the modern world, thereby marking it, and the graveyard Farrukhzād creates out of it, as a particular geography significant to *her*.[38]

Brookshaw provides a useful overview of Farrukhzād's development of garden themes in his chapter "Places of Confinement, Liberation, and Decay: The Home and the Garden in the Poetry of Forugh Farrokhzād," which focuses on two poems: "*Fatḥ-i bāgh*" ("The Conquest of the Garden") and "*Dilam barā-yi bāghchah mīsūzad*" ("I Feel Sorry for the Garden").[39] While Farrukhzād sets earlier poems in garden scenes as well, these two come from her final two collections, *Another Birth* and *Let Us Believe in the Beginning of the Cold Season*. In his analysis of the first, Brookshaw points out how Farrukhzād plays on the premodern Persian tradition's understanding of "the ominous image of a crow flying over the heads of two lovers," "used to symbolize the malicious gossip monger" who might "disclose the lovers' secret union [in the garden] to the inhabitants of the town."[40] Hillman explains further that "[t]he crow seems here to represent people determined to maintain and enforce conventional morality."[41] Brookshaw concludes his discussion of "The Conquest of the Garden" by arguing that its "garden idyll is unadulterated by society's controlling normative attitudes" because of its distance from the city. Moving on to "I Feel Sorry for the Garden," Brookshaw informs us that the "garden depicted in this poem is located in an urban setting, at the centre of the family home, and at the heart of the family itself," such that "the garden acts as the repository of the collective memory of the family."[42] The garden of this second poem, then, is not a place for a lovers' tryst outside the city – a familiar scene in premodern Persian poetry – but rather a symbol of "degeneration" as it goes untended by the family and thus also a representation of modern Iranian society.[43] Brookshaw understands this second poem as an example of Farrukhzād's poetic growth toward the end of her career, by which time she "had succeeded in harnessing her energies to produce poetry with a broad, human perspective that transgressed that of the individual woman; a perspective that went beyond gender itself."[44]

Continuing this line of critical inquiry, we now turn to Farrukhzād's reimagining of the premodern garden scene in "Let Us Believe." Consider the role of passing time in the poem's second stanza, which brings together the regimented time of the modern day, the natural changing of the seasons, and the eternal time of the afterlife, stalled in the body of a savior dead and buried in a grave.

Time passed
Time passed and the clock struck four
the clock struck four
Today is the first day of winter
I know the secrets of the seasons
and understand the words of the moments
The Redeemer sleeps in the grave (*najāt dihandah dar gūr khuftah ast*)
and the dust, the receptive dust
gives away his repose.

Time passed and the clock struck four.[45]

The doubled repetition of "time passed / time passed" and "the clock struck four / the clock struck four" in the first three lines sonically represents the four strikes of the hour. The striking clock in the poem echoes the intrusion of capitalism into modern life, with its unnatural ordering of the day. However, the persona here also links the four strikes of the clock signaling the end of the workday to the coming of the first day of winter and points to the oncoming cold season after which the poem is titled. The lyric "I" then intervenes to tell the reader more about her role in the poem: she "know[s] the secrets of the seasons / and understand[s] the words of the moments." That is, she recognizes the reality of modern existence, where the only thing we can be sure of is death and the only one who can save us is already sleeping in the ground. I have chosen to translate *najāt dihandah* (literally "rescue-giver") as "Redeemer" to indicate the allusion to Christ, which is not as clear should one choose to use "savior."[46] In a fully modernist move, the lines deny the Redeemer's divinity and suggest that His body remains in the grave where its decay into dust "gives away his repose," which is, once again, interrupted by the striking clock in the repeated line "Time passed and the clock struck four." The poem begins by stripping away hope for an eternal afterlife and subordinating worldly life both to the cycle of nature and capitalism's unnatural regulation of time.

The world the persona imagines in the poem, then, is one where God is already dead. In place of the Divine, we have the hands of a clock, which regulate peoples' lives instead. Later in the poem, the speaker again condemns modernity's strict arrangement of time, which replaces the natural progression of the seasons.

What is silence? – what, what, O dearest only one?
What is silence but unspoken words
I refrain from speaking, but the language of sparrows
is one of life in the flowing sentences of nature's celebration.

The language of sparrows: Spring. Leaves. Spring.
The language of sparrows: Breeze. Fragrance. Breeze.
In factories the language of sparrows dies.[47]

The symptoms of capitalism manifest themselves once more "in the factory, where the language of sparrows dies."[48] The lines suggest that as capital reorders society according to its needs, it interrupts "the flowing sentences of nature's celebration," drowned out in the crush of factory gears. However, despite the disassociation of human from nature that compounds with technological advancement, these lines also suggest that, should one "refrain from speaking," they would still hear "the flowing sentences of nature's celebration." Even though technology ("factories") might drown out the sounds of nature, the progression of time continues, here represented by the repetitions of "Spring. Leaves. Spring" (that is, the change of seasons) and "Breeze. Fragrance. Breeze" (the persistence of natural phenomenon). In short, these lines tell us that technology cannot overcome nature, no matter how many of its sounds technology might make impossible to hear.

Continuing to the poem's direct invocation of garden themes, in the third stanza we find the following lines, where Farrukhzād's *flâneuse* persona plays on the intimate natural relationship of life and death, decay and growth, after catching a glimpse of a man passing by.

In the street the wind is blowing
In the street the wind is blowing
and I think of the pollination of the flowers
of the buds with their thin anemic stems
and this tired, consumptive time
A man is passing by the wet trees
a man, the lines of whose bluish veins
have crept up both sides of his throat
like dead snakes
and in his throbbing temples
those sanguine syllables are repeated:
– hello
– hello
and I think of the pollination of the flowers.[49]

These lines, like so many others throughout the poem, directly reference Eliot and many other modernists' ambivalent and at times highly pessimistic view of the utility of the death and rebirth myths that drove their poetry. When Farrukhzād's speaker says, "I think of the pollination of the flowers," the line recalls for us Eliot's famous opening to *The Waste Land*, perhaps the best-known invocation of a garden scene in modernist poetry. "April is the cruellest month, breeding / Lilacs out of the dead land, mixing / Memory and desire, stirring / Dull roots with spring rain."[50] But, more than making a simple reference to the European tradition, Farrukhzād here combines Eliot's poetic vision with her own. Faced with death in the image of the man passing with his blue, lifeless veins like de-oxygenated ropes strangling him, the speaker can only "think of the pollination of the flowers." The Persian word used for "pollination" here is *juft'gīrī*, which is also used to mean "mating" and thus creates a grotesque sexual image linking death and life that parallels Eliot's sprouting corpse and transmogrifies the erotic figure of the *flâneuse* into a prophet. In Eliot's Unreal City, one World War I veteran asks another, "That corpse you planted last year in your garden, / Has it begun to sprout? Will it bloom this year? / Or has the sudden frost disturbed its bed?"[51] As time comes to its end for the passing man in Farrukhzād's poem, the speaker-turned prophet looks into the future when the man's body will reinvigorate the "thin, anemic stems" with nutrients as it decays.[52] The persona further highlights the cyclical process of life and death here by repeating, "I think of the pollination of the flowers." By connecting these moments of reproduction and death, Farrukhzād's modernist imagination transforms the garden into a graveyard.

"Let Us Believe in the Beginning of the Cold Season" and the Death of Modernism

In its engagement of central modernist tropes as it reimagines the pre-modern Persian poetic garden, "Let Us Believe" shows us again the transnational movement of modernist themes across poetic traditions. Farrukhzād's sustained reflections on the theme of death and rebirth and her portrayal of the speaker as a *flâneuse* in the poem show us how she goes about using the European tradition to build her own particular version of Persian modernist poetry, one which remains indebted to the modernist tradition Nīmā began but openly addresses itself to European modernism as well, particularly Eliot's poetry. As Farrukhzād explored the world of art, poetry, and cinema toward the end of her career, her sources of poetic inspiration began to migrate beyond the borders of Iran. After she started working with the film director Ibrāhīm Gulistān (b. 1922) in 1958, opportunities for international travel opened up to her. She and Gulistān carried on a lasting romantic relationship – another machine in the Farrukhzād rumor mill – and she traveled to England, Holland, and

Germany with the support of his film production company, Golestan Studios.[53] During the winter of 1963, when she was in Germany, she produced a collection of modern German poetry in Persian translation.[54] The collection is yet another example of Farrukhzād's interest in modern European poetry, which had previously led her to Eliot's work.[55] Eliot's poetry had an enduring impact on her late poems. In them, we can locate the presence of Eliot's pessimism about the future through Farrukhzād's intertextual references to his poetry, which she uses to create her own poetics of death.

Other than the poem's overall dependence on the cycle of life and death that we also find in *The Waste Land*, it specifically references "The Hollow Men" (1925) as well. Farrukhzād's English translators have pointed out her paraphrase of Eliot when she writes "*miyān-i panjarah va dīdan / hamīshah fāṣilah īst*" ("Between the window and the seeing / always lies a distance").[56] However, more than simply referencing Eliot's poem, Farrukhzād fully integrates its driving theme into her own: the loss of meaning, absence of hope, and pessimism about the future that defines the modernist view of the world. Consider Farrukhzād's lines:

> Hollow man (*insān-i pūk*)
> Hollow man filled with confidence
> Look (*nigāh kun*) how while chewing
> his teeth sing a song
> and while staring
> his eyes are torn
> and he, how he passes by the wet trees:
> patiently,
> gravely,
> lost.[57]

Farrukhzād includes a direct reference to Eliot's hollow man (*insān-i pūk*), signaling us to the transnational movement of modernist tropes. However, her nod to Eliot in these lines is only one element of a broader engagement with modernist themes in her later poetry. Farrukhzād's lyric "I" invites us into the poem as her equal, her compatriot in the fallen modern world. The imperative "Look" (*nigāh kun*) brings the reader into the poem to share the vision of Farrukhzād's *flâneuse*, a witness to desperate attempts to find meaning in the quick flashes of city life she sees.[58] The passing man is a constant reminder of death, as we have already seen in the poet's ruminations on the meaning of life in "Another Birth": "the mindless transit of a passer-by / who tips his hat / and with a meaningless smile says 'good morning' to another passer-by."[59] Death is everywhere in the modern city, where Farrukhzād's *flâneuse* disappears in the crowd to observe modern life.

Elsewhere in the poem, we find:

> Happy corpses
> despondent corpses
> silent, thoughtful corpses
> well-mannered, well-dressed, well-eating corpses
> in the stations of scheduled times
> and the dubious background of temporary lights
> greedily buying futility's rotten fruits.
> Ah,
> how people stare at accidents in the intersections
> and the sound of traffic whistles to stop
> in an instant a man must, must, must
> be crushed beneath the wheels of time
> the man passing beside the wet trees . . .[60]

In these lines as elsewhere, Farrukhzād's *flâneuse* criticizes the rigid structure of modern life "in the stations of scheduled times" that has turned people into walking corpses, just like the walking dead in Eliot's Unreal City. Contrary to her engagements with nature, which we saw some aspects of in the previous section about the garden, Farrukhzād presents how modernity opens up new, terrible, and mundane ways to die. For instance, car accidents cause minor inconveniences during a morning commute but force onlookers to consider their own mortality for at least a moment. "In an instant a man must, must, must / be crushed beneath the wheels of time." Farrukhzād's poetics of death is informed by the experience of modernity, and her ambivalence about death alternatively casts it as meaningless and the only thing that means. Death structures every aspect of life to such an extent that people become corpses while they are still alive, in a direct reversal of Bayātī's revolutionary poetics of death from Chapter 5 that we also found in Shāmlū's *Manifesto* poems. The living dead populate Farrukhzād's modern city, where the "man passing beside the wet trees" leads the speaker's thoughts to the inevitable end.

"Let Us Believe" takes up these ideas in its overarching themes of loneliness, death-in-life, and mortality. In the flashes of city life Farrukhzād's *flâneuse* offers us, we are confronted by the unhappy realities of modern existence. "The Renaissance, it lied; the Enlightenment, it lied: the truth, the only truth, is bad mortality and complete loneliness while we live through the death we call life. [. . .] All men are brothers, but, in another way, all men are alone."[61] Farrukhzād intervenes to assert that all women too are alone in the end. "And this is me / a woman alone." Later in the poem, she writes,

> I am cold
> I am cold, as if I'll never be warmed
> O friend, O most singular friend, how old was that wine?
> Look what a weight
> time has here
> and how the fish chew my flesh
> Why do you always keep me at the bottom of the sea?
>
> I am cold, and I hate these mother-of-pearl earrings
> I am cold, and I know
> that nothing will remain
> from all the red illusions of a wild poppy
> but a few drops of blood.[62]

The lyric "I" here complains to a friend (a lover?) about being left alone to fend for itself "at the bottom of the sea." In these lines, the speaker crosses from the realm of the living to that of the dead, where she contemplates the end of the body ("the fish chew my flesh") and the hubris of those who imagine remaining present in the world after death, declaring, "I know / that nothing will remain / from all the red illusions of a wild poppy / but a few drops of blood." Farrukhzād's subtle reference to *The Waste Land* imbues her own poem with Eliot's pessimism to challenge it, if only slightly. She alludes to these lines in the fourth section of Eliot's poem, "Death by Water."

> Phlebas the Phoenician, a fortnight dead,
> Forgot the cry of gulls, and the deep sea swell
> And the profit and loss.
> A current under sea
> Picked his bones in whispers. As he rose and fell
> He passed the stages of his age and youth
> Entering the whirlpool.
> Gentile or Jew
> O you who turn the wheel and look to windward,
> Consider Phlebas, who was once handsome and tall as you.[63]

By using the first person rather than the third in her version of the same story, Farrukhzād makes personal Eliot's admonition to those who deny the power of time. The lyric "I" in "Let Us Believe" thinks of her body after its death, its eventual, inescapable fate, thus calling attention to the importance of what she does while alive. Therefore, her persona here admits that only "a few drops of blood," a faint trace, will remain after the flower of "red illusions" fades away.

"Let Us Believe" depends on this ambivalent relationship between the lyric "I" and the world it describes. Scott Brewster elaborates,

> The detachment of the lyric "I" is exacerbated by the sense of poetry's marginalisation in the modern world. While this marginalisation seems to confirm Baudelaire's view that the modern is "antilyrical," the provocative challenge to the staleness of everyday language, to mass culture and to bourgeois attitudes in the modernist lyric suggests confrontation with, rather than evasion of, this inhospitable climate.[64]

While we may not be able to say that poetry was (or is) as marginal in Iran as it has been in Europe or America following the modernist turn, we can recognize a similar detachment of Farrukhzād's lyric "I" from her subjects, who appear only in short flashes. This detachment carries with it political meaning, as Brewster argues about the modern lyric "I" more generally, precisely because of its ambivalence, which is not at all an "evasion of" reality but a "provocative challenge" to it.

To stress how the poem so functions, in the final lines we read:

> Perhaps the truth was those two young hands, those two young hands
> buried beneath the never-ending snow
> and next year, when Spring
> makes love to the sky behind the window
> and shoots thrust from its body
> green shoots of carefree branches
> will blossom, O dear one, O dearest only one.
>
> Let us believe in the beginning of the cold season . . .[65]

Although the poem has until this point offered us a series of modern life's depressing scenes: the detached *flâneuse*, capital's reorganization of time and the natural world, the loss of meaning in life symbolized by a stranger's nonchalant doffing of his hat, etc., in these final lines a glimmer of hope flickers. Instead of an ironic invocation of the endless cycle of death and rebirth, the speaker sincerely commands the reader (and herself) to believe in the beginning of the cold season, the only way forward to a truly new birth in spring.[66] Of course, the speaker remains pessimistic about her own survival through the winter and appeals to Eliot once again by imagining the "green shoots" of tomorrow bursting forth from the body of today. The tomorrow she dreams of is not hers but ours, her readers. As Benjamin might put it, "The last journey of the *flâneuse*: death. Her destination: the new."[67]

Beginnings and Ends in Farrukhzād's Late Poetry

Farrukhzād's poetry from late in her career converges on modernist poetry's obsession with mortality. In a few pithy lines from another poem in her last collection, she writes, "No one will introduce / me to the sun / No one will take me to the sparrows' feast / hold on to the memory of flight / the bird is mortal."[68] The final line here reminds us of Shāmlū's *Quqnūs dar bārān* (*Phoenix in the Rain*), a collection that first appeared in late 1966 – the year before Farrukhzād died – and also marks the coming end of Persian modernism.[69] The lines are initially despondent, despairing both of reaching heaven and of being able to appreciate earthly life. Stuck between eternity and existence, all the speaker can hold on to is the hope of freedom, here as elsewhere represented by a bird in flight. However, pessimism takes over in the final line of the poem as the persona remembers that even the bird's freedom must have an end in death. This is not the hopeful end Nīmā's Phoenix meets in "*Quqnūs*" but rather a recognition of the inevitability of death and an attempt to extract an ounce of freedom out of the course of one's life.

With *Another Birth* and *Let Us Believe*, Farrukhzād's lyric "I" completes Nīmā's project as representative of Iranian modernity. These two collections realize Nīmā's modernist vision by bringing together the experience of modern life with elements of the premodern Persian literary tradition, ancient Mesopotamian mythological themes, and the ongoing interaction of Persian poetry with European literature and culture. In its combination of flashes of city life with its solid foundation in mythical allusions, "Let Us Believe" offers a sustained engagement with the gamut of modernist themes found within the movement as a transnational phenomenon – not only as they appeared in Iran but also in Europe and elsewhere. In fact, Farrukhzād's outsize popularity has even brought her to the attention of readers in the Arab world, unlike the other (still quite popular, at least in Iran) Iranian poets we have addressed. Selected lines from "Let Us Believe" grace the first page of the Egyptian author Mīrāl al-Ṭaḥāwī's *Brooklyn Heights* (2010),[70] and the Iraqi translator and poet Maryam al-ʿAṭṭār has recently published a complete translation of Farrukhzād's collected works in Arabic.[71]

Farrukhzād's modernist vision, in its combination of highly innovative metrical experiments still founded in premodern meter with new imaginaries of what it means to live in a modern world, looks beyond the borders of Iran to participate in the wider movement of modernism by putting Persian modernism on the map. Grounded in the Persian poetic tradition, expert in Arabic metrics, and careful with her integration of European modernist poetry into her work, Farrukhzād contributes a crucial pillar to the imaginary edifice of Persian modernism and maps an essential region within our significant modernist geography, even as her untimely death marks one possible end of modernism in Iran.

Conclusion
Reorienting Modernism

The title of Aḥmad Shāmlū's November 1966 collection, *Quqnūs dar bārān* (*Phoenix in the Rain*), represents the stalled project of the earlier modernist poets, the postponed dream of rebirth. Shāmlū metaphorically represents the chilling rain of authoritarianism in his title, which puts out the Phoenix's fire and stops the cycle of death and rebirth. We can extend this metaphor beyond the Persian context to the Arabic one as well, on the cusp of the Six-Day War and the psychological trauma that was to follow. Looking further into the future, Shāmlū also prophesies the ultimate failure of the Third World solidarity movement after the emergence of neoliberalism, which reordered the world system in the 1970s as the USSR fell farther and farther behind the capitalist Western powers. Shāmlū questions the real-world use value of a poetry that had, for the most part, failed to spur the masses to revolution, forcing the poet to become much more self-contemplative and move his gaze inward. In a continuation of previous modernist invocations of Christ (regarded in both the Arab and Iranian modernist traditions as a progenitor of the death-rebirth cycle), Shāmlū – ever so humble – puts the committed poet in the place of the Messiah in his poem "*Marg-i Nāṣirī*" ("The Death of the Nazarene"). As the executioners torture Christ ("'*Shitāb kun Nāṣirī, shitāb kun*!'"; "'Hurry up Nazarene, get on with it!'"), Shāmlū brings us back to Nīmā's comparison of the poet and the swan in 1926's "The Swan." While the ungrateful crowd, including even Lazarus, stands aside in silence, Christ looks inward for strength as he dies. "*Az raḥmī kih dar jān-i khᵛīsh yāft / sabuk shud / va chūnān qū-ī-'ī / maghrūr / dar zulālī-'i khᵛīshtan nigarīst*" ("[Christ] found peace / from the mercy in His soul / and like a proud / swan / He regarded His own purity").[1]

Phoenix in the Rain represents a wider shift among the Persian and Arabic modernists from a poetry of collective commitment – however ambivalent this commitment may have been – during the first two decades after World War II to an individualistic poetry of humanist universalism, often informed by Western Liberalism. Robyn Creswell locates this shift within the group of Arab poets who came together around the *Shiʿr* journal in Beirut in the late 1950s. I especially appreciate his use of the term "late modernism" to refer to this stage of Arabic poetic modernism in *City of Beginnings*. Thinking in comparison with my analyses in this book, we have here addressed the early and middle phases of the same tradition. Among our subjects, the early modernists in Arabic – and we are here thinking in terms of the historically grounded modernist poetic movement, not "the Moderns" broadly conceived – would be poets like Awad, Sayyāb, and Malāʾikah. All three continued writing into the middle period, which we can locate in time after 1953. Disillusionment with local politics eventually led to the late modernist period, which overlapped with the themes and styles of the middle period for some years before taking over almost completely. We find a similar shift with the Iranian modernists in the years following the coup, when disillusionment with Communism ran rife and the Shah consolidated power after retaking the throne. A space then opened up within the political sphere for Islamists to take advantage of, and a new opposition against local despots took shape not between authoritarian leaders and the Left but rather pitting the state and political Islamism against each other.[2] While this shift has manifested in myriad ways across the Arab world, in Iran it led directly to the Islamic Revolution, after which state patronage of revolutionary poets steered them away from the modernist forms of Nimaic poetry and back to those of the premodern *qaṣīdah*.[3]

To return to the beginning of the book, we started out from a relativist perspective inspired by Einstein's special theory of relativity, situating ourselves within the center of a modernist map projecting outward from the border between Iraq and Iran. From here, we pondered the formation of a transnational unconscious that flowed across national borders to bring together the people living in the developing nations of the decolonial and postcolonial world. We then looked to the shared transnational consciousness that emerged across the Global South and sought out alternative futures during the early years of the Cold War. As despotism returned following the heady times that saw some initial progressive successes during the decolonial moment, the subjects of our study began engaging with existentialist themes as they continued to imagine alternative futures. This shift inward, compounded by the disastrous events of the late 1960s and early 1970s, marks the end of our timeline.

Looking back at the history and development of poetry in Arabic and Persian as parts of a significant modernist geography, the chapters in this book take the first steps on a new path for comparative studies of literary modernism. In them, I read Arabic and Persian modernist poetries together as participants in the shared transnational development of a local modernist movement. Rather than understanding these two modernist traditions to be the products of Western colonialism and literary influence, I look to the many connections between them, links in form and content that lay beyond – even against – their interactions with Western modernist poetry. While I do not ignore Western poetry's indelible mark on the development of the modernist Arabic and Persian traditions, I consider the parallel innovations on the premodern Arabic prosodic science that lies at their cores along with their shared incorporations of ancient Mesopotamian myths of death and rebirth. Through such consideration, I further contend that these prosodic links and the modernists' corresponding dependence on mythic foundations transnationally bring the Arab and Iranian modernist poetic traditions together to respond to the Western colonial and neocolonial drive to globalize and homogenize, to complicate the enlightenment project of separation and categorization. By situating the Arabic and Persian modernist traditions as dynamic nodes in a literary polysystem, I argue for a fundamentally different approach to these literatures, one which takes up not only their relationships to their contexts of composition but also – and perhaps more importantly – their internal, reflexive aesthetic features.

Reorienting Modernism pays close attention to the inherently transnational makeup of Arabic modernist poetry, which the Egyptian critic and Marxist Louis Awad recognized as early as 1947 when he wrote his manifesto in *Plutoland*. He started that manifesto by calling fellow poets to *ḥaṭṭimū ʿamūd al-shiʿr*, to "break poetry's back." Despite beginning with this violent, iconoclastic order, Awad went on to explain how Arabic poetry has, in fact, always been changing, ever since it made its way out of the Arabian Peninsula with the Islamic conquests of the seventh century. Awad told us how Arabic poetry developed as it came into contact with the Egyptians, then the Amazigh, and finally the local populations of Andalusia. Thus, the poetry we call "Arabic" was in a dialectical exchange with other cultures for centuries, so there should have been no resistance to the interactions that were going on in the late forties between Arabic and Western poetry. Awad's manifesto marked out our first coordinates as we began mapping the concept of a significant modernist geography in Arabic and Persian poetry.

The readings of Arabic and Persian modernist poetry I offered center around prolonged analyses of how my subjects use premodern poetic form to craft their modernist visions. In Chapter 1, I took up the building blocks of foot, rhyme, and meter as essential tools of poetic craft. Then we looked at Nīmā Yūshīj's invention of new poetic forms that placed the foot rather than the entire line at their structural base to reorient our view of modernist poetry in Iran. In Chapter 3, we addressed Nīmā's compatriot Aḥmad Shāmlū and his move to forge connections across national borders. I proposed referring to this type of pre-Bandung literary solidarity as proto-Third Worldism. Following Shāmlū's committed poetry, I analyzed the complicated transnational history that formed Badr Shākir al-Sayyāb's long poem "Weapons and Children." With it, we noted how Sayyāb's poetry harbors an internal tension between Soviet transnationalism from above and the poet's nascent feelings of Iraqi nationalism, which were thrown into direct conflict following his experience of the 1953 coup against Mosaddegh in Iran. In Chapter 5, I showed how ʿAbd al-Wahhāb al-Bayātī imbued his poetry with premodern poetic voices through his use of *taḍmīn* quoting and by putting on poetic masks. We considered how Bayātī combines existentialism with the Islamic mystical tradition in a poetics of transnational commitment. In Chapter 6, we continued to explore existentialist peregrinations across Arab and Iranian modernisms in Furūgh Farrukhzād's posthumous poetry. We saw how Farrukhzād combined new innovations on premodern Arabic prosodic science with direct influences from Western modernist poetry (especially that of Eliot) to create a subtle modernist masterpiece with her final poem, "Let Us Believe in the Beginning of the Cold Season." Farrukhzād's tragic early death brought us to the end of our study and heralded Shāmlū's announcement of the end of modernism in *Phoenix in the Rain*.

Modernist poetry in Arabic and Persian by its very nature calls us to work comparatively: across the linguistic divide between Arabic and Persian and across the chronological one between the modern and the premodern. Once we begin doing this type of comparative work, we get a much clearer picture of Arab and Iranian modernisms. Instead of simply tracing out and focusing in on lines of influence moving from Western modernism to the East, instead of doing this kind of work that leaves Europe or the West or the Global North at the center of our modernist map, I argue for the necessity of East-East comparison, for comparative work across these minor, marginalized modernisms. Of course, we have to remain attuned to European modernism's presence in global modernism – we cannot simply bracket it off – but we do not have to leave it at the center of our considerations. The examples of modern Arabic and Persian literature I present in this book show just how much this type of East-East comparative work has to tell us about the story of modernism across the planet, about how the movement developed in ways independent of traditional modernist centers in the West. We have more work to do, especially when we acknowledge how marginal Persian literature remains within the canon of world literature – even in comparison to Arabic literature, which can at least boast of the Egyptian Naguib Mahfouz's Nobel Prize from 1988. And we have not even addressed the incredible parallels Arabic and Persian modernist poetry share with Kurdish, Turkish, and Hebrew poetry, yet other cases waiting for the type of East-East comparison *Reorienting Modernism* calls for. That Arabic modernism finds its source in the work of poets from Iraq like Sayyāb, Malā'ikah, Bayātī, and others also has much to tell us, because Baghdad – during the Ottoman period and through the end of the Hashemite monarchy there in 1958 – was thought of as a relative backwater when compared to Cairo or Beirut. Even in the Arab world, then, modernism comes from the margins, and it is time for us, therefore, to reorient our understanding of modernism.

While we cannot deny the impact Western modernist poetry had on the Arab and Iranian modernist poets, reading their poetry solely as a result of colonial intervention gives us only part of the story. Instead, we must account for the dialectical relationship that exists between these multi-sited modernisms and understand their transnational dynamics of poetic exchange. To do so, *Reorienting Modernism* uses a transnational paradigm of analysis to discover how two non-Western modernist traditions interact with each other, often subverting modernist centers in the West. As we have seen, despite the obvious changes these modernist poets' engagements with Western poetry brought to their respective traditions, their continued incorporation into their poems of premodern Arabic poetic form and the vast reserve of Mesopotamian myth brings Arab and Iranian modernist poetry together as a transnational response to Western interventions. That the broader Arabic and Persian modernist traditions developed in concert with one another, as well as out of their interactions with European modernist poetry, leads us to wonder: Where did modernism really begin? The Arabic and Persian traditions are neither wholly the results of Western influence, nor is Western modernism a *sui generis* product of Western literary development. The poems we read in this book help us to tell a more complete story about the world of modernism. To return to the thesis I introduced at the start, *Reorienting Modernism*'s relativist perspective imagines Arabic and Persian poets as creators of a significant modernist geography to argue that the East is already modernist, and modernism reverts to the East.

In conclusion, this book demonstrates not only the possibilities transnational analysis opens up for the study of Arabic and Persian poetry but also reveals many of the constituent elements of these poetries that lay beyond our reach without such analysis. Notwithstanding the newfound interest within the academy in innovative approaches to minor literatures under the rubric of world literature, there remains an all-too-apparent lack of attention to Arabic and Persian literatures and how they found their own way within modernism. By imagining them as producers of a significant modernist geography, we have a starting point for further investigation of the undeniable but as yet mostly unstudied connections of the Arabic and Persian modernist movements, an invitation to reorient our attention to the edges of modernism. Only once we have mapped how far modernism has gone can we venture to find its true beginnings.

Notes

Introduction

1 Max Horkheimer and Theodor Adorno, "Preface," *Dialectic of Enlightenment: Philosophical Fragments*, ed. Gunzelin Schmid Noerr, trans. Edmund Jephcott (Stanford, CA: Stanford University Press, 2002 [1947]), xviii.

2 Kevin Jackson lays out in excruciating detail the case for marking 1922 as the advent of (European) modernism in *Constellation of Genius: 1922: Modernism Year One* (New York: Farrar, Straus, & Giroux, 2012).

3 "Middle East" is a fraught and inexact term. Yet it not only remains widely used across European languages like English, French, and German, but has also been translated and adopted in others like Arabic, Persian, and Turkish. Rashid Khalidi's investigation of the history of the term and the problems concomitant with its use remains relevant, despite recent attempts within academia and elsewhere to employ a geographically based alternative with "West Asia." See "The 'Middle East' as a Framework of Analysis: Re-Mapping a Region in the Era of Globalization," *Comparative Studies of South Asia, Africa, and the Middle East* 28, no. 1 (1998): 74–80. In this book, I avoid using the term "Middle East" and instead highlight the linguistic map I am investigating by preferring the adjectives and nouns "Arabic" and "Persian" and the place names "the Arab world" and "Iran." I am aware of the problems that the phrase "the Arab world" raises in terms of non-Arabs living in the area it purportedly describes. As I am employing it in reference to a part of the globe where Arabic is spoken by the majority of people and because my analysis moves across several majority-Arab countries, I hope that more discerning readers will forgive my use of it as a necessary shorthand.

4 My approach is thus informed by Karima Laachir, Sara Marzagora, and Francesca Orsini's recent formulation of "significant geographies" as a literary-critical concept in "Significant Geographies: In Lieu of World Literature," *Journal of World Literature* 3 (2018): 290–301 and "Multilingual Locals and Significant Geographies: For a Ground-Up and Located Approach to World Literature," *Modern Languages Open* 19, no. 1 (2018): 1–8.

5 This study does not take up some relevant linguistic and poetic contexts that, were I able to include them, could further establish the region of the globe I analyze here as an even broader significant modernist geography. For instance, I have had to leave aside relevant formal and contextual links that Arabic and Persian share with Hebrew, Turkish, Kurdish, and other regional languages due to my inability to read them. I look forward to future scholarship that ventures where I am as yet unable to tread.

6 *From Modernists to Muḥdathūn* (Leiden: E. J. Brill, 2015), 2.

7 *Planetary Modernisms: Provocations on Modernity across Time*, Modernist Latitudes, eds. Jessica Berman and Paul Saint-Amour (New York: Columbia University Press, 2015), 7. Italics original.

8 *City of Beginnings: Poetic Modernism in Beirut* (Princeton, NJ: Princeton University Press, 2019), 198 and Adūnīs, *Dīwān al-shiʿr al-ʿarabī*, 3 vols. (Bayrūt: al-Maktabah al-ʿAṣriyyah, 1964–1968).

9 Tarek El-Ariss, *Trials of Arab Modernity: Literary Affects and the New Political* (New York: Fordham University Press, 2013), 170. Parentheses original.

10 "G: Relative Genius," Pat Walters interviewing Peter Galison, *Radiolab*, 28 June 2019. www.wnycstudios.org/story/g-relative-genius. Italics added.

11 Peter Galison, *Einstein's Clocks, Poincaré's Maps: Empires of Time* (New York: W. W. Norton & Company, 2003), 30.

12 Galison, *Einstein's Clocks*, 14.

13 Martin Heidegger, "The Thing," *Poetry, Language, Thought*, trans. Albert Hofstadter (New York: HarperCollins, 2001 [from lectures originally given in 1949 and 1950]), 163.

14 Qtd. in Paul M. Laporte, "Cubism and Relativity with a Letter of Albert Einstein," trans. Paul M. Laporte and Max Gould with an introduction by Rudolf Arnheim, *Leonardo* 21, no. 3 (1988): 314. Italics removed.

15 "Art and Relativity," *The Dial; A Semi-Monthly Journal of Literary Criticism, Discussion, and Information* XVV (May 1921), 535.

16 Roman Jakobson, *Language in Literature*, eds. Krystyna Pomorska and Stephen Rudy (Cambridge, MA: Belknap Press of Harvard University Press, 1987), 285.

17 Jessica Berman, *Modernist Commitments: Ethics, Politics, and Transnational Modernism*, Modernist Latitudes, eds. Jessica Berman and Paul Saint-Amour (New York: Columbia University Press, 2011), 31.

18 El-Ariss, *Trials of Arab Modernity*, 170.

19 Shengqing Wu, *Modern Archaics: Continuity and Innovation in the Chinese Lyrics Tradition, 1900–1937* (Cambridge, MA: Harvard University Press, 2013), 9.

20 El-Ariss, *Trials of Arab Modernity*, 170.

21 James A. Hijiya, "The *Gita* of J. Robert Oppenheimer," *Proceedings of the American Philosophical Society* 144, no. 2 (2000): 123–167.

22 *Abyssinia's Samuel Johnson: Ethiopian Thought in the Making of an English Author* (New York: Oxford University Press, 2012), 1. Italics added.

23 2 vols. (al-Qāhirah: Dār al-Maʿārif, 1938). Translated by Sidney Glazer as *The Future of Culture in Egypt*, American Council of Learned Societies Near Eastern Translation Program, no. 9 (New York: Octagon Books, 1975).

24 *Maʿnā al-nakbah* (Bayrūt: Dār al-ʿIlm li-l-Malāyīn, 1948). Translated by R. Bayly Winder as *The Meaning of the Disaster* (Beirut: Khayat's College Book Cooperative, 1956).

25 Ṣādiq Jalāl al-ʿAẓm, *al-Naqd al-dhātī baʿda al-hazīmah* (Bayrūt: Dār al-Ṭalīʿah, 1968). Translated by George Stergios as *Self-Criticism after the Defeat* (London: Saqi Books, 2011).

26 Ali Mirsepassi, *Transnationalism in Iranian Political Thought: The Life and Times of Ahmad Fardid* (Cambridge: Cambridge University Press, 2017), 6. Italics added.

27 Jalāl Āl-i Aḥmad, *Gharbzadagī* (Costa Mesa, CA: Mazda Publishers, 1997 [1962]). The title has been translated into English a few ways: *Occidentosis*, *Weststruckness*, and *Westoxification*. For a full translation, see Jalal Al-i Ahmad, *Occidentosis: A Plague from the West*, trans. R. Campbell, annotations and introduction by Hamid Algar (Berkeley, CA: Mizan Press, 1984).

28 *The Transnational Unconscious: Essays in the History of Psychoanalysis and Transnationalism*, The Palgrave Macmillan Transnational History Series, eds. Joy Damousi and Mariano Ben Plotkin (New York: Palgrave Macmillan, 2009), xi. Italics original.

29 El-Ariss, *Trials of Arab Modernity*, 1. Scholar of Arabic literature Roger Allen likewise uses the term "posture" to describe Adūnīs's approach to the modern. *The Arabic Novel: An Historical and Critical Introduction*, 2nd ed. (Syracuse, NY: Syracuse University Press, 1995 [1983]), 5. Cf. also Huda J. Fakhreddine's consideration of the Arabic prose poem as a "posture or an attitude" throughout her analysis in *The Arabic Prose Poem: Poetic Theory and Practice*, Edinburgh Studies in Modern Arabic Literature, ed. Rasheed El-Enany (Edinburgh: Edinburgh University Press, 2021), 6 and *passim*.

30 "And by 'attitude,'" Foucault writes, "I mean a mode of relating to contemporary reality; a voluntary choice made by certain people; in the end, a way of thinking and feeling; a way, too, of acting and behaving that at one and the same time marks a relation of belonging and presents itself as a task. A bit, no doubt, like what the Greeks called an *ethos*." "What Is Enlightenment?" ("*Qu'est-ce que les Lumières?*") *The Foucault Reader*, trans. Catherine Porter, ed. Paul Rabinow (New York: Pantheon Books, 1984), 39.

31 I use the term "planetary" instead of "global" here following Susan Stanford Friedman's suggestion in *Planetary Modernisms*.

32 *Textual Transactions in Nineteenth-Century Arabic, English, and Persian Literatures*, Routledge Studies in Middle Eastern Literatures, eds. James E. Montgomery et al. (New York: Routledge, 2007).

33 Rastegar, *Literary Modernity*, 11.

34 Rastegar, *Literary Modernity*, 19–26.

35 Rastegar, *Literary Modernity*, 19.

36 *Global Matters: The Transnational Turn in Literary Studies* (Ithaca, NY: Cornell University Press, 2010), 1.
37 *Minor Transnationalism*, eds. Françoise Lionnet and Shu-mei Shih (Durham, NC: Duke University Press, 2005*)*, 3.
38 *Global Matters*, 3.
39 "Another Turn for the Transnational: Empire, Nation, Imperium in Early Modern Studies," *PMLA* 130, no. 2 (March 2015): 417.
40 *Planetary Modernisms*, 3. Mao and Walkowitz coined the phrase "the transnational turn" in "The New Modernist Studies," *PMLA* 123, no. 3 (2008): 737–748.
41 *Planetary Modernisms*, 5.
42 Columbia University Press, Modernist Latitudes, https://cup.columbia.edu/series/modernist-latitudes. Arabic literature goes almost unmentioned in the following books that address modernism more globally, to say nothing of Persian literature (which the series has not yet dealt with so far as I can tell): Aarthi Vadde, *Chimeras of Form: Modernist Internationalism Beyond Europe, 1914–2016,* Modernist Latitudes, eds. Jessica Berman and Paul Saint-Amour (New York: Columbia University Press, 2016); *A New Vocabulary for Global Modernism*, eds. Eric Hayot and Rebecca L. Walkowitz, Modernist Latitudes, eds. Jessica Berman and Paul Saint-Amour (New York: Columbia University Press, 2016); and Steven S. Lee, *The Ethnic Avant-Garde: Minority Cultures and World Revolution*, Modernist Latitudes, eds. Jessica Berman and Paul Saint-Amour (New York: Columbia University Press, 2015). Other books in the series examine particular national and/or linguistic contexts, none of which are located in the Arabic- or Persian-speaking regions of the globe.
43 Michael Beard, *Hedayat's "Blind Owl" as a Western Novel* (Princeton, NJ: Princeton University Press, 2014 [1990]).
44 Franco Moretti, "Conjectures on World Literature," *New Left Review* 1 (January–February 2000), 54–68.
45 Efraín Kristal, "Considering Coldly … A Response to Franco Moretti," *New Left Review* 15 (May–June 2002): 62. Italics added.
46 They cite the Warwick Research Collective's work as the latest example of this approach. *Combined and Uneven Development: Towards a New Theory of World Literature* (Liverpool: Liverpool University Press, 2015).
47 An approach developed out of social science and Immanuel Wallerstein's world systems theory that Franco Moretti adapted for literary analysis. "Evolution, World-Systems, *Weltliteratur*," *Studying Transcultural Literary History*, ed. Gunilla Lindberg-Wada (Berlin: Walter de Gruyter, 2006), 113–121. We find a similar approach in Pascale Casanova, *The World Republic of Letters*, trans. M. B. DeBevoise, Convergences: Inventories of the Present, ed. Edward Said (Cambridge: Harvard University Press, 2004).
48 Laachir, Marzagora, and Orsini, "Significant Geographies," 293. Italics added.
49 Laachir, Marzagora, and Orsini, "Significant Geographies," 294. Parentheses and italics original.
50 Laachir, Marzagora, and Orsini, "Significant Geographies," 295. Italics original.

51 Berman, *Modernist Commitments*, 29.
52 *Postcolonial Thought and Historical Difference* (Princeton, NJ: Princeton University Press, 2000). Chakrabarty challenges our conception of Europe as the source and center of political modernity while never ignoring the foundational place of European thought in the development of political modernity in other areas of the globe.
53 Friedman, *Planetary Modernisms*, 6.
54 Aamir Mufti, *Forget English! Orientalisms and World Literatures* (Cambridge, MA: Harvard University Press, 2016), 19.
55 Lionnet and Shih, *Minor Transnationalism*, 5–6, quoting Sarah J. Mahler, "Theoretical and Empirical Contributions toward a Research Agenda for Transnationalism," *Transnationalism from Below*, eds. Michael Peter Smith and Luis Eduardo Guarzino (London: Transaction, 1998): 64–100.
56 I deal with this issue in more detail in Levi Thompson, "An Iraqi Poet and the Peace Partisans: Transnational Pacifism and the Poetry of Badr Shākir al-Sayyāb," *College Literature*, special issue on poetry networks, eds. Kamran Javadizadeh and Robert Volpicelli 47, no. 1 (2020): 65–88. doi:10.1353/lit.2020.0008.
57 Itamar Even-Zohar, "Polysystem Theory," *Polysystem Studies*, [= *Poetics Today* 11:1] (1990), 9. Italics original.
58 Even-Zohar, "Polysystem Theory," 12.
59 Even-Zohar, "Polysystem Theory," 14. Italics original.
60 Adūnīs [ʿAlī Aḥmad Saʿīd Isbir], *al-Thābit wa-l-mutaḥawwil: baḥth fī al-ibdāʿ wa-l-ittibāʿ ʿinda al-ʿarab*, 4 vols., 10th ed. (Bayrūt: Dār al-Sāqī, 2011 [1974]).
61 On the role of shared language in creating the modern nation state, see Benedict Anderson, *Imagined Communities* (New York: Verso, 2006 [1983]).
62 Lionnet and Shih, *Minor Transnationalism*, 8.
63 *Formations of the Secular: Christianity, Islam, Modernity*, Cultural Memory in the Present, eds. Mieke Bal and Hent de Vries (Stanford, CA: Stanford University Press, 2003), 4.
64 My use of the concept of sublation in this book comes from the German tradition of continental philosophy. "Sublation" is the English translation of the German term "*Aufhebung*" as it has been employed by G. W. F. Hegel and his intellectual followers; the infinitive form of the related verb is *aufheben*.
65 Khalīl Ḥāwī, *Dīwān Khalīl Ḥāwī* (Bayrūt: Dār al-ʿAwdah, 2001), 169. I have consulted the translation in and made some changes to Salma Khadra Jayyusi, *Trends and Movements in Modern Arabic Poetry*, 2 Vols., Studies in Arabic Literature: Supplements to the *Journal of Arabic Literature* [*JAL*], Vol. VI, eds. M. M. Badawi et al. (Leiden: Brill, 1977), Vol. 2, 733.

Chapter 1

1 Luwīs ʿAwaḍ, *Blūtūlānd wa-qaṣāʾid ukhrā min shiʿr al-khāṣṣah* (al-Qāhirah: al-Hayʾah al-Miṣriyyah al-ʿĀmmah li-l-Kitāb, 1989 [1947]), 9.

2 s.v. "*ʿamūd,*" in E. W. Lane, *Arabic-English Lexicon* (Cambridge: Islamic Texts Society, 1984 [1863–1893]).
3 Fakhreddine provides a succinct analysis of the origin of the phrase "*ʿamūd al-shiʿr*" in the Arabic tradition in her *Metapoesis in the Arabic Tradition*, 71–74.
4 Fakhreddine, *Metapoesis in the Arabic Tradition*, 2. Italics added.
5 Fakhreddine, *Metapoesis in the Arabic Tradition*, 73, 72.
6 Fakhreddine, *Metapoesis in the Arabic Tradition*, 74, 72. Parentheses original. She quotes Abū al-Qāsim al-Ḥasan ibn Bishr al-Āmidī, *al-Muwāzanah bayna shiʿr Abī Tammām wa-l-Buḥturī*, ed. Aḥmad Ṣaqr, Vol. 1, 2nd ed. (al-Qāhirah: Dār al-Maʿārif, 1972), 8–9.
7 ʿAwaḍ, *Blūtūlānd*, 10.
8 ʿAwaḍ, *Blūtūlānd*, 9.
9 ʿAwaḍ, *Blūtūlānd*, 10.
10 ʿAwad, *Blūtūlānd*, 10.
11 G. Schoeler, "*Muwashshaḥ*," *Encyclopaedia of Islam, Second Edition* [*EI2*]. http://dx.doi.org/10.1163/1573-3912_islam_COM_0826; G. Schoeler and W. Stoetzer, "*Zadjal*," *EI2*. http://dx.doi.org/10.1163/1573–3912_islam_COM_1373.
12 Awad is not alone in recognizing the central place of Andalusian developments in poetic form within Arabic modernism during the late 1940s and 1950s. The Iraqi modernist Shādhil Ṭāqah likewise highlights the Andalusians in the polemical introduction to his first collection *al-Masāʾ al-akhīr* (*The Final Night*, 1950), where he writes that his modernist poetry "is not entirely novel, for its roots stretch back to Andalusian poetry. In turn, the poets of Andalusia inspired those of the *Mahjar* [Arab diaspora] [...] ." *Shādhil Ṭāqah: al-majmūʿah al-shiʿriyyah al-kāmilah*, jamʿ wa-iʿdād Saʿd al-Bazzāz, Silsilat Dīwān al-Shiʿr al-ʿArabī al-Ḥadīth 77 ([Baghdād]: Manshūrāt Wizārat al-Iʿlām, al-Jumhūriyyah al-ʿIrāqiyyah, 1977), 23.
13 ʿAwad, *Blūtūlānd*, 15.
14 ʿAwad, *Blūtūlānd*, 21.
15 ʿAwad, *Blūtūlānd*, 21, 24.
16 For more extensive treatments of Awad's poetic project, see Fadel K. Jabr, "The Children of Gilgamesh: A Half Century of Modern Iraqi Poetry," *Metamorphoses: A Journal of Literary Translation* 19, nos. 1–2 (Spring/Fall 2011): 341–344 and Abdul-Nabi Isstaif, "Forging a New Self, Embracing the Other: Modern Arabic Critical Theory and the West – Luwīs ʿAwaḍ," *Arabic and Middle Eastern Literatures* 5, no. 2 (2002): 161–180.
17 Stephen Wild, "*Zur Geschichte der Arabischen Metrik*," Abū ʾl-Ḥasan ʿAlī b. ʿIsā ar-Rabaʿī an-Naḥwī, *Kitāb al-ʿarūḍ*, ed. Muḥammad Abū ʾl-Faḍl Badrān, *Bibliotheca Islamica*, Vol. 44 (Beirut: Das Arabische Buch, 2000), 11–16.
18 For further information on Arabic metrics, see G. Weil and G. M. Meredith-Owens, "*ʿArūḍ*," *EI2*. Available: http://dx.doi.org/10.1163/1573-3912_islam_COM_0066. I say "ideal" here because the *buḥūr* frequently appear in scientifically "imperfect" forms. This should be no surprise because the extant meters predate al-Khalīl's science of prosody.

19 For variants on the meter, see W. Wright, *A Grammar of the Arabic Language*, W. Robertson Smith and M. J. De Goeje eds., Vol. 2 (New Delhi: Munshiram Manoharlal Publishers, Pvt. Ltd., 2004 [1862]), 364.

20 "The Parthian 'Gōsān' and Iranian Minstrel Tradition," *Journal of the Royal Asiatic Society of Great Britain and Ireland*, nos. 1/2 (April, 1957), 40.

21 L. P. Elwell-Sutton explains that there has been "serious confusion among prosodists, both ancient and modern, as to the true source and nature of the Persian meters, the most obvious error being the assumption that they were copied from the Arabic. This misconception arises solely from the use of the Arabic terminology to describe the Persian meters, but is no sounder evidence for an Arabic origin than is, say, the use of Greek terminology proof of a Greek origin for the meters of English verse." "*ʿArūż*," *Encyclopædia Iranica* [*EIr*], II/6–7, 670–679. www.iranicaonline.org/articles/aruz-the-metrical-system. Cf. Finn Thiesen's comments in *A Manual of Classical Persian Prosody: With Chapters on Urdu, Karakhanidic and Ottoman Prosody* (Wiesbaden: Otto Harrassowitz, 1982), xiv–xv, where he speculates, "A comparison of the prosodical *and* phonological systems of the two languages could probably settle the controversy as to whether Persian prosody is derived from Arabic prosody or, as I am inclined to think, it was only the Arabic terminology that was adapted to a basically native Persian system." Italics original. While the prosodic foundations of Arabic and Persian are almost certainly unrelated due to them being in different language families, I think it would also be quite difficult to prove that there has been no change to how Persian poets have thought about meter following the importation of the Arabic *ʿarūḍ* system into Persian metrical analysis more than a millennium ago. Clearly, many features of Arabic form, like rhyme placement and the number of feet per line in certain meters, have affected the shape of poetry in Persian.

22 On the metrical developments of modernist Arabic poetry, see Iḥsān ʿAbbās, *Ittijāhāt al-shiʿr al-ʿarabī al-muʿāṣir* (Kuwayt: al-Majlis al-Waṭānī li-l-Thaqāfah wa-l-Funūn wa-l-Adab, 1978); M. M. Badawi, *A Critical Introduction to Modern Arabic Poetry* (Cambridge: Cambridge University Press, 1975); Issa J. Boullata, "Badr Shakir al-Sayyab and the Free Verse Movement," *International Journal of Middle East Studies* 1, no. 3 (July, 1970): 248–258; Jayyusi, *Trends and Movements*; Nāzik al-Malā'ikah, *Qaḍāyā al-shiʿr al-muʿāṣir* (Baghdād: Maktabat al-Nahḍah, 1967 [1962]); and Shmuel Moreh, *Modern Arabic Poetry 1800–1970: The Development of Its Forms and Themes under the Influence of Western Literature*, Studies in Arabic Literature: Supplements to *JAL* 5, eds. M. M. Badawi, P. Cachia, M. C. Lyons, J. N. Mattock, and J. T. Monroe (Leiden: E. J. Brill, 1976). For the role of metrics in the Persian modernist tradition, see Amr Taher Ahmad, *La "Révolution littéraire": Étude de l'influence de la poésie française sur la modernisation des formes poétiques persanes au début de XXe siècle* (Wien [Vienna]: Verlag der Österreichischen Akademie der Wissenschaften, 2012); Mahdī Akhavān S̱āliṡ [M. Umīd], *Bidʿat-hā va badāyiʿ-i Nīmā Yūshīj,* 1st ed.

(Tihrān: Tūkā, 1357 [1978]); Yaḥyā Āryanpūr, *Az Ṣabā tā Nīmā: tarīkh-i 150 sāl-i adab-i fārsī*, 5th ed. (Tihrān: Intishārāt-i Zavvār, 1372 [1993; 1350 (1971)]); and Ahmad Karimi-Hakkak, *Recasting Persian Poetry: Scenarios of Poetic Modernity in Iran* (London: Oneworld, 2012 [1995]). For a comparative study of modernist forms in each language, see Muḥammad Khāqānī and Rūḥallāh Maṭlabī, "*Buḥūr qaṣīdat al-taf'īlah fi al-adabayn al-'arabī wa-l-fārisī*," *Buḥūth fi al-lughah al-'arabiyyah wa-ādābihā, Nisf sanawiyyah li-qism al-'arabiyyah wa-ādābihā bi-jāmi'at Iṣfahān* 1 (Pāyīz/Zamistān 1388 [Fall/Winter, 2009/2010]): 51–61.

23 (Bayrūt: Dār al-'Awdah, 1971 [1949]), 27.

24 Al-Malā'ikah, *Shaẓāyā wa-ramād*, 7–10.

25 Al-Malā'ikah, *Shaẓāyā wa-ramād*, 26.

26 Muhsin J. al-Musawi, *Reading Iraq: Culture and Power in Conflict* (New York: I. B. Tauris, 2006), 123–124.

27 I am not suggesting that premodern Arabic poetry was limited by its formal requirements. As we have already seen, Fakhreddine has recently argued for the consideration of the *muḥdathūn* poets who wrote during the Abbasid period as modernists (she prefers "modernizers") in their own right in light of their self-conscious use of metapoesis and the innovations they introduced into the Arabic *qaṣīdah*, metered and monorhymed as it may have been. *Metapoesis in the Arabic Tradition*, 2.

28 *Memories of State: Politics, History, and Collective Identity in Modern Iraq* (Berkeley: University of California Press, 2005), 92–93. Italics added.

29 15 May marks the day after Israel was founded and Israel's ethnic cleansing of hundreds of thousands of Palestinians from their homes and land. It is called the "catastrophe" in Arabic.

30 *Trends and Movements in Modern Arabic Poetry*, Vol. 2, 557–558.

31 *Modern Arabic Poetry: Revolution and Conflict* (South Bend, IN: University of Notre Dame Press, 2017), 8. Cf. my review: Levi Thompson, "Review of Waed Athamneh, *Modern Arabic Poetry: Revolution and Conflict*," *JAL* 48, no. 3 (2017): 340–344.

32 *Modern Arabic Poetry*, 8.

33 *Recasting Persian Poetry*, 235.

34 'Awaḍ, *Blūtūlānd*, 26–27. Awad writes about himself in the third person throughout the introduction, perhaps in an attempt to distance himself from the provocative ideas he proposes within it. Cf. Isstaif's translation of the same passage in "Forging a New Self," 162.

35 *"What Is Enlightenment?"* 39.

36 *"What Is Literature?" and Other Essays*, introduction by Steven Ungar (Cambridge, MA: Harvard University Press, 1988), 25–47.

37 Sartre, *"What Is Literature?"* 37.

38 Raymond Williams, *Marxism and Literature*, Marxist Introductions, ed. Steven Lukes (Oxford: Oxford University Press, 1977), 202.

39 Sartre, *"What Is Literature?"* 29. Italics original.

40 As I am referring to Joan Stambaugh's translation, I have included her translations along with the more frequently used terms "readiness-to-hand" and "presence-at-hand." For instances of each of these terms in *Being and Time*, see Martin Heidegger, *Being and Time*, State University of New York Series in Contemporary Continental Philosophy, ed. Dennis J. Schmidt, trans. Joan Stambaugh, revised and with a foreword by Dennis J. Schmidt (Albany: State University of New York Press, 2010), 439, 453.

41 *Marxism and Form: Twentieth-Century Dialectical Theories of Literature* (Princeton, NJ: Princeton University Press, 1974), 234.

42 Heidegger, *Being and Time*, 69. Parentheses added. For the German, see Martin Heidegger, *Sein und Zeit*, 11th ed. (Tübingen: Max Niemeyer Verlag, 1967 [1927]), 69.

43 Heidegger, *Being and Time*, 73. *Sein und Zeit*, 74. Italics original; parentheses added.

44 *Putting Modernism Together: Literature, Music, and Painting 1872–1927* (Baltimore: Johns Hopkins University Press, 2015), 5 and 242.

45 Sartre, *"What Is Literature?"* 38.

46 The later proponents of which were largely associated with the Lebanese journal *Shiʿr* (*Poetry*), established by Yūsuf al-Khāl in 1957. Al-Khāl shared editing duties with Adūnīs. The journal was published until 1964 and again from 1967–1969. For a useful recent study of *Shiʿr* and the writers associated with the journal, see Creswell, *City of Beginnings*.

47 See Yoav Di-Capua's analysis of Ḥusayn's comments as well as a broader treatment of the reception of commitment in the Arab world in "The Intellectual Revolt of the 1950s and the 'Fall of the *Udabāʾ*'," *Commitment and Beyond: Reflections on/of the Political in Arabic Literature since the 1940s*, Friederike Pannewick, Georges Khalil, and Yvonne Albers eds., Literatures in Context: Arabic – Persian – Turkish, Vol. 41, eds. Verena Klemm, Sonja Mejcher-Atassi, Friederike Pannewick, and Barbara Winckler (Weisbaden: Reichert Verlag Wiesbaden, 2015).

48 Ṭāhā Ḥusayn, "*Mulāḥaẓāt*," *al-Kātib al-Miṣrī* 6, no. 21 (Rajab 1366; June 1947): 9–21.

49 Ḥusayn, "*Mulāḥaẓāt*," 14.

50 For a thorough review of the development of committed literature in the eastern Arabic context, see Verena Klemm, "Different Notions of Commitment (*Iltizām*) and Committed Literature (*al-adab al-multazim*) in the Literary Circles of the Mashriq," *Arabic and Middle Eastern Literatures* 3, no. 1 (2000): 51–62.

51 *Al-Ādāb* 1, no. 1 (January, 1953). Translation found in Mohammad Mustafa Badawi, *Modern Arabic Literature and the West* (London: Ithaca Press, 1985), 13. For a recent review of the role *al-Ādāb* played in the elaboration of *iltizām* in the Arab world, see Qussay Al-Attabi, "The Polemics of Iltizām: *Al-Ādāb*'s Early Arguments for Commitment," *JAL* 52, nos. 1–2 (2021): 124–146.

52 Badawi, *A Critical Introduction*, 209.

53 For another detailed analysis of commitment in modern Persian literature in Iran, see Hamid Dabashi, "The Poetics of Politics: Commitment in Modern Persian Literature," *Iranian Studies* 18, no. 2 (Spring–Autumn, 1985): 147–188.

54 Samad Alavi, "The Poetics of Commitment in Modern Persian: A Case of Three Revolutionary Poets in Iran," PhD diss. University of California, Berkeley, 2013, vii.

55 Alavi, "The Poetics of Commitment," viii.

56 Alavi's term, by which he means the view that "corresponds most closely with commitment debates in Europe and the Americas." Alavi, "The Poetics of Commitment," xi.

57 (Tihrān: Kitāb-i Zamān, 1347 [1968]). For an overview of Baraheni's life and turbulent career, see Michael C. Hillman, "Rezā Barāheni: A Case Study of Politics and the Writer in Iran, 1953–1977," *Literature East & West* 20, nos. 1–4 (1976): 304–313.

58 *Ṭalā dar mis*, 19. Italics added.

59 Peyman Vahabzadeh, "Rebellious Action and 'Guerrilla Poetry': Dialectics of Art and Life in 1970s Iran," *Persian Language, Literature, and Culture: New Leaves, Fresh Looks*, ed. Kamran Talattof (New York: Routledge, 2015), 107.

60 Consider "*Ay marz-i pur guhar . . .* " ("O Bejewelled Land . . . ") in particular. Furūgh Farrukhzād, *Tavalludī dīgar*, 11th ed. (Tihrān: Intishārāt-i Murvārīd, 2536 [1977; originally published in 1963]), 148–157. Translation in *Forugh Farrokhzad: Another Birth and Other Poems*, trans. Hasan Javadi and Susan Salleé (Washington, DC: Mage Publishers, 2010), 99–107.

61 Badawi, *Modern Arabic Literature and the West*, 1, 2. Badawi also informs us that al-Masʿadī's speech was later published in Suhayl Idrīs's *al-Ādāb* 6, no. 1 (January, 1958).

62 These debates are far from over, as evidenced by the recently published conference proceedings on "Commitment and Dissent in Arabic Literature since the 1950s," collected in *Commitment and Beyond: Reflections on/of the Political in Arabic Literature since the 1940s*. Participants in the conference, including authors writing in Arabic such as Elias Khoury and Sinan Antoon, and contributors to the volume not only review the development of the commitment debates in the Arab world but also extend their analyses of the phenomenon through to the twenty-first century, thereby highlighting its continued relevance today.

63 Sayyāb's Communist comrades complained about his reading Edith Sitwell (d. 1964) and even Shakespeare. Al-Sayyāb, *Kuntu shuyūʿiyyan*, aʿaddahā li-l-nashr Walīd Khālid Aḥmad Ḥasan (Kūlūnīyā [Cologne]: Manshūrāt al-Jamal, 2007 [1959]), 105, 174, 218.

64 Luwīs ʿAwaḍ, "*T. S. Iliyūt*," *al-Kātib al-Miṣrī: al-majmūʿah al-kāmilah*, Vol. 1, ed. ʿAbd al-ʿAziz Sharaf (al-Hayʾah al-Miṣriyyah al-ʿĀmmah li-l-Kitāb, 1998), 557–568. Awad's article is in the May 1946 issue. Terri DeYoung, *Placing the Poet: Badr Shakir al-Sayyab and Postcolonial Iraq* (Albany: State University of New York Press, 1998), 68–69.

65 *Al-Adab al-ʿarabī al-muʿāṣir: aʿmāl muʾtamar Rūmā al-munʿaqid fī Tishrīn al-awwal sanat 1961* (Manshūrāt Aḍwāʾ, 1961), 248–249. Italics added. Also see Sayyāb, *Kuntu shuyūʿiyyan*, 127.
66 "Commitment," Theodor Adorno, Ernst Bloch, Walter Benjamin, Bertolt Brecht, and Georg Lukács, *Aesthetics and Politics*, trans. Francis McDonagh, trans. ed. Ronald Taylor (London: NLB, 1977), 177. Italics added.
67 Adorno, "Commitment," 193–194.
68 Berman, *Modernist Commitments*, 24. Italics original.
69 *The Politics of Aesthetics*, trans. Gabriel Rockhill (New York: Continuum, 2011), 22. Italics original.
70 Jacques Rancière, "The Politics of Literature," *SubStance #103* 33, no. 1 (2004): 10. Italics added.
71 Rancière, "The Politics of Literature," 10.
72 Jacques Rancière, *Dissensus: On Politics and Aesthetics*, ed. and trans. Steven Corcoran (New York: Continuum, 2010), 38. Parentheses and italics original.
73 Rancière, *Dissensus*, 37.
74 Joseph J. Tanke, "What Is the Aesthetic Regime?" *Parrhesia* 12 (2011), 71.
75 Cleanth Brooks, *The Well Wrought Urn: Studies in the Structure of Poetry* (New York: Harcourt Brace & Company, 1975 [1947]), 196.
76 Stanley Fish, *Is There a Text in This Class? The Authority of Interpretive Communities* (Cambridge, MA: Harvard University Press, 1980), 11.
77 Persuasion features prominently in Fish's work. "The business of criticism," he tells us, "[is] not to decide between interpretations by subjecting them to the test of disinterested evidence but to establish by *political and persuasive* means (they are the same thing) the set of interpretive assumptions from the vantage of which the evidence (and the facts and the intentions and everything else) will hereafter be specifiable [. . .] . I claimed the right, along with everyone else, to argue for *a way of reading*, which, if it became accepted, would be, for a time at least, the true one." *Is There a Text in This Class?*, 16. Brackets and italics added; parentheses original.

Chapter 2

1 Nīmā Yūshīj, *Majmūʿah-ʾi kāmil-i ashʿār-i Nimā Yushij: fārsī va ṭabarī* (Tihrān: Intishārāt-i Nigāh, 1370 [1991]) 37. Cf. the translation in Firoozeh Papan-Matin, "Love: Nima's Dialogue with Hafez," *Essays on Nima Yushij: Animating Modernism in Persian Poetry*, eds. Ahmad Karimi-Hakkak and Kamran Talattof (Leiden: E. J. Brill, 2004), 174.
2 Perhaps a friend of his, though he mentions no name. See Papan-Matin, "Love: Nima's Dialogue with Hafez," 173.
3 On Pound's use of the phrase, see Michael North, "The Making of 'Make It New,'" *Guernica*, August 15, 2013, www.guernicamag.com/the-making-of-making-it-new/.
4 This metaphor appears in the 1938 poem "*Quqnūs*" ("The Phoenix").

5 T. S. Eliot, "Tradition and the Individual Talent," *The Sacred Wood: Essays on Poetry and Criticism* (London: Methuen & Co. 1934), 49. I also see significant parallels between the modernists' sublation of earlier literature into their poetry and Eliot's "analogy [. . .] of the catalyst," in which a shred of platinum catalyzes the reaction of oxygen and sulphur dioxide so that they form sulphurous acid. In the analogy, "the newly formed acid contains no trace of platinum, and the platinum itself is apparently unaffected; has remained inert, neutral, and unchanged. The mind of the poet is the shred of platinum," 53–54.

6 Eliot, "Tradition and the Individual Talent," 49.

7 In applying Foucault's thought to conceive of Nīmā's self-fashioning and turning to the work of Bruno Latour, I am led by Rastegar's comments in a footnote from *Literary Modernity*, 149.

8 Bruno Latour, *We Have Never Been Modern*, trans. Catherine Porter (Cambridge, MA: Harvard University Press, 1993 [1991]), 50–51. Italics original.

9 *Recasting Persian Poetry*, 242.

10 See Albright's comments on these two systems in the chapter "Communism, Fascism, and Later Modernism," in *Putting Modernism Together: Literature, Music, and Painting 1872–1927* (Baltimore: Johns Hopkins University Press, 2015), 291–310.

11 *Dialectic of Enlightenment*, 6.

12 A reader of Nīmā's *Arzish-i iḥsāsāt va panj maqālah dar shiʿr va namāyish* (*The Value of Feelings and Five Articles on Poetry and Drama*) (Tihrān: Intishārāt-i Gūtinbirg, 2535 [1976/1977]) cannot miss his frequent citations and discussions of Western thinkers and artists.

13 *Recasting Persian Poetry*, 240. Parentheses original.

14 *Nakhustīn kungirah-'i nivīsandigān-i Īrān* (Tihrān: 1326 [1947]), 64.

15 Talinn Grigor, "Recultivating 'Good Taste': The Early Pahlavi Modernists and Their Society for National Heritage," *Iranian Studies* 37, no. 1 (2004): 18, 25.

16 Grigor, "Recultivating 'Good Taste'," 18. Italics added.

17 Yūshīj, *Majmūʿah*, 55.

18 Hushang Philsooph, "Book Review: *Essays on Nima Yushij: Animating Modernism in Persian Poetry*," *Middle Eastern Literatures* 12, no. 1 (April 2009): 103.

19 Philsooph, "Book Review," 102–103.

20 W. Geoffrey Arnott, "Swan Songs," *Greece & Rome* 24, no. 2 (October 1977): 149–153, 152. See also Mark Brazil, *The Whooper Swan* (London: T. & A. D. Poyser, 2003), especially chapter 2, "Swan Culture."

21 Ibn Sīnā uses the same spelling ʿAṭṭār does (*qugnus*, with a *ḍammah* in place of the second *wāw*) but is certainly referencing a swan – not the Phoenix – in his *al-Shifāʾ*. See Ibn Sīnā, *al-Shifāʾ*, *al-Manṭiq*, 4, *al-Qiyās*, rājaʿahu wa-qaddama la-hu Ibrāhīm Madkūr, bi-taḥqīq Saʿīd Zāyid (al-Qāhirah: al-Hayʾah al-ʿĀmmah li-Shuʾūn al-Amīriyyah, 1384; 1964), 217, 222, and 505.

22 Muḥāmmad Rizā Shafīʿī-Kadkanī, Farīd al-Dīn Muḥammad ibn Ibrāhīm Nīshābūrī [ʿAṭṭār], *Manṭiq al-ṭayr*, muqaddamah, taṣḥīḥ va taʿlīqāt Muḥammad Rizā Shafīʿī-Kadkanī (Tihrān: Sukhan, 1388 [2010]), 649–651.

23 For ʿAṭṭār's whole account of the *quqnus*'s story, see Farīd al-Dīn ʿAṭṭār, *Manṭiq al-ṭayr*, bi-taṣḥīḥ va ihtimām-i Muḥammad Javād Mashkūr, bā muqaddimah va taʿlīqāt, 2nd ed. (Tihrān: Kitābfurūshī-'i Tihrān, 1341 [1962]), 153–155. Translation by Afkham Darbandi and Dick Davis, 1984. www.laphamsquarterly.org/magic-shows/ashes.

24 The Whooper (*Cygnus cygnus*) is the swan associated with the "swan song." Furthermore, its range extends to the Caspian region where Nīmā was from. *The Handbook of British Birds*, H. F. Witherby, F. C. R. Jourdain, Norman F. Ticehurst, and Bernard W. Tucker, Vol. 3 (London: H. F. & G. Witherby 1939), 171. In Persian, the Whooper is appropriately called *qū-yi faryādkash*. *Fihrist-i pīshnihādī-'i asāmī-'i parandigān-i Īrān*, ed. Sāymūn Jirvīs Rīd [Simon Jervis Read] (Tihrān: Dānishgāh-i Tihrān, 1337 [1958/1959]), 3.

25 Thiesen, *A Manual of Classical Persian Prosody*, 243. See also Wright, *A Grammar of the Arabic Language*, Vol. 2, 367–368.

26 *La "Révolution littéraire,"* 378.

27 Yūshīj, *Majmūʿah*, 115.

28 Karimi-Hakkak, "Nima Yushij: A Life," 16.

29 Karimi-Hakkak, "Nima Yushij: A Life," 34.

30 Al-Malāʾikah, *Qaḍāyā al-shiʿr al-muʿāṣir*, 34.

31 Yūshīj, *Majmūʿah*, 222. I have consulted translations by Kaveh Bassiri and Hamid Dabashi in rendering these lines into English. See www.catranslation.org/online-exclusive/phoenix/ and "Nima Yushij and the Constitution of a National Subject," *The World Is My Home: A Hamid Dabashi Reader*, eds. Andrew Davison and Himadeep Muppidi (New Brunswick, NJ: Transaction Publishers, 2011), 163.

32 In Dabashi's version, the Sphinx is male. "The solitary stance of the Sphinx is the location of his rise [. . .] ." "Nima Yushij," 163.

33 My heartfelt appreciation to Susan Slyomovics for pressing me with an excellent question about gender in the poem at the 2018 meeting of the American Comparative Literature Association in Los Angeles.

34 ʿAttār, *Manṭiq al-ṭayr*, 153. The translation is mine, and I have consulted other versions in Farīd al-Dīn ʿAṭṭār, *The Speech of the Birds: Manṭiq't-Tair*, presented by Peter Avery (Cambridge: The Islamic Texts Society, 2001), 208 and Darbandi and Davis.

35 For a concise definition of *muʿāraḍah*, see A. Schippers, "*Muʿāraḍa*," *EI2*, http://dx.doi.org/10.1163/1573-3912_islam_SIM_5276. For a study of poetic imitation in the premodern Persian tradition, see Paul E. Losensky, *Welcoming Fighānī: Imitation and Poetic Individuality in the Safavid-Mughal* Ghazal (Costa Mesa, CA: Mazda Publishers, 1998).

36 Amr Taher Ahmed gives the entire metrical breakdown of the poem in *La "Révolution littéraire,"* 423–427, along with a translation into French.

37 Charles Baudelaire, *The Flowers of Evil*, eds. Marthiel and Jackson Mathews (New York: New Directions, 1989), 337. Translation in the same edition by C. F. MacIntyre, 118. The poem was first published in 1855.

38 T. S. Eliot, *The Waste Land*, ed. Michael North (New York: W. W. Norton & Company, 2001), 7. North notes that Eliot's description of London here is in fact based on another of Baudelaire's poems, "*Le septs vieillards*" ("The Seven Old Men," 1859), which opens "*Fourmillante cité, cité pleine de rêves, / Où le spectre en plein jour raccroche le passant!*" ("Ant-seething city, city full of dreams, / Where ghosts by daylight tug the passer's sleeve."). Baudelaire, *The Flowers of Evil*, 331. Trans. by Roy Campbell, 111.

39 Paul Losensky outlines this critical approach in the initial pages of his "'To Tell Another Tale of Mournful Terror': Three of Nima's Songs of the Night," (*Essays on Nima Yushij*, 139–172) after which he proceeds to challenge such binary readings and suggest other ways we might understand the meaning of Nīmā's night poems.

40 Trans. Darbandi and Davis, www.laphamsquarterly.org/magic-shows/ashes.

41 S. Hessampour and S. F. Sadat Sharifi explore the concept of solitude as elaborated in "*Quqnūs*" at length in "*Barrasī-'i ʿanāṣir-i mudirnism dar shiʿr-i Quqnūs*," *Majallah-'i shiʿr-pazhūhī* (*Būstān-i adab*) *Dānishgāh-i Shīrāz* 5, no. 1 (Bahār, 1392 [Spring 2013]): 1–28.

42 For more on the *radīf* and the rhyme letter (*rāwī*), see L. P. Elwell-Sutton, "'*Arūż*."

43 "*Tarṣīʿ* is a stylistic feature of a word combination based on the principle of equivalence of sound. It is attested in Arabic literature from the earliest stages and can be found in Ḳur'ān, *Ḥadīth*, poetry, and prose. A figure of style explicitly called *tarṣīʿ* was described for the first time, as far as we know, by Ḳudāma b. Dj̲aʿfar [. . .], who only requires agreement in metre or rhyme and who allows assonance instead of pure rhyme [. . .] ." G. Schoeler, "*Tarṣīʿ*," *EI2*. http://dx.doi.org/10.1163/1573-3912_islam_COM_1186. Magdi Wahba defines the English equivalent of *al-tarṣīʿ* (also called *al-sajʿ al-mutawāzī*) as "isocolon," or "structuring the parts of a sentence, or paragraph, so as to balance each part in accordance with length, number of parts, and words. This very much resembles what is called *al-tarṣīʿ*." My translation of the given Arabic definition. "*Isocolon*," Magdi Wahba, *A Dictionary of Literary Terms (English, French, Arabic)* (Beirut: Librairie du Liban, 1974), 263–264. See also "*Isocolon*," *The New Princeton Encyclopedia of Poetry and Poetics*. http://gateway.proquest.com/openurl?ctx_ver=Z39.88-2003&xri:pqil:res_ver=0.2&res_id=xri:lion&rft_id=xri:lion:ft:ref:R00793756:0. The word *tarṣīʿ* literally means "embellishing with jewels or gold." For more on its use in the Persian tradition, see N. Chalisova, "*Rhetorical Figures*," *EIr*. www.iranicaonline.org/articles/rhetorical-figures.

44 The Persian critical tradition calls antithesis *taḍādd* (*tażādd*) or follows the Arab use of the term *ṭibāq*. W. P. Heinrichs, "*Ṭibāḳ*," *EI2*, http://dx.doi.org/10.1163/1573-3912_islam_COM_1215.

45 "The hearth fire, providing warmth, light and comfort, was regarded by the ancient Iranians as the embodiment of the divinity Ātar, who lived among men as their servant and master." M. Boyce, "Ātaš," *EIr*, III/1, 1-5, www.iranicaonline.org/articles/atas-fire; M. Boyce, "Ahura Mazdā," *EIr*, I/7, 684–687, www.iranicaonline.org/articles/ahura-mazda.

46 Trans. Darbandi and Davis, www.laphamsquarterly.org/magic-shows/ashes. ʿAṭṭār, *Manṭiq al-ṭayr*, 154.

47 I am following Louis Massignon's use of the term in the title of his wide-ranging study of al-Ḥallāj: *La Passion de Husayn Ibn Mansûr Hallâj: martyr mystique de l'Islam, exécuté à Bagdad le 26 mars 922: étude d'histoire religieuse* ([Paris]: Gallimard, 1975 [1922]); *The Passion of al-Hallāj: Mystic and Martyr of Islam*, foreword by trans. Herbert Mason, 4 Vols. (Princeton, NJ: Princeton University Press, 1982).

48 It is worth pointing out that although "Sufism" and "Sufi" are useful terms for referencing "Islamic mysticism" and a "mystic" generally, there are many different types of Sufis, Sufi practices, and Sufi beliefs. While Ḥallāj is venerated by some Sufis, he is (and was) rejected by others. Interested readers can find a useful dramatization of Ḥallāj's story in Ṣalāh ʿAbd al-Ṣabūr, *Murder in Baghdad*, trans. Khalil I. Semaan, Arabic Translation Series of the *Journal of Arabic Literature* 1 (Leiden: E. J. Brill, 1972). The original Arabic is Ṣalāḥ ʿAbd al-Ṣabūr, *Maʾsāt al-Ḥallāj* (al-Qāhirah: al-Hayʾah al-Miṣriyyah al-ʿĀmmah li-l-Kitāb, 1996 [1965]).

49 Jawid Mojaddedi, "Ḥallāj," *EIr*, XI/6, 589–592; www.iranicaonline.org/articles/hallaj-1. For ʿAṭṭār's entry on Ḥallāj, see *Tadhkiratu 'l-awliya ("Memoirs of the Saints") of Muḥammad ibn Ibrahim Faridu'd-Din ʿAṭṭar*, ed. Reynold A. Nicholson, Part II, Persian Historical Texts, Vol. V (London: Luzac & Co., 1907), 135–145.

50 "A Study of 'Elegy for al-Ḥallāj' by Adūnīs," *JAL* 25, no. 3 (1994): 247.

51 Al-Ḥusayn ibn Manṣūr Ḥallāj, *Hallaj: Poems of a Sufi Martyr*, trans. Carl. W. Ernst (Evanston, IL: Northwestern University Press, 2018), 5.

52 The spectacle of Ḥallāj's execution only intensified his fame and reminds us of Foucault's analysis of the unintended consequences of corporal punishment that breaks body but not soul. Michel Foucault, *Discipline & Punish: The Birth of the Prison* (New York: Vintage Books, 1995 [1975]).

53 Mojaddedi, "Ḥallāj."

54 Cf. Mojaddedi, "Ḥallāj" and Massignon, *The Passion of al-Hallāj*, Vol. I, *The Life of al-Hallāj*, 622–624.

55 ʿAṭṭār, *Manṭiq al-ṭayr*, 258–259.

56 Annemarie Schimmel, *Mystical Dimensions of Islam* (Chapel Hill: University of North Carolina Press, 1978), 70. See also Mahmoud Omidsalar and J. T. P. de Bruijn, "Candle," *EIr*, IV/7, 748–751; www.iranicaonline.org/articles/candle-pers: "[W]hen the candle represents the beloved, then the lover is the moth (*parvāna*), which cannot resist the light and is drawn into the flame and consumed."

57 Annmarie Schimmel, *A Two-Colored Brocade: The Imagery of Persian Poetry* (Chapel Hill: University of North Carolina Press, 1992), 198. Translation modified.

58 Line 6 of *ghazal* 174. *Sharḥ-i ghazaliyyāt-i Ḥāfiẓ*, Bihrūz S̱arvatiyyān, Daftar-i Duvvum (Tihrān: Pūyandagān-i Dānishgāh, 1380 [2001]), 1867.

59 Lines 48 and 49 are closely linked due to the presence of a *radīf* (*"ast murgh"*), which I have attempted to mirror in my English translation by repeating the

word "up" with the preceding consonance of "b's" and "c's" in place of the Persian rhyme "*ūkht.*" The Persian is, "*bād-i shadīd mīdamad u sūkht-ast murgh / khākistar-i tan-ash-rā andūkht-ast murgh.*"

60 See Patrick Laude, *Pathways to an Inner Islam: Massignon, Corbin, Guenon, and Schuon* (Albany: State University of New York Press, 2010), 187.

61 Ru'ūbīn Sanīr [Reuven Snir], *Rakʿatān fī al-ʿishq: dirāsah fī shiʿr ʿAbd al-Wahhāb al-Bayātī* (Bayrūt: Dār al-Sāqī, 2002).

62 ʿAṭṭār, *Tadhkiratu 'l-awliya*, 144. Translation is modified from Laude, *Pathways to an Inner Islam*, 187.

Chapter 3

1 Because I want to highlight Shāmlū's contemporary Communist commitments here, I prefer to translate the title as "*The Manifesto*" throughout the chapter, though the 2000 edition of the text published in Tehran by Zamānah (*Qaṭʿnāmah: majmūʿah-yī shiʿr, 1329–1330*) gives the English translation "*The Resolution*," another viable option. My sincere thanks to Navid Naderi for pointing this out to me, along with many other insights about Shāmlū's literary engagements in the 1950s that I do not have the space to fully address here but will gesture to again later on.

2 *Planetary Modernisms*, 7–8. Italics original.

3 For a sustained account of the will for independence that spawned the Bandung Conference, see Richard Wright, *The Color Curtain: A Report on the Bandung Conference*, foreword by Gunnar Myrdal (Cleveland, OH: World Publishing Company, 1956).

4 While I would not necessarily exclude Anglophone literature from the proto-Third Worldist category, I am more interested in finding ways to make literature from less commonly taught languages part of our discussions about world literature, even if they must be mediated through English translations. This may be an unsatisfactory position for some who worry about the unfettered ascendance of English as a global language, but at the very least it acknowledges the presence and importance of literature not originally written in English and allows for an engagement with it.

5 "Speaking Back to Orientalist Discourse," in *Orientalism's Interlocutors: Painting, Architecture, Photography*, eds. Jill Beaulieu and Mary Roberts (Durham, NC: Duke University Press, 2002), 20. This chapter also appears in 2014's *Empires of Vision: A Reader*, eds. Martin Jay and Sumathi Ramaswamy (Durham, NC: Duke University Press, 2014), 395–414.

6 "Seoul City Sue and the Bugout Blues: Black American Narratives of the Forgotten War," in *Afro Asia: Revolutionary Political and Cultural Connections Between African Americans and Asian Americans*, eds. Fred Ho and Bill V. Mullen (Durham, NC: Duke University Press, 2008), 77.

7 *Neither Peace Nor Freedom: The Cultural Cold War in Latin America* (Cambridge, MA: Harvard University Press, 2015), 60.

8 You can find a trenchant critique of the formulation of world literature in the shadow of the colonial and decolonial experience and with the rise of "local bourgeoisies at least elements of which now consider themselves part of the global ruling class" in Aamir Mufti, *Forget English!* 243.

9 Lionnet and Shih, *Minor Transnationalism*, 5–6. Their use of the term initially comes from Sarah J. Mahler's "Theoretical and Empirical Contributions toward a Research Agenda for Transnationalism," *Transnationalism from Below*, eds. Michael Peter Smith and Luis Eduardo Guarzino (London: Transaction, 1998), 64–100.

10 *Minor Transnationalism*, 6.

11 Aarthi Vadde, *Chimeras of Form*, 30. Italics original.

12 Laachir, Marzagora, and Orsini, "Multilingual Locals," 5.

13 "Third World" has its roots in an article written by Alfred Sauvy, in French, in the newspaper *L'Observateur* (August 14, 1952), where he referred to "*ce Tiers Monde ignoré, exploité, méprisé*" ("this ignored, exploited, scorned Third World") in a comparison between the exploited nations of the world and the dispossessed Third Estate at the beginning of the French Revolution. "Seeing the World Differently; Rethinking the 'Third World'," *The Economist* (London) 395, no. 8686 (June 12, 2010). The Non-Aligned Movement began under the leadership of Yugoslavia's Josip Broz Tito (d. 1980) and India's Jawaharlal Nehru (d. 1964) at a conference held during September 1961 in Belgrade. William Potter and Gaukhar Mukhatzhanova, "Chapter One: NAM [Non-Aligned Movement] Origins, Structure, Policymaking and Politics," Adelphi Series, Nuclear Politics and the Non-Aligned Movement: Principles vs. Pragmatism 51, no. 427 (2011): 17–18. "Global South" is a newer term that scholars have employed against the hierarchical delineation of the First, Second, and Third Worlds. For a recent definition of the term's use, see Anne Garland Mahler, "Global South," *Oxford Bibliographies in Literary and Critical Theory*, ed. Eugene O'Brien (2017), https://globalsouthstudies.as.virginia.edu/what-is-global-south.

14 A formulation recently found in the polemical title of conservative Scottish historian Niall Ferguson's *Civilization: The West and the Rest* (London: Allen Lane, 2011).

15 Vadde, *Chimeras of Form*, 30. Parentheses original.

16 *Worldmaking after Empire: The Rise and Fall of Self-Determination* (Princeton, NJ: Princeton University Press, 2019), 2.

17 For a thorough analysis of this link and specific attention to Shāmlū's thoughts on literary commitment, see Alavi, "The Poetics of Commitment in Modern Persian."

18 Laachir, Marzagora, and Orsini, "Multilingual Locals," 5. Italics original.

19 Shāmlū, *Qaṭʿnāmah*, 37–38.

20 Firoozeh Papan-Matin, *The Love Poems of Ahmad Shamlu*, trans. Firoozeh Papan-Matin and Arthur E. Lane (Bethesda, MD: Ibex, 2005), 26–27.

21 *Recasting Persian Poetry*, 262.

22 ʿAskarī Pāshāʾī elaborates on the interconnection of Shāmlū's "I" and "you" in the May 1981 introduction he wrote for the second edition of the *Qaṭʿnāmah*. "The search for 'you' [*tū*]," he concludes, "is a theme throughout all of Shāmlū's poetry from 1951, and it makes up the broader theme of all his poetry." "*Faryād-hā-yi ʿāṣī āẕarakhsh*," in Shāmlū, *Qaṭʿnāmah*, 18.

23 Laachir, Marzagora, and Orsini, "Multilingual Locals," 6.

24 Shāmlū, *Qaṭʿnāmah*, 57.

25 Shāmlū, *Qaṭʿnāmah*, 58.

26 Shāmlū, *Qaṭʿnāmah*, 61.

27 Ikhtiyārī, "*Az āghāz, pāyān rā mīdīd*," *Āhang-hā-yi farāmūsh shudah*, 209. Urmia (Urūmiyyah in Persian) is a city in far northwestern Iran where Shāmlū spent time as a teenager during the uncertain final years of World War II. After being held in an Allied prison, Shāmlū and his father were arrested in Urmia during the time of the Azerbaijan People's Government, which separated from Iran for a year from December 1945 until December 1946. Sentenced to death, "[t]hey were left waiting for execution in front of a firing squad for hours before being freed." Sadiq Saba, "Obituary: Ahmad Shamlu"; see also 2:30–2:45 of Voice of America's Last Page episode "*Aḥmad Shāmlū rā bihtar bishināsīm,*" YouTube video, 35:47, posted by "VOA Last Page," July 28, 2013, www.youtube.com/watch?v=Ho4ilBUWvOI&t=1s. For more about the separatist movement in Azerbaijan, see Lousie L'Estrange Fawcett, *Iran and the Cold War: The Azerbaijan Crisis of 1946* (Cambridge: Cambridge University Press, 1992), especially chapter 3, "The Year of Crisis: 1946," 53–82.

28 Riżāʾiyyah being another name for Urmia deriving from Riżā Shāh Pahlavi's name.

29 Readers who know Persian will notice that I have departed from poetic transcription with my rendering of "*tū*" throughout this chapter. I recognize that the long *vāv* is merely an indicator of a short "o" sound ("u" in my transliterations) and should not show up in an exact transcription. However, I want to render the original Persian word with English characters the same way wherever it occurs. Since there is always a written *vāv* in the Persian, I have chosen to retain it even though the vowel may scan as either a long or a short syllable. As my analysis does not emerge from Shāmlū's treatment of meter, this should be acceptable to most readers, and I ask clemency from others who object. For those who do not know Persian, "*tū*" is pronounced much in the same way most English speakers would say the homophones "toe" or "tow."

30 Shāmlū, *Āhang-hā-yi farāmūsh shudah*, 165–168.

31 Shāmlū, *Qaṭʿnāmah*, 59.

32 Lorca was not the only Western poet whose works inspired Shāmlū at the time. The Iranian filmmaker and poet Farīdūn Rahnamā (d. 1975), writing under his pen name Chūbīn, mentions in his introduction to the first printing of *Qaṭʿnāmah* many other poets important to this moment in Iranian literary history and for Shāmlū's poetic development, including but not limited to

Walt Whitman, Pablo Neruda, Langston Hughes, Tristan Tzara, Nâzım Hikmet, and several others. Chūbīn, "*Shiʿr zindagī-st. Buzurgtarīn zindagī-hā.*" in Shāmlū, *Qaṭʿnāmah*, 19–35. While we still await a thorough reckoning with the role these poets played in shifting Persian poetics in the 1950s, I choose to follow Shāmlū's poetic persona here and focus on Lorca alone, as he does.

33 Shāmlū, *Qaṭʿnāmah*, 62–63.

34 Not only was Germany Iran's top trading partner by the end of the decade, but also Heideggerean notions of authenticity entered Iranian philosophical and political discourse around the same time. On the intricate history of antimodernism, hermeneutics, and *gharbzadagī* ("westoxification") in mid-twentieth century Iran, see Mirsepassi, *Transnationalism in Iranian Political Thought*.

35 Sadiq Saba, "Obituary: Ahmad Shamlu," *The Guardian*, July 28, 2000, www.theguardian.com/news/2000/jul/28/guardianobituaries.books; Firoozeh Papan-Matin, *The Love Poems of Ahmad Shamlu*, 30. For examples of Shāmlū's Lorca projects, see Federico García Lorca, *ʿArūsī-ʾi khun: namāyishnāmah dar sih pardah va haft majlis*, tarjamah-ʾi Aḥmad Shāmlū (Tihrān: Intishārāt-i Tūs, 1356 [1978]); Federico García Lorca, *Tarānah-ʾi sharqī va ashʿār-i dīgar*, tarjamah-ʾi Aḥmad Shāmlū ([Sweden]: Havādarān-i Sāzmān-i Vaḥdat-i Kumūnīstī dar Sūʾīd, [198?]); Federico García Lorca, *Sih namāyishnāmah az Lūrkā: ʿArūsī-ʾi khūn, Yirmā, Khanah-ʾi Birnardā Ālbā*, tarjamah-ʾi Aḥmad Shāmlū, chāp-i 2 ([Tihrān]: Nashr-i Chashmah, 1382 [2003]); and *Fidirikū Kārsiyā Lūrkā*, compact disc, tarjamah va ṣidā-yi Aḥmad Shāmlū (n.d.; Tihrān: Muʾassasah-ʾi Intishārātī-ʾi Farhangī Hunarī-ʾi Ibtikār). There is even an audio recording of Shāmlū reciting his Persian translation of Lorca's "Romance sonámbulo" available on YouTube. "Federico García Lorca-Ahmad Shamlou," YouTube video, 6:22, posted by "Bijanfazli," February 21, 2012, www.youtube.com/watch?v=6t-TKIGfr5Y.

36 *Iran without Borders: Towards a Critique of the Postcolonial Nation* (New York: Verso, 2016), 93. "Shamlou, the Iranian national poet laureate," Dabashi adds, "was *entirely beholden* to Lorca [. . .] ." 94. Italics added.

37 *The God That Failed*, foreword by David C. Engerman, introduction by ed. Richard Crossman (New York: Columbia University Press, 2001), 249.

38 Rasheed El-Enany provides a useful overview of Lorca's role in modern Arabic poetry in "Poets and Rebels: Reflections of Lorca in Modern Arabic Poetry," *Third World Quarterly* 11, no. 4 (1989): 252–264. Aḥmad ʿAbd al-ʿAzīz thoroughly investigates Lorca's influence on modern Arabic poetry in "*Athar Fīdīrīkū Jārthiya Lūrkā fī al-adab al-ʿarabī al-muʿāṣir*," *Fuṣūl: majallat al-naqd al-adabī*, al-Adab al-Muqārin 2, 3, no. 4 (1983): 271–299. Muhsin al-Musawi likewise discusses the Arab modernists' frequent "identification with [Lorca as] their dedicatee" in a section titled "Addressing Lorca" in *Arabic Poetry: Trajectories of Modernity and Tradition*, Routledge Series in Middle Eastern Literature, eds. James E. Montgomery, Roger Allen, and Philip F. Kennedy (London: Routledge, 2006), 144–146. Cf. also Robyn Creswell's recent

comment on the "re-politicizing" of the elegy genre, where he points to "'Abdalwahab al-Bayati's 'Elegies for Lorca,' [. . .]" which "elegize his Spanish confrere through the meditations of Gilgamesh's lament for Enkidu and Lorca's own elegy for the bullfighter, 'Llanto por Ignacio Sánchez Mejías'." *City of Beginnings*, 235.

39 As another example of Lorca's transnational reach beyond Europe, the Americas, North Africa, and West Asia, Dai Wangshu (d. 1950) – who was "sympathetic with the anti-fascist Communist cause both in China and worldwide" – translated Lorca's poetry into Chinese. Jesús Sayols Lara, "Translating as Transculturating: A Study of Dai Wangshu's Translation of Lorca's Poetry from an Integrated Sociological-Cultural Perspective," PhD diss., Hong Kong Baptist University, 2015, 128.

40 El-Enany, "Poets and Rebels," 260.

41 *The Tamarit Poems: A Version of* Diván del Tamarit, trans. Michael Smith, afterword by Emilio García Gómez (Dublin: Dedalus Press, 2007 [first published posthumously in 1940]).

42 Federico Garcia Lorca, *Poet in New York: A Bilingual Edition*, trans. Mark Statman and Pablo Medina, foreword by Edward Hirsch (New York: Grove Press, 2008 [originally published as *Poeta en Nueva York* in 1940]); Roberto González Echevarría, "The Master of Modernismo," *The Nation* (February 13, 2006), published online January 25, 2006, www.thenation.com/article/archive/master-modernismo/;*Spanish Poetry; Poesía Española: A Dual-Language Anthology 16th–20th Centuries*, ed. Angel Flores (Mineola, NY: Dover Publications, 1998), 378. For a brief treatment of *modernismo* and Darío, see *Selected Poems of Rubén Darío: A Bilingual Anthology*, eds. and trans. Alberto Acerada and Will Derusha (Lewisburg, PA: Bucknell University Press, 2001), 15–17.

43 Efraín Kristal, "'Considering Coldly. . .': A Response to Franco Moretti," *New Left Review* 15 (May–June 2002), 66, 63.

44 *Modernism, Rubén Darío, and the Poetics of Despair* (Lanham, MD: University Press of America, 2004), 67.

45 For the Spanish, see Federico García Lorca, *Selected Poems*, trans. Martin Sorrell, introduction and notes by D. Gareth Walters, Oxford World's Classics (Oxford: Oxford University Press, 2007), 156; a translation is on 157. For more information about the events that led to Lorca's composition of the poem, see "The Death of a Bullfighter," in Ian Gibson, *Federico García Lorca: A Life* (New York: Pantheon Books, 1989), 387–391. Shāmlū would later include a Persian translation of the entire poem in his collection of translated world poetry, *Hamchūn kūchah-'ī bī-intihā: guzīnah-'ī az ash'ār-i shā'irān-i buzurg-i jahān*, tarjumah-'i Aḥmad Shāmlū, 3rd ed. (Tihrān: Mu'assasah-'i Intishārāt-i Nigāh, 1374 [1995]; originally published in Tābistān 1352 [Summer 1973]), 181–195.

46 *Iran without Borders*, 93.

47 "The Blood of a Genius," *The New York Times Book Review*, October 8, 1989, available online at www.nytimes.com/1989/10/08/books/the-blood-of-a-genius.html?pagewanted=all.

48 Gibson, *Federico García Lorca*, 446–470.

49 On the Iranian reading public's later reception of Shāmlū, see the chapter "A Weapon of the Masses: Ahmad Shamlu and the Poetics of Humanism," in Alavi, "The Poetics of Commitment in Modern Persian," 90–121.

50 For a cogent analysis of the tension between authorial intent and language as alternative sources of a literary text's meaning in contemporary literary theory, which ultimately privileges neither, see Antoine Compagnon, *Literature, Theory, and Common Sense*, trans. Carol Cosman, New French Thought, eds. Thomas Pavel and Mark Lilla (Princeton, NJ: Princeton University Press, 2004 [1998]), 30–33, 68.

51 Shāmlū, *Qaṭʿnāmah*, 63–64.

52 Discussing the roles of the lyric "I" and "You" in terms of the development of poetic modernism, W. R. Johnson writes, "Since its romantic flowering meditative verse has itself changed in various ways, but common to these changes are the isolation, the self-sufficiency, of the lyric I and the virtual disappearance of the lyric You." *The Idea of Lyric: Lyric Modes in Ancient and Modern Poetry* (Berkeley: University of California Press, 1982), 8. Shāmlū's poetic development goes in the opposite direction. As his lyric "I" becomes aware of the realities of existence, he becomes more interested in the experiences of those he speaks to.

53 Shāmlū, *Qaṭʿnāmah*, 66–67.

54 Wheeler M. Thackston, *An Introduction to Persian*, 4th ed. (Bethesda, MD: Ibex, 2009 [1978]), 44. Italics added.

55 Shāmlū, *Qaṭʿnāmah*, 89.

56 Fatemeh Keshavarz, *Lyrics of Life: Saʿdi on Love, Cosmopolitanism, and Care of the Self* (Edinburgh: Edinburgh University Press, 2015), 21.

57 Shāmlū, *Qaṭʿnāmah*, 69.

58 Shāmlū uses the term "*zardpūst*" (literally "yellow-skinned"), which I translate as "Asian" in order to avoid what would now come off as absurdly racist language in English. Considering the rest of the poem, its tone, and its valorization of Shen-Cho, Shāmlū likely meant it as a term of endearment.

59 Shāmlū, *Qaṭʿnāmah*, 69–70.

60 The reference is either to the Bergen-Belsen concentration camp in Germany (supported to some extent by Shāmlū's note that each place in the line is a Nazi *kushtārgāh*, or slaughterhouse [*Qaṭʿnāmah*, 91]) or perhaps to the 1939 transfer of the Jewish citizens of Plzeň to the Dachau concentration camp and subsequent anti-Jewish violence from the local German population during the Nazi occupation of Czechoslovakia in World War II (Kim Wünschmann, *Before Auschwitz: Jewish Prisoners in the Prewar Concentration Camps* [Cambridge, MA: Harvard University Press, 2015], 218). In this second case, the transliteration should instead be *Blzin*.

61 On June 10, 1944, Nazis slaughtered 642 people in the central French department of Haute-Vienne "in what was the single worst massacre carried out by German troops during the four years of occupation." Alan Riding,

"Generation of Mourning: An Account of the Nazi Massacre at Oradour-sur-Glane and the Town's Fight for Justice," *The New York Times Book Review* (February 28, 1999), 7 6:2, available online at https://archive.nytimes.com/www.nytimes.com/books/99/02/28/reviews/990228.28riding.html. Shāmlū provides a note on what he means by "*Vīyūn*" (*Qaṭʿnāmah*, 91), saying that it is "an old prison in the north of France," but I have not found a prison by this name or one similar to it there. Haute-Vienne is located in west central France, not the north.

62 The Nazis executed more than one thousand members of the French Resistance by firing squad at Fort Mont-Valérian between 1941 and 1944.

63 Shāmlū, *Qaṭʿnāmah*, 74–75.

64 The poem thus exploits a trope found in anti-German propaganda postcards created in 1942 by the artist Kimon Evan Marengo (d. 1988; pen name Kem) at the request of the Allies and with the encouragement of Mujtabā Minuvī (d. 1977), who "edit[ed] the pro-Allied newspaper *Ruzgar-i Naw*." For more information and to see examples of Hitler as Żaḥḥāk on these postcards, see Nur Sobers-Khan, "The Shahnameh as propaganda for World War II," Asian and African Studies Blog, The British Library (May 31, 2013), http://blogs.bl.uk/asian-and-african/2013/05/the-shahnameh-as-propaganda-for-world-war-ii.html.

65 For a narrative translation of this section of the epic, see Ferdowsi, *The Epic of the Kings: Shāh-nāma, the National Epic of Persia*, trans. Reuben Levy, forward by Ehsan Yarshater, preface by Amin Banani, introduction by Dick Davis (Costa Mesa, CA: Mazda, 1996), 11–25.

66 E. Abrahamian and B. Alavi, "Arānī, Taqī," *Encyclopaedia Iranica*, II/3, 263–265, available online at www.iranicaonline.org/articles/arani-taqi.

67 Shāmlū, *Qaṭʿnāmah*, 82–83.

68 Aḥmad Shāmlū va Āyidā Sarkīsiyān, *Kitāb-i kūchah: farhang-i lughāt, iṣṭilāḥāt, taʿbīrāt, żarb al-maṣal-hā-yi fārsī* (Tihrān: Intishārāt-i Māzyār, 1998–).

69 Mīkhāʾīl Shūlūkhūf, *Dun-i ārām*, bargardān-i Aḥmad Shāmlū, tarjamah az bargardān-i farānsavī-ʾi Āntwān Vītiz (Tihrān: Intishārāt-i Māzyār, 1391 [2012/2013]; originally published 1382 [2003/2004]).

70 Langstūn Hiyūz, *Siyāh hamchūn aʿmāq-i Āfrīqā-yi kh*^{v}*ūdam*, bargardān-i Aḥmad Shāmlū [va Ḥasan Fayyād, uncredited], 1st ed. (Tihrān: Sāzmān-i Intishārāt va Farhangī-ʾi Ibtikār, 136? [198?]).

71 For several other examples, see Shāmlū, *Hamchūn kūchah-ʾī bī-intihā*.

72 Alavi, "The Poetics of Commitment," 90.

73 "Third-World Literature in the Era of Multinational Capitalism," *Social Text*, no. 15 (Autumn 1986): 65–88.

74 See also Steven S. Lee's presentation of the vibrant minority literature that flourished in the USSR until the institution of socialist realism as state policy in 1934. *The Ethnic Avant-Garde: Minority Cultures and World Revolution*, Modernist Latitudes, eds. Jessica Berman and Paul Saint-Amour (New York: Columbia University Press, 2018 [2015]), 41.

Chapter 4

1 From "Weapons and Children," Badr Shākir al-Sayyāb, *al-Aʿmāl al-shiʿriyyah al-kāmilah*, 4th ed. (Baghdād: Dār al-Ḥurriyah li-l-Ṭibāʿah wa-l-Nashr, 2008), 296–310; lines excerpted from 307–310.

2 For my analysis of his 1950 long poem *Fajr al-salām* (*The Dawn of Peace*), see Levi Thompson, "An Iraqi Poet."

3 On the distinction between "*qawmi* (pan-Arab) and *watani* (national or democratic)" nationalism in Iraq, see Abdul-Salaam Yousif, "The Struggle for Cultural Hegemony during the Iraqi Revolution," *The Iraqi Revolution of 1958*, eds. Robert A Fernea and Wm. Roger Louis (London: I. B. Tauris & Co., 1991), 172. Many Iraqis shifted between these two trends, and many Communists likewise took up parts of nationalist ideology. Throughout the 1950s, the borders separating these different political positions remained quite porous in Iraq. See also Kevin Jones's discussion of these political trends in relation to Iraqi poetry during the period in his chapter "Poetry of Public Spaces: Mass Politics and New Horizons, 1946–1958" in *The Dangers of Poetry* (Stanford, CA: Stanford University Press, 2020), 130–158.

4 *Minor Transnationalism*, 5–6, quoting Sarah J. Mahler, "Theoretical and Empirical Contributions."

5 Al-Sayyāb, *Kuntu shuyūʿiyyan*, 248, 146–148.

6 Terri DeYoung, *Placing the Poet*, 45; al-Sayyāb, *Kuntu shuyūʿiyyan*, 11.

7 Fellow Iraqi poet ʿAbd al-Wahhāb al-Bayātī writes that a posting to al-Ramādī, west of Baghdad and the capital of the Anbar governorate, was an especially difficult one reserved for recent graduates of the Teachers College who had fiery political views that the government wanted to stamp out. *Yanābīʿ al-shams: al-sīrah al-shiʿriyyah*, 1st ed. (Dimashq: Dār al-Farqad li-l-Ṭabāʿah wa-l-Nashr wa-l-Tawzīʿ, 1999), 89.

8 DeYoung, *Placing the Poet*, 221.

9 Al-Sayyāb, *Kuntu shuyūʿiyyan*, 105, 174, 218–219.

10 For the proceedings, see *al-Adab al-ʿarabī al-muʿāṣir*.

11 For more on the CCF and CIA's roles in Arabic letters, see both Elizabeth Holt, "'Bread or Freedom': The Congress for Cultural Freedom, the CIA, and the Arabic Literary Journal *Hiwar* (1962–1967)," *JAL* 44, no. 1 (2013): 83–102 and Elliott Colla, "Badr Shākir al-Sayyāb, Cold War Poet." *Middle Eastern Literatures* 18, no. 3 (2015): 247–263.

12 Al-Sayyāb, "*al-Iltizām wa-l-lāiltizām*," *al-Adab al-ʿarabī al-muʿāṣir*, 247.

13 Al-Sayyāb, "*al-Iltizām wa-l-lāiltizām*," 246–247.

14 Al-Sayyāb, "*al-Iltizām wa-l-lāiltizām*," 248–249.

15 For "his [1946] leadership of a student strike protesting the lengthening of the teacher training program from four to five years." DeYoung, *Placing the Poet*, 69.

16 Al-Sayyāb, *Kuntu shuyūʿiyyan*, 53–54.

17 "The People's Republic of Letters: Towards a Media History of Twentieth Century Socialist Internationalism," PhD diss., Yale University, 2011, 6.

18 Al-Sayyāb, *Kuntu shuyūʿiyyan*, 253–254.
19 See Wright, *A Grammar of the Arabic Language*, Vol. 2, 363–364.
20 The final *d* and *ṣ* of the words scan long due to the vocalization they get in Arabic, a pronounced *ḍummah tanwīn* (*un*) indicating that they are in a standard nominal state when the words are non-final in a line.
21 Majīd al-Samarrāʾī, *Rasāʾil al-Sayyāb* (Bayrūt: al-Muʾassasah al-ʿArabiyyah li-l-Dirāsāt wa-l-Nashr, 1994), 130; *Badr Shakir Al-Sayyab: Three Letters*, trans. Terri DeYoung, *Jadaliyya*, December 24, 2014, www.jadaliyya.com/pages/index/20362/badr-shakir-al-sayyab_three-letters.
22 For a thorough analysis of al-Sayyāb's encounter with Eliot's poetry, see Nazeer El-Azma, "The Tammūzī Movement and the Influence of T. S. Eliot on Badr Shākir al-Sayyāb," *Journal of the American Oriental Society* 88, no. 4 (October–December, 1968): 671–678.
23 See ʿĪsā Bullāṭah, *Badr Shākir al-Sayyāb: Ḥayātuh wa-shiʿruh* (Bayrūt: Dār al-Nahār li-l-Nashr, 1971), 81. Jabrā mentions that Sayyāb read a manuscript of his translation in the introduction to its second edition. Jayms Frīzir, *Adūnīs aw Tammūz: Dirāsah fī al-asāṭīr wa-l-adyān al-sharqiyyah al-qadīmah*, tarjamat Jabrā Ibrāhīm Jabrā (Bayrūt: al-Muʾassasah al-ʿArabiyyah li-l-Dirāsāt wa-l-Nashr, 1979), 11. See also Jabrā Ibrāhīm Jabrā, *al-Riḥlah al-thāminah: dirāsāt naqdiyyah* (Ṣaydā: al-Maktabah al-ʿAṣriyyah, 1967), 24. The source text is James Frazer, *The Golden Bough: A Study in Magic and Religion* (New York: MacMillan, 1922 [1890]; bartleby.com 2000), www.bartleby.com/196/.
24 T. S. Eliot, *The Annotated Waste Land with Eliot's Contemporary Prose*, Lawrence Rainey ed., 2nd ed. (New Haven, CT: Yale University Press, 2006), 71.
25 Frazer, *The Golden Bough*, www.bartleby.com/196/79.html.
26 Terri DeYoung offers a nuanced reading of al-Sayyāb's *Unshūdat al-maṭar* ("Rain Song") by tracing this pessimistic line of thought throughout the poem. My understanding of Sayyāb's poetics is indebted to her article "A New Reading of Badr Shākir al-Sayyāb's 'Hymn of the Rain,'" *JAL* 24, no. 1 (March 1993): 39–61.
27 These lines are also translated by DeYoung in *Placing the Poet*, 102. I have consulted her translation here, departing from it in some cases.
28 "Sayyab's poems represent Jaykur (his home village in southern Iraq) as an almost utopian space related to emotionality, memory, lost childhood, and the source of a sense of identity threatened by exile. Jaykur, with its river, Buwayb, and palm trees, was also linked to motherly warmth and a sense of nostalgia evoked by the loneliness and strangeness of the city." Orit Bashkin, *The Other Iraq: Pluralism and Culture in Hashemite Iraq* (Stanford, CA: Stanford University Press, 2009), 226.
29 DeYoung, *Placing the Poet*, 103.
30 For a detailed analysis of the structure of the Sindbad tales and other information on the text, see Mia I. Gerhardt, *The Art of Story-Telling:*

A Literary Study of the Thousand and One Nights (Leiden: E. J. Brill, 1963), 236–263.

31 Iḥsān ʿAbbās, *Badr Shākir al-Sayyāb: Dirāsah fī ḥayātih wa-shiʿrih* (Bayrūt: Dār al-Thaqāfah, 1969), 220.

32 The translation is from *The Koran*, trans. J. M. Rodwell, foreword and introduction by Alan Jones (London: Orion Publishing Group, 1996 [1909]).

33 The note in the edition of the poem used here reads, "Shakespeare: *Romeo and Juliet*." The exact lines are not given, but they are 3.5.1, 5, and 12. Sayyāb, who studied English, probably engaged with the text in the original, either during his school days or at the Teachers College in Baghdad. Shakespeare citations refer to *William Shakespeare: The Complete Works*, ed. Alfred Harbage (Baltimore, MD: Penguin Books, 1972).

34 As far as I know, this is the only time al-Sayyāb uses the term *dawālīb* or its singular form *dūlāb* in his entire body of work.

35 W. P. Heinrichs, "*Ṭibāḳ*," *EI2*, http://dx.doi.org/10.1163/1573-3912_islam_COM_1215.

36 W. P. Heinrichs, "*Tadjnīs*," *EI2*, http://dx.doi.org/10.1163/1573–3912_islam_COM_1144.

37 Specifically, this is called a *tajnīs muṣaḥḥaf*: paronomasia based on a difference in diacritical markings. Heinrichs, "*Tadjnīs*."

38 Indicating he was from the poor peasant class of the countryside and almost certainly not a policeman. On tattooing in Iraq, see Winifred Smeaton, "Tattooing among the Arabs of Iraq," *American Anthropologist* 39, no. 1 (January–March 1937): 53–61.

39 Al-Sayyāb, *Kuntu shuyūʿiyyan*, 208.

40 Al-Sayyāb's full account of the day's events is in *Kuntu shuyūʿiyyan*, 207–209. See also Kevin Jones, "The Poetics of Revolution: Cultures, Practices, and Politics of Anti-Colonialism in Iraq, 1932–1960," PhD diss., The University of Michigan, 2013, 254–255 and a different, longer translation of this passage in Colla, "Badr Shākir al-Sayyāb," 253–254. Instead of "one or two rifles," Hanna Batatu reports that the protestors faced a "fierce fusillade" from the police, which "brought death to twelve of their comrades. With revenge in their heart, they seized a policeman, who had had no time to escape from the station, dragged him to the street, and burned him." *The Old Social Classes and the Revolutionary Movements of Iraq: A Study of Iraq's Old Landed and Commercial Classes and of its Communists, Baʿthists and Free Officers* (Princeton, NJ: Princeton University Press, 1978), 669. The second police officer and the tattooed man go unmentioned in Batatu's records.

41 Al-Sayyāb, *Kuntu shuyūʿiyyan*, 211.

42 Al-Sayyāb, *Kuntu shuyūʿiyyan*, 216–217.

43 Al-Sayyāb, *Kuntu shuyūʿiyyan*, 222.

44 Al-Sayyāb, *Kuntu shuyūʿiyyan*, 15–16. Cf. Jones, "The Poetics of Revolution," 284–285.

45 Al-Sayyāb, *Kuntu shuyūʿiyyan*, 17.

46 Al-Sayyāb, *Kuntu shuyūʿiyyan*, 211. Colla translates parts of this passage in "Badr Shākir al-Sayyāb," 255–256.
47 One of al-Sayyāb's biographers, Iḥsān ʿAbbās, refers to it as such. *Badr Shākir al-Sayyāb*, 179.
48 ʿAbbās, *Badr Shākir al-Sayyāb*, 187.
49 Al-Sayyāb, *al-Aʿmāl*, 302.
50 ʿAbbās, *Badr Shākir al-Sayyāb*, 191.
51 ʿAbbās, *Badr Shākir al-Sayyāb*, 192.
52 ʿAbbās, *Badr Shākir al-Sayyāb*, 220.
53 The Prime Minister of Iraq during the British Mandate and after who was killed in ʿAbd al-Karīm Qāsim's 1958 coup.
54 *Kuntu shuyūʿiyyan*, 82. Colla also offers a translation of this passage in "Badr Shākir al-Sayyāb," 250.

Chapter 5

1 G. J. H. van Gelder, "*Taḍmīn*," *EI2*. http://dx.doi.org/10.1163/1573-3912_islam_SIM_7284.
2 For instance, he edited the popular Iraqi leftist cultural journal *al-Taqāfah al-jadīdah* (*The New Culture*).
3 This interest is not without its critics. Saadi Simawe grumbles,

> Obsessively self-promoting all his life, al-Bayātī had a shrewd talent for effective networking to promote his poetry, as can be seen from the hundreds of studies written on him. Still another reason is the tendency of the international left and of the socialist realist school to inflate any exiled mediocre poet from the Third World, evaluating his or her poetry according to political commitment. And lastly, some of the problem may be attributable to the tendency of Western scholars to become fascinated with exotic foreign writers without adequate understanding of the cultural contexts. (Saadi A. Simawe, "The Lives of the Sufi Masters in ʿAbd al-Wahhāb al-Bayātī's Poetry," *JAL* 32, no. 2 (2001): 120)

Simawe is right to note that Bayātī actively tried to insert himself into the literary sphere of the international Left, as can be seen in his frequent allusions to and invocations of famous Leftists in his poetry. I am not interested in judging the quality of Bayātī's poetry (a subjective exercise of little use in any case), but rather in investigating how Bayātī goes about bringing premodern poetry, philosophy, and myth into his politically committed modernist poetry.
4 ʿAbd al-Wahhāb al-Bayātī, *Yanābīʿ al-shams: al-sīrah al-shiʿriyyah*, 1st ed. (Dimashq: Dār al-Farqad li-l-Ṭabāʿah wa-l-Nashr wa-l-Tawzīʿ, 1999), 97. That the funeral took place in Moscow shows, again, the central role the Soviets played in forging connections among poets coming from the Global South to the USSR.
5 Nāṣir Muḥsinī'niyā and Sipīdah Akhavān Māsūlah, "*Bāztāb-i farhang va adab-i Īrān dar shiʿr-i ʿAbd al-Wahhāb al-Bayātī*," *Kāvishnāmah-'i adabiyyāt-i taṭbīqī (muṭālaʿāt-i taṭbīqī-'i ʿarabī — fārsī)*, Dānishkadah-'i Adabiyyāt va

ʿUlūm-i Insānī, Dānishgāh-i Rāzī Kirmānshāh 3, no. 12 (Zamistān [Winter], 1392; 2014): 97.

6 Al-Bayātī, *Yanābīʿ al-shams*, 27.

7 "A secret Bayātī kept for over fifty years, Furūzandah: the spark of lost love," Qāsim al-Buraysīm wrote in the pages of *al-Raʾī*. Quoted in ʿAbd al-Riḍā ʿAlī, *Alladhī akalat al-qawāfī lisānahu wa-ākharūn: shakhṣiyyāt wa-mawāqif fī al-shiʿr wa-l-naqd wa-l-kitābah* (Bayrūt: al-Muʾassasah al-ʿArabiyyah li-l-Dirāsāt wa-l-Nashr, 2009), 58. Bayātī dedicated his final poem, *Bukāʾiyyah ilā Ḥāfiẓ al-Shīrāzī* (1st ed. [Bayrūt: Dār al-Kunūz al-Adabiyyah, 1999]) to Furūzandah, finally exposing his secret. See also Muḥsinīʾniyā and Māsūlah, "*Bāztāb*," 101–102.

8 See Aḥmad Nuhayrāt, "*Shakhṣiyyāt Īrāniyyah fī dīwān ʿAbd al-Wahhāb al-Bayātī*," *Majallat al-jamʿiyyah al-ʿilmiyyah al-Īrāniyyah li-l-lughah al-ʿarabiyyah wa-ādābihā* 9, no. 26 (al-Rabīʿ [Spring] 1392; 2013): 1–28; ʿĪsā Mutaqqāʾzādah and ʿAlī Bashīrī, "*al-Athr al-fārisī fī shiʿr ʿAbd al-Wahhāb al-Bayātī*," *Iḍāʾāt naqdiyyah* 2, no. 6 (Ṣayf [Summer] 1391; Ḥazīrān [June] 2012): 129–150; Nāhidah Fawzī, Maryam Amjad, and Kubrā Rawshanfikr, "*Barrasī-ʾi shiʿr-i Muḥammad Riżā Shafīʿī-Kadkanī va ʿAbd al-Wahhāb al-Bayātī az manẓar-i adabiyyāt-i taṭbīqī*," *Pazhūhash-hā-yi adabiyyāt-i taṭbīqī* 1, nos. 1–3 (Bahār va Tābistān [Spring and Summer] 1393 [2014]): 79–97; and Kubrā Rawshanfikr and Sajjād Ismāʿīlī, "*Barrasī-ʾi taṭbīqī-ʾi nūstālzhī dar shiʿr-i ʿAbd al-Wahhāb al-Bayātī va Shafīʿī-Kadkanī*," *Pazhūhash-hā-yi adabiyyāt-i taṭbīqī* 2, nos. 2–4 (Pāyīz va Zamistān [Fall and Winter] 1393 [2014–2015]): 27–55. Nāhidah Fawzī has also individually written "*Hājis al-ightirāb wa-l-tarḥāl ʿinda ʿAbd al-Wahhāb al-Bayātī*," *Majallat Markaz Dirāsāt al-Kūfah* 1, no. 21 (2011): 25–44, and *ʿAbd al-Wahhāb al-Bayātī ḥayātuh wa-shiʿruh (dirāsah naqdiyyah)* (Tihrān: Intishārāt-i S̱ār Allāh, 1383 [2004/05]). Additionally, Muḥammad Riżā Shafīʿī-Kadkanī has translated Bayātī in *Avāz-hā-yi Sindibād*, 2nd ed. ([Tihrān]: Intishārāt-i Nīl, 2536 [1976/77]; originally published in 1348 [1969/1970]). Bayātī knew about Shafīʿī-Kadkanī's translation and mentions that it "received lots of attention in the Persian literary scene" for its second printing that followed the Islamic Revolution, after which "other books [of his] were published in Persian translation, including *ʿUyūn al-kilāb al-mayyitah* (*Eyes of Dead Dogs*), *Ashʿār fī al-manfā*, and *Qamar Shīrāz*." ʿAbd al-Wahhāb al-Bayātī, *Mudun wa-rijāl wa-matāhāt* (Bayrūt: Dār al-Kunūz al-Adabiyyah, 1999), 112.

9 ʿAbd al-Wahhāb al-Bayātī, *Sifr al-faqr wa-l-thawrah: shiʿr*, 1st ed. (Bayrūt: Dār al-Ādāb, 1965), 9–30.

10 Al-Bayātī, *al-Aʿmāl al-shiʿriyyah*, Vol. 2, 203–204. See Bassam K. Frangieh's translation, Abdul Wahab Al-Bayati, *Love, Death and Exile: Poems Translated from the Arabic* (Washington, DC: Georgetown University Press, 1990), 35–37.

11 Al-Bayātī, *al-Aʿmāl al-shiʿriyyah*, Vol. 2, 205–206.

12 Al-Bayātī, *al-Aʿmāl al-shiʿriyyah*, Vol. 2, 359–392; Frangieh's translation is *Love, Death and Exile*, 209–217.

13 Al-Bayātī, *al-Aʿmāl al-shiʿriyyah*, Vol. 2, 405–408; Frangieh's translation is *Love, Death and Exile*, 249–255.

14 "Your eyes are Isfahan (*ʿaynāk 'Iṣfahān'*)" Bayātī writes in "To Hind," a poem to his wife. Al-Bayātī, *al-Aʿmāl al-shiʿriyyah*, Vol. 2, 55–56. Nishapur figures prominently in Bayātī's work, most obviously in his 1962 play *Muḥākamah fī Nīsābūr* (Tūnis: al-Dār al-Tūnisiyyah li-l-Nashr, 1973). "At the gates of Tehran, we saw him . . ." is the opening line to "*al-Rajul alladhī kāna yughannī*," *al-Aʿmāl al-shiʿriyyah*, Vol. 1, 280.

15 H. Ziai, "Illuminationism," *EIr*, XII/6, 670–672 and XIII/1, 1–2, www.iranicaonline.org/articles/illuminationism. Although there is not space for a long analysis of Bayātī's engagements with Suhrawardī alongside the other Persians of interest to us here, I ought to mention that Bayātī opens his first autobiographical work with an epigraph from Suhrawardī's *Ḥikmat al-ishrāq* (*The Philosophy of Illumination*). He considered Suhrawardī a revolutionary figure because he was compelled to involve himself and his Philosophy of Illumination in the political realm. According to Bayātī, Suhrawardī's philosophy "establishes a connection between political authority, just rule, and the ruler's access to divine light." Al-Bayātī, *Tajribatī al-shiʿriyyah*, 1st ed. (Bayrūt: Manshūrāt Nizār al-Qabbānī, 1968), 7. Like Ḥallāj, Suhrawardī was also executed by the ruling dynasty of his time, the Ayyūbids (r. 1171–1260), due to his philosophical commitments, leading to his appellation as *al-Maqtūl* (The Slain). C. Cahen, "Ayyūbids," *EI2*. http://dx.doi.org/10.1163/1573-3912_islam_SIM_0934. Regarding the chain of thinkers I am linking into Bayātī's philosophical genealogy, Muhsin al-Musawi helpfully suggests that "Al-Bayātī's major source on Sufism [...] may be Henry Corbin's study *Creative Imagination in the Sufism of Ibn Arabi* [1958]." *Islam on the Street: Religion in Modern Arabic Literature* (Lanham, MD: Rowman & Littlefield, 2009), 214.

16 Yoav Di-Capua, "Arab Existentialism: An Invisible Chapter in the Intellectual History of Decolonization," *American Historical Review* 117, no. 4: 1068.

17 Heidegger, *Being and Time*, 253. Italics original.

18 Di-Capua, "Arab Existentialism," 1066–1067. Italics, parentheses, and brackets original.

19 Heidegger, *Being and Time*, 254.

20 For more on the connection between Heidegger's and Albert Camus's engagements with anxiety, see Julian Young, "A Life Worth Living," *A Companion to Phenomenology and Existentialism*, eds. Hubert L. Dreyfus and Mark A. Wrathall (Oxford: Wiley-Blackwell, 2009), 526. For a study of the courses Sartre's philosophy took in the Arab world, see Yoav Di-Capua, *No Exit: Arab Existentialism, Jean-Paul Sartre, and Decolonization* (Chicago: University of Chicago Press, 2018).

21 Di-Capua, "Arab Existentialism," 1066.

22 Di-Capua, "Arab Existentialism," 1077.

23 Ḥusayn, "*Mulāḥaẓāt*."

24 Di-Capua, "Arab Existentialism," 1068, quoting R. Arnaldez, "*al-Insān al-Kāmil*," *EI2*, http://dx.doi.org/10.1163/1573-3912_islam_COM_0375. Transliterations amended and words in ellipsis replaced. For a recent explanation of the Arabic root *ḥā' - dāl – thā'*, which we find here in "*ḥidthān*" but which also lies at the core of "modernity" (*ḥadāthah*) and "modernist" (*muḥdath*), see El-Ariss, 2–3.

25 Di-Capua, "Arab Existentialism," 1081, quoting al-Bayātī, *Tajribatī al-shi'riyya*, 31.

26 Al-Bayātī, *al-A'māl*, Vol. 2, 132.

27 The Arabic is "*arā 'l-'anqā'a takburu an tuṣādā // fa-'ānid man tuṭīqu la-hu 'inādan*." *Dīwān Abī al-'Alā' al-Ma'arrī al-mashhūr bi-saqṭ al-zand*, ed. Shākir Shuqayr (Bayrūt: al-Maktabah al-Waṭaniyyah, 1884), 35.

28 Bayātī uses an accepted variant of the word, sometimes also voweled as *ufuq*, due to the meter.

29 Al-Bayātī, *al-A'māl*, Vol. 1, 113.

30 Wright, *A Grammar of the Arabic Language*, Vol. 2, 362–363.

31 Reuven Snir (Ru'ūbīn Sanīr) gives a full metrical analysis of the poem in his comprehensive study of Bayātī's work. *Rak'atān fī al-'ishq*, 27.

32 For the rest of the poem and its explanation, see *Sharḥ dīwān al-Mutanabbī*, waḍa'ah 'Abd al-Raḥmān al-Barqūqī, rāja'ah wa-fahrasah Dr. Yūsuf al-Shaykh Muḥammad al-Buqā'ī, Vol. 1 (Bayrūt: Dār al-Kātib al-'Arabī, 2010), 391–392.

33 Wright, *A Grammar of the Arabic Language*, Vol. 2, 363.

34 Levi Thompson, "A Transnational Approach to 'Abd al-Wahhāb al-Bayātī's 'Umar Khayyām," *Transnational Literature* 11, no. 1 (2018): 1–14. https://dspace.flinders.edu.au/xmlui/bitstream/handle/2328/38761/Thompson%20_A_Transnational_Approach.pdf.

35 There is simply not enough space for us to fully cover Ḥallāj's presence throughout Arabic modernism. I am, for instance, leaving out a discussion of Ṣalāḥ 'Abd al-Ṣabūr's versified play *Ma'sāt al-Ḥallāj*, translated to English by Khalil I. Semaan as *Murder in Baghdad*.

36 For al-Musawi's discussion of "satanic" love and Bayātī's engagement of the Ḥallāj myth, see *Islam on the Street*, 211–222.

37 Mojaddedi, "Ḥallāj."

38 Snir explains, "al-Ḥallāj was considered [...] by moderate Sufis to have deviated from Sufism when he revealed the secret [i.e., when he said, 'I am the Truth']." *Rak'atān fī al-'ishq*, 87.

39 Sanīr, *Rak'atān fī al-'ishq*, 86.

40 Al-Bayātī, *Yanābī' al-shams*, 166–167.

41 Laachir, Marzagora, and Orsini, "Significant Geographies," 295.

42 Those of us partial to Walter Benjamin's work might even see Bayātī's *dunyā* as a world ripe for Messianic intervention. See Walter Benjamin, "Theses on the Philosophy of History," *Illuminations: Essays and Reflections*, ed. Hannah Arendt, trans. Harry Zohn (New York: Shocken Books, 1968), 253–264.

43 Laura Doyle, "Toward a Philosophy of Transnationalism," *Journal of Transnational American Studies* 1, no. 1 (2009): 2. Italics original.

44 I am here again answering the question – at least in terms of Bayātī's poetry – that Laachir, Marzagora, and Orsini pose regarding the problem of relativism that the concept of significant geographies produces, "a relativism that issues not from the macro- or meta-categories chosen by the critic/scholar but from the texts and authors; it is a point-of-view relativism based on historically concrete literary actors. What geographies are significant to *them*?" Laachir, Marzagora, and Orsini, "Significant Geographies," 295. Italics original.

45 For the original poem, see Bayātī, *al-Aʿmāl*, Vol. 2, 9–20. A full English translation can be found in Khalil I. Semaan, "'Al-Ḥallāj': A Poem by ʿAbd al-Wahhāb al-Bayātī," *JAL* 10 (1979): 65–69.

46 Al-Bayātī, *al-Aʿmāl*, Vol. 2, 15.

47 Al-Bayātī, *al-Aʿmāl*, Vol. 2, 15–16.

48 Al-Bayātī, *Tajribatī al-shiʿriyyah*, 21–22. Partially quoted also in Sanīr, *Rakʿatān fī al-ʿishq*, 48.

49 Al-Bayātī, *al-Aʿmāl al-shiʿriyyah*, Vol. 1, 421.

50 Di-Capua, "Arab Existentialism," 1084. Consider the continued interest in existentialism in Iraq reflected in the title of ʿAlī Badr's novel, *Bābā Sartr* (Bayrūt: Riyāḍ al-Rayyis, 2001), translated into English as Ali Bader, *Papa Sartre* (Cairo: American University in Cairo Press, 2009).

51 Di-Capua, "Arab Existentialism," 1084.

52 For example, see Simawe, "The Lives of the Sufi Masters"; Aida O. Azouqa, "Al-Bayyātī [*sic*] and W. B. Yeats at Mythmakers: A Comparative Study," *JAL* 30, no. 3 (1999): 258–290; and Aida O. Azouqa, "Defamiliarization in the Poetry of ʿAbd al-Wahhāb al-Bayātī and T. S. Eliot: A Comparative Study," *JAL* 32, no. 2 (2001): 167–211.

53 Ṣādiq Hidāyat, *Tarānah-hā-yi Khayyām: bā shish majlis-i taṣvīr az Darvīsh Naqqāsh* ([Tihrān]: Intishārāt-i Māh, [1982?; originally published in 1934]), 18–19. Parentheses original.

54 (Garden City, NY: Doubleday, Doran & Company, 1934). See also Issa J. Boullata, 'The Masks of ʿAbd al-Wahhāb al-Bayātī,' *JAL* 32, no. 2 (2001): 107. An Arabic translation of Lamb's book was undertaken under the auspices of the Franklin Book Program that Sayyāb attempted to work for when he needed money after he shifted his allegiances from Communism to Western Liberalism. The Franklin edition came out sometime in the 1960s, but it is undated and does not show up in the Franklin book lists, available online here: www.loc.gov/rr/rarebook/coll/franklinbookprogram.html, so we cannot be sure whether Bayātī read the English original or the Arabic translation. The Arabic translation is Hārūld Lām, *Qiṣṣat ḥayāt al-Khayyām*, tarjamat Muḥammad Tawfīq Muṣṭafā (al-Qāhirah: Dār al-Qalam, 196?). Franklin also had the book translated into Persian as Hārūld Lamb, *ʿUmar Khayyām*, tarjamat Dr. Muḥammad ʿAlī Islāmī (Tihrān: Amīr Kabīr, 1957).

55 Al-Bayātī, *Muḥākamah*, 41. It is worth nothing that the line breaks only result in three lines rather than the usual four and there does not seem to be any

regular meter, which we would normally expect to find. This should not be surprising, as the Professor may have made up the verse himself in order to ascribe it to Khayyām and accuse him of *kufr*, thereby betraying his lack of literary critical ability and ignorance of even basic poetic standards.

56 Al-Bayātī, *Muḥākamah*, 40–41.

57 The Khayyām in Bayātī's play here reminds us of the Khayyām mythos found in Persian literary history. "It is clear that by the 15th century at the latest the name of the famous philosopher and scientist had become a collective pseudonym for authors of *rubā'īyāt*, especially those of hedonistic, fatalistic and more or less overtly anti-Islamic content [. . .] ." François de Blois, *Persian Literature: A Bio-Bibliographical Survey, Volume V: Poetry of the Pre-Mongol Period*, 2nd ed. (London: RoutledgeCurzon in association with The Royal Asiatic Society of Great Britain and Ireland, 2004), 305.

58 Al-Bayātī, *Muḥākamah*, 41–42.

59 Al-Bayātī, *Muḥākamah* 42. Ghazālī is well-known for his *Incoherence of the Philosophers*, where he argues against the influence of the Neoplatonism in Farābī's (d. 950) and Ibn Sīnā's thought on Islamic philosophy. He studied and taught in the newly instituted *madrasahs* (schools) founded by the Saljuq grand-vizier Niẓām al-Mulk. For more on him, see Frank Griffel, 'Al-Ghazali,' *The Stanford Encyclopedia of Philosophy* (2016), ed. Edward N. Zalta, http://plato.stanford.edu/archives/sum2016/entries/al-ghazali/.

60 For a detailed study of the Assassins, see Marshall G. S. Hodgson, *The Order of Assassins: The Struggle of the Early Nizârî Ismâ'îlîs against the Islamic World* (Philadelphia: University of Pennsylvania Press, 2005). For a brief discussion of the political, religious, and historical context in Iran at the time, see *The Rubā'īyāt of 'Umar Khayyām,* with an introduction by trans. Parichehr Kasra, UNESCO Collection of Representative Works Persian Series, no. 21, ed. Ehsan Yar-Shater (Delmar, NY: Scholar's Facsimiles & Reprints, 1975), xi–xxxvii.

61 Al-Bayātī, *Muḥākamah*, 75.

62 Al-Bayātī, *Muḥākamah*, 78.

63 Al-Bayātī, *Muḥākamah*, 79.

64 Al-Bayātī, *Muḥākamah*, 79–81.

65 In his famous rejection of nihilism, Camus wrote, '*La lutte elle-même vers les sommets suffit à remplir un cœur d'homme. Il faut imaginer Sisyphe heureux.*' Albert Camus, *Le Mythe de Sisyphe: Essai sur l'absurde* (Paris: Gallimard, 1942), 166.

66 'Abd al-Wahhāb al-Bayātī, *Nuṣūṣ sharqiyyah* (Dimashq: al-Madā, 1999), 63. Ḥusayn Fāṭimī, Mosaddegh's Minister of Foreign Affairs, was executed by firing squad on November 10, 1954. Makkāwī (d. 1997) was an Egyptian radio personality, composer, and singer.

67 Al-Bayātī, *Nuṣūṣ sharqiyyah*, 64.

68 This feeling of disillusionment with Arab socialism among the Arab Left is in no way limited to Bayātī. We find an almost parallel scene of an intellectual, the character Yūsuf al-Najjār, escaping into alcohol during the 1977 Egyptian

Bread Riots in Ibrāhīm Aṣlān's *Mālik al-ḥazīn* (Bayrūt: Dār al-Ādāb, 1992 [1983]), 81–82. The English translation is Ibrahim Aslan, *The Heron*, trans. Elliott Colla (Cairo: American University in Cairo Press, 2005), 72–73.

69 Al-Bayātī, *Nuṣūṣ sharqiyyah*, 76.

70 Al-Bayātī, *Nuṣūṣ sharqiyyah*, 88.

Chapter 6

1 *Qaṭʿnāmah*, 67.

2 Furūgh Farrukhzād, *Īmān biyāvarīm bih āghāz-i faṣl-i sard*, 7th ed. (Tihrān: Intishārāt-i Murvārīd, 1368 [1989]), 23. Cf. the translation in Hillman, *A Lonely Woman: Forugh Farrokhzad and Her Poetry* (Washington, DC: Three Continents & Mage, 1987), 125. The poem was first published in part in a fall 1965 issue of the journal *Ārash* but did not appear in a collection until the release of a posthumous volume carrying the name of the same poem in 1974. While I depend on a version found in a 1989 edition, some scholars add a final (but incomplete) section. The theme of the additional section does not, to my mind, fit with the rest of the poem, so I will leave it aside in my analysis. For a facing-page translation with the original Persian, see *Forugh Farrokhzad: Another Birth and other poems*, trans. Hasan Javadi and Susan Salleé (Washington, DC: Mage, 2010), 134–139. For the translations of the poem in this chapter, I have relied for the most part on the version just mentioned, making changes where necessary. Javadi and Salleé's translations are also published as *Another Birth: Selected Poems of Forugh Farrokhzad*, Middle Eastern Series 1 (Emeryville, CA: Albany Press, 1981). I have consulted other translations as well: "Let's Believe in the Beginning of the Cold Season," trans. Mohammad Hadi Kamyabee, "The Waste Land Vision in T. S. Eliot and Forugh Farrokhzad," Master's thesis, Pahlavi University, 1978, 138–143; "Let Us Believe in the Oncoming Season of Cold," *Bride of Acacias: Selected Poems of Forugh Farrokhzad*, trans. Jascha Kessler and Amin Banani, introduction by Amin Banani, afterword by Farzaneh Milani (Delmar, NY: Caravan Books, 1982), 95–102; a partial translation in Hillman, *A Lonely Woman*, 125–128; and "Let Us Believe in the Dawn of the Cold Season," *Sin: Selected Poems of Forugh Farrokhzad*, trans. Sholeh Wolpé, foreword by Alicia Ostriker (Fayetteville: University of Arkansas Press, 2007), 85–93. This line literally means "a lonely woman." I prefer the cadence of "a woman alone" in my translation, though "a woman, lonely" would make a nice rhyme with the first line and match the original Persian word order.

3 We might also add Mohammad Mosaddegh's March 5, 1967 death under house arrest to this list of events since the royalist coup against his government has played such a pivotal role in our timeline so far. Farrukhzād, being the youngest of the poets we address at length in this book, started writing her modernist poetry after the disillusionment with politics that afflicted our other subjects during the years following the coup had already set in.

4 Rižā Barāhinī, "*Buzurgtarīn zan-i tārīkh-i Īrān,*" *Kasī kih mis̱l-i hīch kas nīst: darbārah-'i Furūgh Farrukhzād,* eds. Pūrān Farrukhzād va Muḥammad Qāsimzādah (Tihrān: Kārvān, 1381 [2001]), 62. In comparing the two, I am following the lead of ʿAlī Sharīʿat Kāshānī, who wrote "*Furūgh va Shāmlū: az nazdīkī-hā tā fāṣilah-hā,*" also in *Kasī kih mis̱l-i hīch kas nīst,* 125–182.

5 See chapter 2 of Hillman's *A Lonely Woman,* 37–72. He quotes Farrukhzād on 37. Italics added.

6 *Forugh Farrokhzad, Poet of Modern Iran: Iconic Woman and Feminine Pioneer of New Persian Poetry,* eds. Dominic Parviz Brookshaw and Nasrin Rahimieh (New York: I. B. Tauris & Co., 2010), 3.

7 "Love and Sexuality in the Poetry of Forugh Farrokhzad: A Reconsideration," *Iranian Studies* 15, no. 1/4 (1982): 120.

8 Farrukhzād, *Īmān biyāvarīm,* 23. Translation in Hillman, *A Lonely Woman,* 125. Translation modified.

9 Walter Benjamin, *The Writer of Modern Life: Essays on Charles Baudelaire,* ed. Michael W. Jennings, trans. Howard Eiland, Edmund Jephcott, Rodney Livingston, and Harry Zohn (Cambridge, MA: Belknap Press of Harvard University Press, 2006), 40.

10 Cf. Haideh Ghomi, "Female Identity in the Poetry of Forugh Farrokhzad," *Identità e appartenenza in Medio Oriente,* eds. Marta Petricioli and Albert Tonini (Florence: Università di Firenze, Dipartimento di Studi sullo Stato, 1998), 207–214.

11 Farrukhzād, *Īmān biyāvarīm,* 21, 32; *Another Birth: Selected Poems of Forugh Farrokhzad,* 65, 68–69.

12 Benjamin, *Writer of Modern Life,* 40.

13 After a woman quickly passes by Baudelaire's *flâneur* in the Parisian streets, he wonders, "A flash . . . then night! – O lovely fugitive / I am suddenly reborn from your swift glance; / Shall I never see you till eternity?" ("*Un éclair . . . puis la nuit! – Fugitive beauté / Dont le regard m'a fait soudainement renaître, / Ne te verrai-je plus que dans l'éternité?*") Charles Baudelaire, *The Flowers of Evil,* trans. C. F. MacIntyre, 118. French on 337.

14 Benjamin, *Writer of Modern Life,* 77. Italics added.

15 Furūgh Farrukhzād, *Tavalludī dīgar,* 164–165; *Another Birth and Other Poems,* 111.

16 Farzaneh Milani addresses the (masculine) Iranian critical reception of Farrukhzād's poetry in "Love and Sexuality in the Poetry of Forugh Farrokhzad." See also Dylan Olivia Oehler-Stricklin, "'And This Is I:' The Power of the Individual in the Poetry of Forugh Farrokhzâd," PhD diss., University of Texas at Austin, 2005; John Zubizarreta, "The Woman Who Sings No, No, No: Love, Freedom, and Rebellion in the Poetry of Forugh Farrokhzad," *World Literature Today* 66, no. 3 (Summer, 1992): 421–426; Farzaneh Milani, "Conflicts between Traditional Roles and Poetry in the Work of Forugh Farrokhzod," *Women and the Family in Iran,* ed. Asghar Fathi (Leiden: E. J. Brill, 1985), 226–237; and chapter 1 of Hillman's *A Lonely Woman,* 5–36, especially 32–33.

17 Jasmin Darznik, "Forough Goes West: The Legacy of Forough Farrokhzad in Iranian Diasporic Art and Literature," *Journal of Middle East Women's Studies* 6, no. 1 (Winter 2010): 104.
18 Nasrin Rahimieh, *Oriental Responses to the West: Comparative Essays in Select Writers from the Muslim World* (Leiden: E. J. Brill, 1990), 44. Italics added.
19 Darznik, "Forough Goes West," 104.
20 Yūshīj, *Majmūʿah*, 222.
21 Eliot, *The Annotated Waste Land*, 59.
22 Hillman, *A Lonely Woman*, 126. Italics original.
23 *Another Birth: Selected Poems of Forugh Farrokhzad*, 96. Ellipsis original.
24 *Another Birth and Other Poems*, 187–188, 198. Ālāshtī and Dilāvar describe Farrukhzād's later work as "poems in meters particular to Farrukhzād, which [initially] appear to be Nīmāic and within which different meters are combined or [poetic] feet are rearranged – a style particular to Furūgh." They add, "The poetry and metrics particular to Furūgh fill the gap between Nīmāic poetry and blank verse poetry (*shiʿr-i sipīd*) or prose poetry (*shiʿr-i manṣūr*)." Ḥusayn Ḥasan'pūr Ālāshtī and Parvānah Dilāvar, "*ʿAnāṣir-i sabk'sāz̠ dar mūsīqī-'i shiʿr-i Furūgh Farrukhzād*," *Faṣl'nāmah-'i takhaṣṣuṣī-'i adabiyyāt-i fārsī-'i Dānishgāh-i Āzād-i Islāmī-'i Mashhad* 5, no. 18 (Tābistān, 1387 [Summer, 2008]), http://fa.journals.sid.ir/ViewPaper.aspx?id=133315: 122–123.
25 For a short analysis of her use of poetic feet in "Let Us Believe," see Ālāshtī and Dilāvar, "*ʿAnāṣir-i sabk'sāz*," 125–126.
26 *Another Birth: Selected Poems of Forugh Farrokhzad*, 112, 113.
27 *Another Birth: Selected Poems of Forugh Farrokhzad*, 99.
28 Consider, for instance, the iambs in the first several lines in section two of *The Waste Land*, "A Game of Chess." Eliot, *The Annotated Waste Land*, 59–60, or the lines from its Unreal City section, particularly the "dead sound" of the extra "nine" in the last line.
29 Wright points out that the Arabic name of the *muḍāriʿ* (the "similar" meter) was so chosen due to its similarity to the *mujtathth* (*mujtas̠s̠* in Persian) meter since we might find a single line fits both by "adopting another mode of scansion." Wright, *A Grammar of the Arabic Language*, Vol. 2, 364–365, 368.
30 Farrukhzād, *Īmān biyāvarīm*, 25–26; *Another Birth: Selected Poems of Forugh Farrokhzad*, 66. Translation modified.
31 The base feet of the *mużāriʿ* here being *mafʿūlu fāʿilātu mafāʿīlu fāʿilun* and of the *mujtas̠s̠*: *mafāʿilun faʿilātun mafāʿilun faʿilun*. Cf. Thiesen's presentation of these meters in *A Manual of Classical Persian Prosody*, 144–148, 153–158. For an extremely detailed analysis of Furūgh's use of meter in "Let Us Believe" and the scansions on which I am depending for my reading here, see Sīrūs Shamīsā, *Nigāhī bih Furūgh Farrukhzād*, 1st ed. (Tihrān: Intishārāt-i Murvārīd, 1382 [2003]), 80–83.
32 Shamīsā, *Nigāhī bih Furūgh*, 82.
33 Shamīsā surmises that the meter could also be in the *mużāriʿ*, in which case the feet would be *mafʿūlu fāʿilun*. *Nigāhī bih Furūgh*, 82.

34 In the edition I am using, the line is so long that it does not fit on a single line, and the words *zandah nabūdahst* are left-justified on the page.
35 For further analysis and more examples, see Shamīsā, *Nigāhī bih Furūgh*, 83.
36 For more on Eliot's use of metrics in *The Waste Land*, see Harvey Gross and Robert McDowell, *Sound and Form in Modern Poetry*, 2nd ed. (Ann Arbor: University of Michigan Press, 1996 [1985]), 175–177.
37 Although *The Waste Land* was translated into Persian by 1955 (Muḥammad Jaʿfar Yāḥaqqī, *Jūybār-i laḥẓah-hā: jaryān-hā-yi adabiyyāt-i muʿāṣir-i fārsī, naẓm va nas̱r* [Tihrān: Jāmī, 1388 (2009/2010)], 103), Farrukhzād remained "very keen on improving her reading skills in English so that she could read T. S. Eliot and other modernist English or American poets in the original," as Karim Emami (d. 2005) remembers it. "Recollections and Afterthoughts," lecture given in Austin, TX (n.d.), www.forughfarrokhzad.org/papers/papers3.htm. See also *Forugh Farrokhzad: Another Birth and Other Poems*, xii.
38 My italics here hark back to Laachir, Marzagora, and Orsini's italics in the question, "What geographies are significant to *them*?" "Significant Geographies," 295.
39 Dominic Parviz Brookshaw, "Places of Confinement, Liberation, and Decay: The Home and the Garden in the Poetry of Forugh Farrokhzād," in *Forugh Farrokhzad, Poet of Modern Iran*, 35–52.
40 Brookshaw, "Places of Confinement," 45.
41 *A Lonely Woman*, 98.
42 Brookshaw, "Places of Confinement," 48.
43 Brookshaw, "Places of Confinement," 48, 51.
44 Brookshaw, "Places of Confinement," 52.
45 Farrukhzād, *Īmān biyāvarīm*, 24; *Another Birth: Selected Poems of Forugh Farrokhzad*, 65. Translation modified.
46 Javadi and Sallée go with "savior" while Kessler and Banani as well as Wolpé use "Messiah." The word "Messiah," however, is a term used also in the Jewish tradition, while Christ is often called "the Redeemer" in Christianity. I prefer "the Redeemer" here because of its more specifically Christian resonance, which contrasts nicely with the lines that follow about His being buried in a grave.
47 Farrukhzād, *Īmān biyāvarīm*, 38–39; *Another Birth: Selected Poems of Forugh Farrokhzad*, 71. Translation modified. Cf. the translation in *Bride of Acacias*, 100.
48 Farrukhzād, *Īmān biyāvarīm*, 39. Cf. the translations found in *Another Birth: Selected Poems of Forugh Farrokhzad*, 71 and *Bride of Acacias*, 100.
49 Farrukhzād, *Īmān biyāvarīm*, 24–25; *Another Birth: Selected Poems of Forugh Farrokhzad*, 65.
50 Eliot, *The Annotated Waste Land*, 57.
51 Eliot, *The Annotated Waste Land*, 59.
52 It is worth noticing how the perspective of Farrukhzād's *flâneuse* changes throughout the poem, moving from the viewpoint of "a lonely woman" to that of a prophet more akin to Eliot's Tiresias, the "legendary blind seer" who

famously experienced life as both a man and a woman. Eliot, *The Annotated Waste Land*, 64, 107.

53 See the timeline of her life in *Another Birth and Other Poems*, 232–233.

54 Furūgh Farrukhzād, *Marg-i man rūzī … : majmūʿah-yī az namūnah-hā-yi āsār-i shāʿirān-i Ālmān dar nīmah-ʾi avval-i qarn-i bīstum*, tarjamah-ʾi Furūgh Farrukhzād va Dr. Masʿūd Farrukhzād (Tihrān: Kitābsarā-yi Tandīs, 1379 [2000]).

55 Dabashi adds, "When she returned to Tehran, she would carry the lasting memories of Europe with her back to her homeland. The effect was not one of ambivalence or confusion, identity crisis or misplaced emotions. Quite to the contrary: the effect was an emotive universe that was *rooted in Iran* but *global in its sentiments*, rooted in the world but effervescent in its worldly conception of her homeland." *Iran without Borders*, 111–112. Italics added.

56 See *Another Birth: Selected Poems of Forugh Farrokhzad*, 132 and *Another Birth and Other Poems*, 123, each by the same translators. They give an incorrect citation of Eliot, "Between the idea and the act / Falls the shadow." Cf. *T. S. Eliot: Collected Poems 1909–1962* (New York: Harcourt, Brace & World, 1963), 81–82. Barbara Fister also points out that "Let Us Believe in the Beginning of the Cold Season" "contains references to – and emulates the mood of – Eliot's 'Hollow Men.'" *Third World Women's Literatures: A Dictionary and Guide to Materials in English* (Westport, CT: Greenwood Press, 1995), 20.

57 Farrukhzād, *Īmān biyāvarīm*, 34–35; *Another Birth: Selected Poems of Forugh Farrokhzad*, 69–70. Translation modified.

58 "The lyric gaze glimpses isolated fragments, in keeping with the episodic rhythms of the street." Scott Brewster writes, discussing the changing role of the lyric "I" in modernist poetry. "The poet is a 'ragpicker,' a sifter of the city's debris: the movement of the boulevard, its transient novelty and fleeting sensory stimuli, becomes a new subject in lyric poetry. In contrast to the static, contemplative look in the Romantic ode or greater lyric, the modernist gaze is fleeting and furtive, mimicking the restless mobility of urban modernity. The lyric moment is now characterised by collisions and chance encounters that allow the 'I' only a temporary vantage point." *Lyric*, The New Critical Idiom, series ed. John Drakakis (New York: Routledge Taylor & Francis Group, 2009), 100.

59 *Another Birth and Other Poems*, 111.

60 Farrukhzād, *Īmān biyāvarīm*, 40–41; *Another Birth: Selected Poems of Forugh Farrokhzad*, 72. Translation modified.

61 Johnson, *The Idea of Lyric*, 10–11.

62 Farrukhzād, *Īmān biyāvarīm*, 29; cf. the translations in *Another Birth: Selected Poems of Forugh Farrokhzad*, 67 and *Bride of Acacias*, 97. Translations modified.

63 Eliot, *The Annotated Waste Land*, 66–67.

64 Brewster, *Lyric*, 100.

65 Farrukhzād, *Īmān biyāvarīm*, 42–43; *Another Birth: Selected Poems of Forugh Farrokhzad*, 73. Translation modified.
66 Kamyabee likewise reads these final lines in an optimistic mode when he compares them with those at the end of Eliot's *The Waste Land*. "Waste land vision," 63.
67 My reformulation of Walter Benjamin, *The Writer of Modern Life*, 41.
68 Farrukhzād, *Īmān biyāvarīm*, 100. I have consulted the translations in Wolpé, *Sin: Selected Poems of Forugh Farrokhzad*, 111; *Forugh Farrokhzad: Another Birth and other poems*, 167; and Hillman, *A Lonely Woman*, 95.
69 Aḥmad Shāmlū, *Quqnūs dar bārān*, 1st ed. (Tihrān: Intishārāt-i Nīl, 1966).
70 Mīrāl al-Ṭaḥāwī, *Brūklīn Hāyits* (al-Qāhirah: Dār Mīrīt, 2010), 5.
71 Furūgh Farrukhzād, *al-Aʿmāl al-shiʿriyyah al-kāmilah*, tarjamat Maryam al-ʿAṭṭār (Baghdād: Dār al-Madā, 2017).

Conclusion

1 *Quqnūs dar bārān*, 46.
2 In fact, in some cases, the state was able to entirely co-opt the Communist Left into the fold. Creswell reminds us that in 1965 "the two largest Communist parties in Egypt met and voted to dissolve themselves, instructing their memberships to enroll in Nasser's newly formed Arab Socialist Union. They hoped to have some influence on the regime's policies by shaping them from the inside, but this was not to be." "Translator's Introduction," Sonallah Ibrahim, *That Smell and Notes from Prison*, ed. and trans. Robyn Creswell (New York: New Directions, 2013), 6.
3 Fatemeh Shams, *A Revolution in Rhyme: Poetic Co-option under the Islamic Republic* (Oxford: Oxford University Press, 2021), 33.

Bibliography

ʿAbbās, Iḥsān. *Badr Shākir al-Sayyāb: Dirāsah fī ḥayātih wa-shiʿrih*. Bayrūt: Dār al-Thaqāfah, 1969.

ʿAbbās, Iḥsān. *Ittijāhāt al-shiʿr al-ʿarabī al-muʿāṣir*. Kuwayt: al-Majlis al-Waṭānī li-l-Thaqāfah wa-l-Funūn wa-l-Adab, 1978.

ʿAbd al-ʿAzīz, Aḥmad. "Athar Fīdīrīkū Jārthiya Lūrkā fī al-adab al-ʿarabī al-muʿāṣir." *Fuṣūl: majallat al-naqd al-adabī. Al-Adab al-Muqārin* 2, 3, no. 4 (1983): 271–299.

ʿAbd al-Ṣabūr, Ṣalāḥ. *Maʾsāt al-Ḥallāj*. Al-Qāhirah: al-Hayʾah al-Miṣriyyah al-ʿĀmmah li-l-Kitāb, 1996 [1965].

ʿAbd al-Ṣabūr, Ṣalāh. "Murder in Baghdad." Translated by Khalil I. Semaan. *Arabic Translation Series of the Journal of Arabic Literature 1*. Leiden: E. J. Brill, 1972.

Adorno, Theodor, Ernst Bloch, Walter Benjamin, Bertolt Brecht, and Georg Lukás. *Aesthetics and Politics*. Edited by Ronald Taylor. Translated by Francis McDonagh. London: NLB, 1977.

Adūnīs [ʿAlī Aḥmad Saʿīd Isbir]. *Dīwān al-shiʿr al-ʿarabī*. 3 vols. Bayrūt: al-Maktabah al-ʿAṣriyyah, 1964–1968.

Adūnīs. *Al-Thābit wa–mutaḥawwil: baḥth fī al-ibdāʿ wa-l-ittibāʿ ʿinda al-ʿarab*. 10th ed. Bayrūt: Dār al-Sāqī, 2011 [1974].

Afro Asia: Revolutionary Political and Cultural Connections between African Americans and Asian Americans. Edited by Fred Ho and Bill V. Mullen. Durham, NC: Duke University Press, 2008.

Ahmed, Amr Taher. *La "Révolution littéraire": Étude de l'influence de la poésie française sur la modernisation des formes poétiques persanes au début de XXe siècle*. Wien [Vienna]: Verlag der Österreichischen Akademie der Wissenschaften, 2012.

Akhavān S̱ālis, Mahdī [M. Umīd]. *Bidʿat-hā va badāyiʿ-i Nīmā Yūshīj*. 1st ed. Tihrān: Tūkā, 1357 [1978].

Al-Adab al-ʿarabī al-muʿāṣir: aʿmāl muʾtamar Rūmā al-munʿaqid fī Tishrīn al-awwal sanat 1961. Manshūrāt al-Aḍwāʾ, 1961.

Āl-i Aḥmad, Jalāl. *Gharbzadagī*. Costa Mesa, CA: Mazda Publishers, 1997 [1962].

Al-i Ahmad, Jalal. *Occidentosis: A Plague from the West*. Translated by R. Campbell. Annotations and introduction by Hamid Algar, Berkeley, CA: Mizan Press, 1984.

Ālāshtī, Ḥusayn Ḥasan'pūr and Parvānah Dilāvar. "'Anāṣir-i sabk'sāz dar mūsīqī-'i shi'r-i Furūgh Farrukhzād." *Faṣl'nāmah-'i takhaṣṣuṣī-'i adabiyyāt-i fārsī-'i Dānishgāh-i Āzād-i Islāmī-'i Mashhad* 5, no. 18 Tābistān, 1387 [Summer, 2008]: 120–137.

Alavi, Samad. "The Poetics of Commitment in Modern Persian: A Case of Three Revolutionary Poets in Iran." PhD diss., University of California, Berkeley, 2013.

Albright, Daniel. *Putting Modernism Together: Literature, Music, and Painting 1872–1927*. Baltimore: Johns Hopkins University Press, 2015.

'Alī, 'Abd al-Riḍā. *Alladhī akalat al-qawāfī lisānahu wa-ākharūn: shakhṣiyyāt wa-mawāqif fī al-shi'r wa-l-naqd wa-l-kitābah*. Bayrūt: al-Mu'assasah al-'Arabiyyah li-l-Dirāsāt wa-l-Nashr, 2009.

Allen, Roger. *The Arabic Novel: An Historical and Critical Introduction*. 2nd ed. Syracuse, NY: Syracuse University Press, 1995 [1983].

Al-Āmidī, Abū al-Qāsim al-Ḥasan ibn Bishr. *Al-Muwāzanah bayna shi'r Abī Tammām wa-l-Buḥturī*. 2nd ed. Edited by Aḥmad Ṣaqr. Vol. 1. Al-Qāhirah: Dār al-Ma'ārif, 1972.

Anderson, Benedict. *Imagined Communities: Reflections on the Origin and Spread of Nationalism*. Revised ed. New York: Verso, 2006 [1983].

Another Birth: Selected Poems of Forugh Farrokhzad. Translated by Hasan Javadi and Susan Sallée. Emeryville, CA: Albany Press, 1981.

Anthology of Modern Arabic Poetry. Edited and translated by Mounah A. Khouri and Hamid Algar. Berkeley: University of California Press, 1974.

Arnott, W. Geoffrey. "Swan Songs." *Greece & Rome* 24, no. 2 (1977): 149–153.

Āryanpūr, Yaḥyā. *Az Ṣabā tā Nīmā: tarīkh-i 150 sāl-i adab-i fārsī*. 5th ed. Tihrān: Intishārāt-i Zavvār, 1372 [1993] (1350 [1971]).

Asad, Talal. *Formations of the Secular: Christianity, Islam, Modernity*. Cultural Memory in the Present. Edited by Mieke Bal and Hent de Vries. Stanford, CA: Stanford University Press, 2003.

Aṣgharī, Muḥammad Ja'far and Nargis Ganjī. "Tajalliyyāt al-intiẓār fī qaṣīdatay 'Unshūdat al-maṭar' wa 'Dārūg' li-Badr Shākir al-Sayyāb wa Nīmā Yūshīj (dirāsah muqāranah)." *Faṣliyyat al-lisān al-mubīn (buḥūth fī al-adab al-'arabī)* 4, no. 10 (Shitā', 1391 [2012/2013]): 21–37.

Aṣlān, Ibrāhīm. *The Heron*. Translated by Elliott Colla. Cairo: American University in Cairo Press, 2005.

Aṣlān, Ibrāhīm. *Mālik al-ḥazīn*. Bayrūt: Dār al-Ādāb, 1992 [1983].

Athamneh, Waed. *Modern Arabic Poetry: Revolution and Conflict*. South Bend, IN: University of Notre Dame Press, 2017.

'Aṭṭār, Farīd al-Dīn. *Manṭiq al-ṭayr, bi-taṣḥīḥ va ihtimām-i Muḥammad Javād Mashkūr, bā muqaddamah va ta'līqāt*. 2nd ed. Tihrān: Kitābfurūshī-'i Tihrān, 1341 [1962].

'Aṭṭār, Farīd al-Dīn Muḥammad ibn Ibrāhīm Nīshābūrī. *Manṭiq al-ṭayr*. Muqaddamah, taṣḥīḥ va ta'līqāt Muḥammad Rizā Shafī'ī-Kadkanī. Tihrān: Sukhan, 1388 [2010].

ʿAṭṭār, Farīdu'd-Dīn. *The Speech of the Birds: Manṭiq't-Tair*. Presented by Peter Avery. Cambridge, UK: The Islamic Texts Society, 2001.

ʿAṭṭār, Farīdu'd-Dīn. *Tadhkiratu 'l-awliya ("Memoirs of the Saints") of Muḥammad ibn Ibrahim Faridu'd-Din ʿAṭṭar*. Edited by Reynold A. Nicholson. Part II. Persian Historical Texts. Vol. V. London: Luzac & Co., 1907.

ʿAwaḍ, Luwīs. *Blūtūlānd wa-qasāʾid ukhrā min shiʿr al-khāṣṣah*. Al-Qāhirah: al-Hay'ah al-Miṣriyyah al-ʿĀmmah li-l-Kitāb, 1989 [1947].

ʿAwaḍ, Luwīs. "T. S. Iliyūt." *al-Kātib al-Miṣrī: al-majmūʿah al-kāmilah*. Vol. 1. Edited by ʿAbd al-ʿAziz Sharaf. Al-Hay'ah al-Miṣriyyah al-ʿĀmmah li-l-Kitāb, 1998: 557–568.

Al-ʿAẓm, Ṣādiq Jalāl. *Al-Naqd al-dhātī baʿda al-hazīmah*. Bayrūt: Dār al-Ṭalīʿah, 1968.

Al-Azm, Sadik. *Self-Criticism after the Defeat*. Translated by George Stergios. London: Saqi Books, 2011.

Azouqa, Aida O. "Al-Bayyātī and W. B. Yeats as Mythmakers: A Comparative Study." *Journal of Arabic Literature* 30, no. 3 (1999): 258–290.

Azouqa, Aida O. "Defamiliarization in the Poetry of ʿAbd al-Wahhāb al-Bayātī and T. S. Eliot: A Comparative Study." *Journal of Arabic Literature* 32, no. 2 (2001): 167–211.

Badawi, Mohammed Mustafa. *A Critical Introduction to Modern Arabic Poetry*. Cambridge: Cambridge University Press, 1975.

Badawi, Mohammed Mustafa. *Modern Arabic Literature and the West*. London: Ithaca Press, 1985.

Badawi, Mohammed Mustafa. *A Short History of Modern Arabic Literature*. Oxford: Clarendon Press, 1993.

Badr, ʿAlī. *Bābā Sartr*. Bayrūt: Riyāḍ al-Rayyis, 2001.

Bader, Ali. *Papa Sartre*. Cairo: American University in Cairo Press, 2009.

Barāhinī, Riżā. *Ṭalā dar mis: dar shiʿr va shāʿrī*. Tihrān: Kitāb-i Zamān, 1347 [1968].

Al-Barqūqī, ʿAbd al-Raḥmān. *Sharḥ dīwān al-Mutanabbī*. Rājaʿah wa-fahrasah Dr. Yūsuf al-Shaykh Muḥammad al-Buqāʿī. 4 vols. Bayrūt: Dār al-Kātib al-ʿArabī, 2010.

Bashkin, Orit. *The Other Iraq: Pluralism and Culture in Hashemite Iraq*. Stanford, CA: Stanford University Press, 2009.

Batatu, Hanna. *The Old Social Classes and the Revolutionary Movements of Iraq: A Study of Iraq's Old Landed and Commercial Classes and of Its Communists, Baʿthists, and Free Officers*. Princeton, NJ: Princeton University Press, 1978.

Baudelaire, Charles. *The Flowers of Evil*. Edited by Marthiel and Jackson Mathews. New York: New Directions, 1989.

Al-Bayātī, ʿAbd al-Wahhāb. *Al-Aʿmāl al-shiʿriyyah*. 2 Vols. Bayrūt: al-Mu'assasah al-ʿArabiyyah li-l-Dirāsāt wa-l-Nashr, 1995.

Al-Bayātī, ʿAbd al-Wahhāb. *Avāz-hā-yi Sindibād*. Tarjamah-'i Muḥammad Riżā Shafīʿī-Kadkanī. 2nd ed. [Tihrān]: Intishārāt-i Nīl, 2536 [1976/1977].

Al-Bayātī, ʿAbd al-Wahhāb. *Bukāʾiyyah ilā Ḥāfiẓ al-Shīrāzī*. 1st ed. Bayrūt: Dār al-Kunūz al-Adabiyyah, 1999.

Al-Bayātī, ʿAbd al-Wahhāb. *Mudun wa-rijāl wa-matāhāt*. Bayrūt: Dār al-Kunūz al-Adabiyyah, 1999.

Al-Bayātī, ʿAbd al-Wahhāb. *Muḥākamah fī Nīsābūr*. Tūnis: al-Dār al-Tūnisiyyah li-l-Nashr, 1973.

Al-Bayātī, ʿAbd al-Wahhāb. *Nuṣūṣ sharqiyyah*. Dimashq: al-Madā, 1999.

Al-Bayātī, ʿAbd al-Wahhāb. *Sifr al-faqr wa-l-thawrah: shiʿr*. 1st ed. Bayrūt: Dār al-Ādāb, 1965.

Al-Bayātī, ʿAbd al-Wahhāb. *Tajribatī al-shiʿriyyah*. 1st ed. Bayrūt: Manshūrāt Nizār al-Qabbānī, 1968.

Al-Bayātī, ʿAbd al-Wahhāb. *Yanābīʿ al-shams: al-sīrah al-shiʿriyyah*. 1st ed. Dimashq: Dār al-Farqad li-l-Ṭabāʿah wa-l-Nashr wa-l-Tawzīʿ, 1999.

Al-Bayati, Abdul Wahab. *Love, Death and Exile: Poems Translated from the Arabic*. Translated by Bassam K. Frangieh. Washington, DC: Georgetown University Press, 1990.

Beard, Michael. *Hedayat's "Blind Owl" as a Western Novel*. Princeton, NJ: Princeton University Press, 2014 [1990].

Benjamin, Walter. "Theses on the Philosophy of History." *Illuminations: Essays and Reflections*. Edited by Hannah Arendt. Translated by Harry Zohn. New York: Shocken Books, 1968.

Benjamin, Walter. *The Writer of Modern Life: Essays on Charles Baudelaire*. Edited by Michael W. Jennings. Translated by Howard Eiland, Edmund Jephcott, Rodney Livingstone, and Harry Zohn. Cambridge, MA: Harvard University Press, 2006.

Belcher, Wendy Laura. *Abyssinia's Samuel Johnson: Ethiopian Thought in the Making of an English Author*. New York: Oxford University Press, 2012.

Berman, Jessica. *Modernist Commitments: Ethics, Politics, and Transnational Modernism*. Modernist Latitudes. Edited by Jessica Berman and Paul Saint-Amour. New York: Columbia University Press, 2011.

Blois, François de. *Persian Literature: A Bio-Bibliographical Survey, Volume V: Poetry of the Pre-Mongol Period*. 2nd ed. London: RoutledgeCurzon in association with The Royal Asiatic Society of Great Britain and Ireland, 2004.

Boullata, Issa J. "Badr Shakir al-Sayyab and the Free Verse Movement." *International Journal of Middle East Studies* 1, no. 3 (July, 1970): 248–258.

Boullata, Issa J. "The Masks of ʿAbd al-Wahhāb al-Bayātī." *Journal of Arabic Literature* 32, no. 2 (2001): 107–118.

Boyce, Mary. "The Parthian 'Gōsān' and Iranian Minstrel Tradition," *Journal of the Royal Asiatic Society of Great Britain and Ireland* no. 1/2 (April, 1957): 10–45.

Brazil, Mark. *The Whooper Swan*. London: T. & A. D. Poyser, 2003.

Brewster, Scott. *Lyric, The New Critical Idiom*. Series editor John Drakakis. New York: Routledge Taylor & Francis Group, 2009.

Bride of Acacias: Selected Poems of Forugh Farrokhzad. Translated by Jascha Kessler and Amin Banani. Delmar, NY: Caravan Books, 1982.

Brooks, Cleanth. *The Well Wrought Urn: Studies in the Structure of Poetry*. New York: Harcourt Brace & Company, 1975 [1942].

Bullāṭah, ʿĪsā. *Badr Shākir al-Sayyāb: Ḥayātuh wa-shiʿruh*. Bayrūt: Dār al-Nahār li-l-Nashr, 1971.

Camus, Albert. *Le Mythe de Sisyphe: Essai sur l'absurde*. Paris: Gallimard, 1942.

Casanova, Pascale. "The World Republic of Letters." Convergences: Inventories of the Present. Series editor Edward Said. Translated by M. B. DeBevoise. Cambridge: Harvard University Press, 2004.

Chakrabarty, Dipesh. *Provincializing Europe: Postcolonial Thought and Historical Difference* Princeton, NJ: Princeton University Press, 2000.

Colla, Elliott. "Badr Shākir al-Sayyāb, Cold War Poet." *Middle Eastern Literatures* 18, no. 3 (2015): 247–263.

Commitment and Beyond: Reflections on/of the Political in Arabic Literature since the 1940s. Friederike Pannewick, Georges Khalil, and Yvonne Albers eds. Literatures in Context: Arabic – Persian – Turkish. Vol. 41. Verena Klemm, Sonja Mejcher-Atassi, Friederike Pannewick, and Barbara Winckler eds. Weisbaden: Reichert Verlag Wiesbaden, 2015.

Compagnon, Antoine. *Literature, Theory, and Common Sense*. Edited by Thomas Pavel and Mark Lilla. Translated by Carol Cosman. New French Thought. Princeton, NJ: Princeton University Press, 2004 [1998].

A Companion to Phenomenology and Existentialism. Edited by Hubert L. Dreyfus and Mark A. Wrathall. Oxford: Wiley-Blackwell, 2009.

Craven, Thomas Jewell. "Art and Relativity." *The Dial; a Semi-Monthly Journal of Literary Criticism, Discussion, and Information* XVV (May 1921): 535–539.

Creswell, Robyn. *City of Beginnings: Poetic Modernism in Beirut*. Princeton, NJ: Princeton University Press, 2019.

Dabashi, Hamid. *Iran without Borders: Towards a Critique of the Postcolonial Nation*. New York: Verso, 2016.

Dabashi, Hamid. "The Poetics of Politics: Commitment in Modern Persian Literature." *Iranian Studies* 18, no. 2 (Spring-Autumn, 1985): 147–188.

Dabashi, Hamid. *The World Is My Home: A Hamid Dabashi Reader*. Edited with an Introduction by Andrew Davison and Himadeep Muppidi. New Brunswick, NJ: Transaction Publishers, 2011.

Darznik, Jasmin. "Forough Goes West: The Legacy of Forough Farrokhzad in Iranian Diasporic Art and Literature." *Journal of Middle East Women's Studies* 6, no. 1 (Winter 2010): 103–116.

Davis, Eric. *Memories of State: Politics, History, and Collective Identity in Modern Iraq*. Berkeley: University of California Press, 2005.

DeYoung, Terri. "A New Reading of Badr Shākir al-Sayyāb's 'Hymn of the Rain.'" *Journal of Arabic Literature* 24, no. 1 (March, 1993): 39–61.

DeYoung, Terri. *Placing the Poet: Badr Shakir al-Sayyab and Postcolonial Iraq*. Albany: State University of New York Press, 1998.

Di-Capua, Yoav. "Arab Existentialism: An Invisible Chapter in the Intellectual History of Decolonization." *American Historical Review* 117, no. 4: 1061–1091.

Di-Capua, Yoav. *No Exit: Arab Existentialism, Jean-Paul Sartre, and Decolonization*. Chicago: University of Chicago Press, 2018.

Djagalov, Rossen. "The People's Republic of Letters: Towards a Media History of Twentieth Century Socialist Internationalism." PhD diss., Yale University, 2011.

Doyle, Laura. "Toward a Philosophy of Transnationalism." *Journal of Transnational American Studies* 1, no. 1 (2009): 1–29.

El-Ariss, Tarek. *Trials of Arab Modernity: Literary Affects and the New Political*. New York: Fordham University Press, 2013.

El-Azma, Nazeer. "The Tammūzī Movement and the Influence of T. S. Eliot on Badr Shākir al-Sayyāb." *Journal of the American Oriental Society* 88, no. 4 (October–December, 1968): 671–678.

El-Enany, Rasheed. "Poets and Rebels: Reflections of Lorca in Modern Arabic Poetry." *Third World Quarterly* 11, no. 4 (1989): 252–264.

Eliot, T. S. *The Annotated Waste Land with Eliot's Contemporary Prose*. Edited by Lawrence Rainey. 2nd ed. New Haven, CT: Yale University Press, 2006.

Eliot, T. S. *Collected Poems 1909–1962*. New York: Harcourt, Brace & World, 1963.

Eliot, T. S. *The Sacred Wood: Essays on Poetry and Criticism*. London: Methuen & Co., 1934.

Eliot, T. S. *The Waste Land*. Edited by Michael North. New York: W. W. Norton & Co., 2001.

Empires of Vision: A Reader. Edited by Martin Jay and Sumathi Ramaswamy. Durham, NC: Duke University Press, 2014.

Encyclopaedia Iranica. Online edition. New York, 1996-. www.iranicaonline.org/.

Encyclopaedia of Islam. Second Edition. Edited by P. Bearman, Th. Bianquis, C. E. Bosworth, E. van Donzel and W. P. Heinrichs. 11 vols. Leiden: E. J. Brill, 1960–2005.

Essays on Nima Yushij: Animating Modernism in Persian Poetry. Edited by Ahmad Karimi-Hakkak and Kamran Talattof. Leiden: E. J. Brill, 2004.

Even-Zohar, Itamar. "Polysystem Theory." *Polysystem Studies, [= Poetics Today 11:1]*. 1990.

Fakhreddine, Huda J. *The Arabic Prose Poem: Poetic Theory and Practice*. Edinburgh Studies in Modern Arabic Literature. Edited by Rasheed El-Enany. Edinburgh: Edinburgh University Press, 2021.

Fakhreddine, Huda J. *Metapoesis in the Arabic Tradition: From Modernists to Muḥdathūn*. Leiden: E. J. Brill, 2015.

Farrukhzād, Furūgh. *Al-Aʿmāl al-shiʿriyyah al-kāmilah*. Tarjamat Maryam al-ʿAṭṭār. Baghdād: Dār al-Madā, 2017.

Farrukhzād, Furūgh. *Īmān biyāvarīm bih āghāz-i faṣl-i sard*. 7th ed. Tihrān: Intishārāt-i Murvārīd, 1368 [1989].

Farrukhzād, Furūgh. *Marg-i man rūzī...: majmūʿah-yī az namūnah-hā-yi āsār-i shāʿirān-i Ālmān dar nīmah-'i avval-i qarn-i bīstum*. Tarjamah-'i Furūgh Farrukhzād va Dr. Masʿūd Farrukhzād. Tihrān: Kitābsarā-yi Tandīs, 1379 [2000].

Farrukhzād, Furūgh. *Tavalludī dīgar*. 11th ed. Tihrān: Intishārāt-i Murvārīd, 2536 [1977].

Fawcett, Lousie L'Estrange. *Iran and the Cold War: The Azerbaijan Crisis of 1946*. Cambridge: Cambridge University Press, 1992.

Fawzī, Nāhidah. *ʿAbd al-Wahhāb al-Bayātī ḥayātuh wa-shiʿruh (dirāsah naqdiyyah)*. Tihrān: Intishārāt-i Sār Allāh, 1383 [2004/2005].

Fawzī, Nāhidah. "Hājis al-ightirāb wa-l-tarḥāl ʿinda ʿAbd al-Wahhāb al-Bayātī." *Majallat Markaz Dirāsāt al-Kūfah* 1, no. 21 (2011): 25–44.

Fawzī, Nāhidah, Maryam Amjad, and Kubrā Rawshanfikr. "Barrasī-'i shiʿr-i Muḥammad Rižā Shafīʿī-Kadkanī va ʿAbd al-Wahhāb al-Bayātī az manẓar-i adabiyyāt-i taṭbīqī." *Pazhūhash-hā-yi adabiyyāt-i taṭbīqī* 1, nos. 1–3 (Bahār va Tābistān [Spring and Summer] 1393 [2014]): 79–97.

Ferdowsi. *The Epic of the Kings: Shāh-nāma, the National Epic of Persia*. Translated by Reuben Levy. Foreword by Ehsan Yarshater. Preface by Amin Banani. Introduction by Dick Davis. Costa Mesa, CA: Mazda Publishers, 1996.

Fihrist-i pīshnihādī-'i asāmī-'i parandigān-i Īrān. Edited by Sāymūn Jirvīs Rīd [Simon Jervis Read]. Tihrān: Dānishgāh-i Tihrān, 1337 [1958/1959].

Fish, Stanley. *Is There a Text in This Class? The Authority of Interpretive Communities*. Cambridge, MA: Harvard University Press, 1980.

Fister, Barbara. *Third World Women's Literatures: A Dictionary and Guide to Materials in English*. Westport, CT: Greenwood Press, 1995.

Forugh Farrokhzad: Another Birth and Other Poems. Translated by Hasan Javadi and Susan Sallée. Washington, DC: Mage Publishers, 2010.

Forugh Farrokhzad: Poet of Modern Iran, Iconic Woman and Feminine Pioneer of New Persian Poetry. Edited by Dominic Parviz Brookshaw and Nasrin Rahimieh. New York: I. B. Tauris, 2010.

Foucault, Michel. *Discipline & Punish: The Birth of the Prison*. Translated by Alan Sheridan. New York: Vintage Books, 1995 [1975].

Foucault, Michel. "What Is Enlightenment?" ("Qu'est-ce que les Lumières?"). Edited by Paul Rabinow. Translated by Catherine Porter. *The Foucault Reader*. New York: Pantheon Books, 1984: 32–50.

Frazer, James. *The Golden Bough: A Study in Magic and Religion*. New York: MacMillan, 1922; Bartleby.com, 2000 [1890]. www.bartleby.com/196/.

Friedman, Susan Stanford. *Planetary Modernisms: Provocations on Modernity across Time*. Modernist Latitudes. Edited by Jessica Berman and Paul Saint-Amosur. New York: Columbia University Press, 2015.

Frīzir, Jayms. *Adūnīs aw Tammūz: Dirāsah fī al-asāṭīr wa-l-adyān al-sharqiyyah al-qadīmah*. Tarjamat Jabrā Ibrāhīm Jabrā. Bayrūt: al-Mu'assasah al-ʿArabiyyah li-l-Dirāsāt wa-l-Nashr, 1979.

Fuchs, Barbara. "Another Turn for the Transnational: Empire, Nation, Imperium in Early Modern Studies." *PMLA* 130, no. 2 (March 2015): 412–418.

Galison, Peter. *Einstein's Clocks, Poincaré's Maps: Empires of Time*. New York: W. W. Norton & Co., 2003.

Gerhardt, Mia I. *The Art of Story-Telling: A Literary Study of the Thousand and One Nights*. Leiden: E. J. Brill, 1963.

Getachew, Adom. *Worldmaking after Empire: The Rise and Fall of Self-Determination*. Princeton, NJ: Princeton University Press, 2019.

Ghomi, Haideh. "Female Identity in the Poetry of Forugh Farrokhzad." *Identità e appartenenza in Medio Oriente*. Edited by Marta Petricioli and Albert Tonini. Florence: Università di Firenze, Dipartimento di Studi sullo Stato, 1998: 207–214.

Gibson, Ian. *Federico García Lorca: A Life*. New York: Pantheon Books, 1989.

The God That Failed. Foreword by David C. Engerman, introduction by editor Richard Crossman. New York: Columbia University Press, 2001.

Grigor, Talinn. *Building Iran: Modernism, Architecture, and National Heritage under the Pahlavi Monarchs*. New York: Periscope Publishing, Ltd., 2009.

Gross, Harvey and Robert McDowell. *Sound and Form in Modern Poetry*. 2nd ed. Ann Arbor: The University of Michigan Press, 1996 [1985].

Ḥallāj, al-Ḥusayn ibn Manṣūr. *Hallaj: Poems of a Sufi Martyr*. Translated by Carl. W. Ernst. Evanston, IL: Northwestern University Press, 2018.

Hamchūn kūchah-'ī bī-intihā: guzīnah-'ī az ash'ār-i shā'irān-i buzurg-i jahān. Tarjumah-'i Aḥmad Shāmlū. 3rd Edition (Tihrān: Mu'assasah-'i Intishārāt-i Nigāh, 1374 [1995]; originally published in Tābistān 1352 [Summer, 1973])

Ḥāwī, Khalīl. *Dīwān Khalīl Ḥāwī*. Bayrūt: Dār al-'Awdah, 2001.

Heidegger, Martin. *Being and Time*. SUNY Series in Contemporary Continental Philosophy. Edited by Dennis J. Schmidt. Translated by Joan Stambaugh. Revised and with a Foreword by Dennis J. Schmidt. Albany: State University of New York Press, 2010.

Heidegger, Martin. *Poetry, Language, Thought*. Translated by Albert Hofstadter. New York: HarperCollins, 2001.

Heidegger, Martin. *Sein und Zeit*. 11th ed. Tübingen: Max Niemeyer Verlag, 1967 [1927].

Hessampour, S. and S. F. Sadat Sharifi. "Barrasī-'i 'anāṣir-i mudirnism dar shi'r-i Quqnūs." *Majallah-'i shi'r-pazhūhī (Būstān-i adab) Dānishgāh-i Shīrāz* 5, no. 1 (Bahār, 1392 [Spring, 2013]): 1–28.

Hijiya, James A. "The *Gita* of J. Robert Oppenheimer." *Proceedings of the American Philosophical Society* 144, no. 2 (2000): 123–167.

Hidāyat, Ṣādiq. *Tarānah-hā-yi Khayyām: bā shish majlis-i taṣvīr az Darvīsh Naqqāsh*. [Tihrān?]: Intishārāt-i Māh, [1982?; 1934].

Hillman, Michael. *A Lonely Woman: Forugh Farrokhzad and Her Poetry*. Washington, DC: Three Continents and Mage, 1987.

Hillman, Michael C. "Rezā Barāheni: A Case Study of Politics and the Writer in Iran, 1953–1977." *Literature East & West* 20:1-4 (January–December 1976): 304–313.

Hiyūz, Langstūn. *Siyāh hamchūn a'māq-i Āfrīqā-yi khᵛūdam*. Bargardān-i Aḥmad Shāmlū. 1st ed. Tihrān: Sāzmān-i Intishārāt va Farhangī-'i Ibtikār, 136? [198?].

Hodgson, Marshall G. S. *The Order of Assassins: The Struggle of the Early Nizârî Ismâ'îlîs Against the Islamic World*. Philadelphia: University of Pennsylvania Press, 2005 [1955].

Holt, Elizabeth. "'Bread or Freedom': The Congress for Cultural Freedom, the CIA, and the Arabic Literary Journal *Hiwar* (1962–1967)." *Journal of Arabic Literature* 44, no. 1 (2013): 83–102.

Horkheimer, Max and Theodor Adorno. *Dialectic of Enlightenment: Philosophical Fragments*. Edited by Gunzelin Schmid Noerr. Translated by Edmund Jephcott. Stanford, CA: Stanford University Press, 2002 [1947].

Ḥusayn, Ṭāhā. The Future of Culture in Egypt. Translated by Sidney Glazer. *American Council of Learned Societies Near Eastern Translation Program*, no. 9. New York: Octagon Books, 1975.

Ḥusayn, Ṭāhā. "Mulāḥaẓāt." *Al-Kātib al-Miṣrī* 6, no. 21 (Rajab 1366; June 1947): 9–21.

Ḥusayn, Ṭāhā. *Mustaqbal al-thaqāfah fī Miṣr*. 2 vols. Al-Qāhirah: Dār al-Maʿārif, 1938.

Iber, Patrick. *Neither Peace Nor Freedom: The Cultural Cold War in Latin America*. Cambridge, MA: Harvard University Press, 2015.

Ibrahim, Sonallah. *That Smell and Notes from Prison*. Edited and translated by Robyn Creswell. New York: New Directions Publishing, 2013.

Isstaif, Abdul-Nabi. "Forging a New Self, Embracing the Other: Modern Arabic Critical Theory and the West – Luwīs ʿAwaḍ." *Arabic and Middle Eastern Literatures* 5, no. 2 (2002): 161–180.

Jabr, Fadel K. "The Children of Gilgamesh: A Half Century of Modern Iraqi Poetry." *Metamorphoses: A Journal of Literary Translation* 19, nos. 1–2 (Spring/Fall 2011): 341–344.

Jabrā, Jabrā Ibrāhīm. *Al-Riḥlah al-thāminah: dirāsah naqdiyyah*. Ṣaydā: al-Maktabah al-ʿAṣriyyah, 1967.

Jackson, Kevin. *Constellation of Genius: 1922: Modernism Year One*. New York: Farrar, Straus, & Giroux, 2012.

Jakobson, Roman. *Language in Literature*. Edited by Krystyna Pomorska and Stephen Rudy. Cambridge, MA: Belknap Press of Harvard University Press, 1987.

Jameson, Fredric. *Marxism and Form: Twentieth-Century Dialectical Theories of Literature*. Princeton, NJ: Princeton University Press, 1974.

Jameson, Fredric. "Third World Literature in the Era of Multinational Capitalism. *Social Text* 15 (Autumn, 1986): 65–88.

Jay, Paul. *Global Matters: The Transnational Turn in Literary Studies*. Ithaca, NY: Cornell University Press, 2010.

Jayyusi, Salma Khadra. *Trends and Movements in Modern Arabic Poetry*. Vol. II. Studies in Arabic Literature: Supplements to the Journal of Arabic Literature VI. Edited by M. M. Badawi, P. Cachia, M. C. Lyons, J. N. Mattock, and J. T. Monroe. Leiden: E. J. Brill, 1977.

Johnson, W. R. *The Idea of Lyric: Lyric Modes in Ancient and Modern Poetry*. Berkeley: University of California Press, 1982.

Jones, Kevin. *The Dangers of Poetry*. Stanford, CA: Stanford University Press, 2020.

Jones, Kevin. "The Poetics of Revolution: Cultures, Practices, and Politics of Anti-Colonialism in Iraq, 1932–1960." PhD diss., University of Michigan, 2013.

Kadhim, Hussein N. *The Poetics of Anti-Colonialism in the Arabic Qaṣīdah.* Leiden: E. J. Brill, 2004.

Kamyabee, M. H. "The Waste Land Vision in T. S. Eliot and Forugh Farrokhzad." Master's thesis, Pahlavi University, 1978.

Karimi-Hakkak, Ahmad. *Recasting Persian Poetry: Scenarios of Poetic Modernity in Iran*. London: Oneworld, 2012 [1995].

Kasī kih mis̱l-i hīch kas nīst: darbārah-'i Furūgh Farrukhzād. Pūrān Farrukhzād va Muḥammad Qāsimzādah. Tihrān: Kārvān, 1381 [2001].

Khalidi, Rashid. "The 'Middle East' as a Framework of Analysis: Re-Mapping a Region in the Era of Globalization." *Comparative Studies of South Asia, Africa, and the Middle East* 28, no. 1 (1998): 74–80.

Khāqānī, Muḥammad and Rūḥallāh Maṭlabī. "Buḥūr qaṣīdat al-taf'īlah fī al-adabayn al-'arabī wa-l-fārisī." *Buḥūth fī al-lughah al-'arabiyyah wa-ādābihā, niṣf sanawiyyah li-qism al-'arabiyyah wa-ādābihā bi-jāmi'at Iṣfahān* 1, (Pāyīz/Zamistān 1388 [Fall/Winter, 2009/2010]): 51–61.

Khayyam, Omar. *The Ruba'iyat of Omar Khayyam.* Translated by Peter Avery and John Heath-Stubbs. London: Penguin Books, 1981.

Khayyam, Omar. *Rubaiyat of Omar Khayyam: English, French, German, Italian, and Danish Translations Comparatively Arranged in Accordance with the Text of Edward FitzGerald's Version with Further Selections, Notes, Biographies, Bibliographies, and Other Material.* Edited by Nathan Haskell Dole. Vol. I. Boston: L. C. Page & Company, 1898.

Khayyām, 'Umar. *The Rubā'īyāt of 'Umar Khayyām.* Translated with an introduction by Parichehr Kasra. UNESCO Collection of Representative Works Persian Series, no. 21. Edited by Ehsan Yar-Shater. Delmar, NY: Scholar's Facsimiles & Reprints, 1975.

Klemm, Verena. "Different Notions of Commitment (*Iltizām*) and Committed Literature (*al-adab al-multazim*) in the Literary Circles of the Mashriq." *Arabic and Middle Eastern Literatures* 3, no. 1 (2000): 51–62.

The Koran. Translated by J. M. Rodwell. Foreword and Introduction by Alan Jones. London: Orion Publishing Group, 1996 [1909].

Kristal, Efraín. "Considering Coldly... A Response to Franco Moretti." *New Left Review* 15 (May–June 2002): 61–74.

Laachir, Karima, Sara Marzagora, and Francesca Orsini. "Multilingual Locals and Significant Geographies: For a Ground-Up and Located Approach to World Literature." *Modern Languages Open,* no. 1, 19 (2018): 1–8.

Laachir, Karima, Sara Marzagora, and Francesca Orsini. "Significant Geographies: In Lieu of World Literature." *Journal of World Literature* 3 (2018): 290–301.

Lām, Hārūld. *Qiṣṣat ḥayāt al-Khayyām.* Tarjamat Muḥammad Tawfīq Muṣṭafā. Al-Qāhirah: Dār al-Qalam, 196?.

Lamb, Harold. *Omar Khayyam: A Life.* Garden City, NY: Doubleday, Doran & Company, 1934.

Lamb, Hārūld. *'Umar Khayyām*. Tarjamat Dr. Muḥammad 'Alī Islāmī. Tihrān: Amīr Kabīr, 1957.

Lane, E. W. *Arabic-English Lexicon*. Cambridge: Islamic Texts Society, 1984 [1863–1893].

Laporte, Paul M. "Cubism and Relativity with a Letter of Albert Einstein." Introduction by Rudolf Arnheim. *Leonardo* 21, no. 3 (1988): 313–315.

Lara, Jesús Sayols. "Translating as Transculturating: A Study of Dai Wangshu's Translation of Lorca's Poetry from an Integrated Sociological-Cultural Perspective." PhD diss., Hong Kong Baptist University, 2015.

Latour, Bruno. *We Have Never Been Modern*. Translated by Catherine Porter. Cambridge, MA: Harvard University Press, 1993 [1991].

Laude, Patrick. *Pathways to an Inner Islam: Massignon, Corbin, Guenon, and Schuon*. Albany: State University of New York Press, 2010.

Lee, Steven S. *The Ethnic Avant-Garde: Minority Cultures and World Revolution*. Modernist Latitudes. Edited by Jessica Berman and Paul Saint-Amour. New York: Columbia University Press, 2015.

Lorca, Federico García. *'Arūsī-'i khun: namāyishnāmah dar sih pardah va haft majlis*. Tarjamah-'i Aḥmad Shāmlū. Tihrān: Intishārāt-i Tūs, 1356 [1978].

Lorca, Federico García. *Selected Poems*. Translated by Martin Sorrell. Introduction and notes by D. Gareth Walters. Oxford World's Classics. Oxford: Oxford University Press, 2007.

Lorca, Federico García. *Sih namāyishnāmah az Lūrkā: 'Arūsī-'i khūn, Yirmā, Khanah-'i Birnardā Ālbā*. Tarjamah-'i Aḥmad Shāmlū. Chāp-i 2. [Tihrān]: Nashr-i Chashmah, 1382 [2003].

Lorca, Federico García. *The Tamarit Poems: A Version of Diván del Tamarit*. Translated by Michael Smith. Dublin: Dedalus Press, 2007 [1940].

Lorca, Federico García. *Tarānah-'i sharqī va ash'ār-i dīgar*. Tarjamah-'i Aḥmad Shāmlū. [Sweden]: Havādarān-i Sāzmān-i Vaḥdat-i Kumūnīstī dar Sū'īd, [198?].

Losensky, Paul E. *Welcoming Fighānī: Imitation and Poetic Individuality in the Safavid-Mughal Ghazal*. Costa Mesa, CA: Mazda Publishers, 1998.

Lūrkā, Fidirikū Kārsiyā. Compact disc. Tarjamah va ṣidā-yi Aḥmad Shāmlū. N.d.; Tihrān: Mu'assasah-'i Intishārātī-'i Farhangī Hunarī-'i Ibtikār.

Al-Ma'arrī, Abū al-'Alā'. *Dīwān Abī al-'Alā' al-Ma'arrī al-mashhūr bi-saqṭ al-zand*. Edited by Shākir Shuqayr. Bayrūt: al-Maktabah al-Waṭaniyyah, 1884.

Al-Malā'ikah, Nāzik. *Qaḍāyā al-shi'r al-mu'āṣir*. Bayrūt: Dār al-Ādāb, 1962; Baghdād: Maktabat al-Nahḍah, 1967.

Al-Malā'ikah, Nāzik. *Shaẓāyā wa-ramād*. Bayrūt: Dār al-'Awdah, 1971 [1949].

Mao, Douglas and Rebecca L. Walkowitz. "The New Modernist Studies." *PMLA* 123, no. 3 (2008): 737–748.

Massignon, Louis. *La Passion de Husayn Ibn Mansûr Hallâj: Martyr mystique de l'Islam, exécuté à Bagdad le 26 mars 922: étude d'histoire religieuse*. [Paris]: Gallimard, 1975 [1922].

Massignon, Louis. *The Passion of al-Hallāj: Mystic and mMartyr of Islam*. Translated with a Foreword by Herbert Mason. 4 Vols. Princeton, NJ: Princeton University Press, 1982.

Milani, Farzaneh. "Love and Sexuality in the Poetry of Forugh Farrokhzad: A Reconsideration." *Iranian Studies 15* 1, no. 4 (1982): 117–128.

Minor Transnationalism. Edited by Françoise Lionnet and Shu-mei Shih. Durham, NC: Duke University Press, 2005.

Mirsepassi, Ali. *Transnationalism in Iranian Political Thought: The Life and Thought of Ahmad Fardid*. Cambridge: Cambridge University Press, 2017.

Moretti, Franco. "Conjectures on World Literature." *New Left Review* 1 (January–February 2000): 54–68.

Moreh, Shmuel. "Modern Arabic Poetry 1800–1970: The Development of Its Forms and Themes under the Influence of Western Literature." Studies in Arabic Literature: Supplements to the Journal of Arabic Literature, 5. Edited by M. M. Badawi, P. Cachia, M. C. Lyons, J. N. Mattock, and J. T. Monroe. Leiden: E. J. Brill, 1976.

Muḥsinī'niyā, Nāṣir and Sipīdah Akhavān Māsūlah. "Bāztāb-i farhang va adab-i Īrān dar shiʿr-i ʿAbd al-Wahhāb al-Bayātī." *Kāvish-nāmah-'i adabiyyāt-i taṭbīqī (muṭālaʿāt-i taṭbīqī-'i ʿarabī —fārsī)*. Dānishkadah-'i Adabiyyāt va ʿUlūm-i Insānī, Dānishgāh-i Rāzī Kirmānshāh 3, no. 12 (Zamistān [Winter], 1392; 2014): 95–119.

Mumtaḥan, Mahdī and Mihīn Ḥājī Zādah. "Barrasī-'i sayr-i taḥavvul-i shiʿr-i naw dar zabān-i ʿarabī va fārsī." *Muṭāliʿāt-i adabiyyāt-i taṭbīqī* 5, no. 16: 153–180.

Al-Musawi, Muhsin Jassim. "ʿAbd al-Wahhāb al-Bayātī's Poetics of Exile." *Journal of Arabic Literature* 32, no. 2 (2001): 212–238.

Al-Musawi, Muhsin Jassim. *Arabic Poetry: Trajectories of Modernity and Tradition*. Routledge Studies in Middle Eastern Literature. Edited by James E. Montgomery, Roger Allen, and Philip F. Kennedy. New York: Routledge, 2006.

Al-Musawi, Muhsin Jassim. "Engaging Tradition in Modern Arab Poetics." *Journal of Arabic Literature* 33, no. 2 (2002): 172–210.

Al-Musawi, Muhsin Jassim. *Islam on the Street: Religion in Modern Arabic Literature*. Lanham, MD: Rowman & Littlefield Publishers, 2009.

Al-Musawi, Muhsin Jassim. *Reading Iraq: Culture and Power in Conflict*. New York: I. B. Tauris, 2006.

Mutaqqā'zādah, ʿĪsā and ʿAlī Bashīrī. "Al-Athr al-fārisī fī shiʿr ʿAbd al-Wahhāb al-Bayātī." *Iḍāʾāt naqdiyyah* 2, no. 6 (Ṣayf [Summer] 1391; Ḥazīrān [June] 2012): 129–150.

A New Vocabulary for Global Modernism. Edited by Eric Hayot and Rebecca L. Walkowitz. Modernist Latitudes. Edited by Jessica Berman and Paul Saint-Amour. New York: Columbia University Press, 2016.

North, Michael. "The Making of 'Make It New.'" *Guernica*. 15 August 2013. www.guernicamag.com/the-making-of-making-it-new/.

Nuhayrāt, Aḥmad. "Shakhṣiyyāt Īrāniyyah fi dīwān ʿAbd al-Wahhāb al-Bayātī." *Majallat al-jamʿiyyah al-ʿilmiyyah al-Īrāniyyah li-l-lughah al-ʿarabiyyah wa-ādābihā* 9, no. 26 (al-Rabīʿ [Spring] 1392; 2013): 1–28.

Oehler-Stricklin, Dylan Olivia. "'And This Is I:' The Power of the Individual in the Poetry of Forugh Farrokhzâd." PhD diss., University of Texas at Austin, 2005.

Orientalism's Interlocutors: Painting, Architecture, Photography. Edited by Jill Beaulieu and Mary Roberts. Durham, NC: Duke University Press, 2002.

Papan-Matin, Firoozeh. *The Love Poems of Ahmad Shamlu*. Translated by Firoozeh Papan-Matin and Arthur E. Lane. Bethesda, MD: Ibex Publishers, 2005.

Persian Language, Literature, and Culture: New Leaves, Fresh Looks. Edited by Kamran Talattof. New York: Routledge, 2015.

Philsooph, Hushang. "Book Review: Essays on Nima Yushij: Animating Modernism in Persian Poetry," *Middle Eastern Literatures* 12, no. 1 (April, 2009): 100–105.

Rahimieh, Nasrin. *Oriental Responses to the West: Comparative Essays in Select Writers from the Muslim World*. Leiden: E. J. Brill, 1990.

Rancière, Jacques. *Dissensus: On Politics and Aesthetics*. Edited and translated by Steven Corcoran. New York: Continuum, 2010.

Rancière, Jacques. *The Politics of Aesthetics*. Translated by Gabriel Rockhill. New York: Continuum, 2011.

Rancière, Jacques. "The Politics of Literature." *SubStance #103* 33, no. 1 (2004): 10–24.

Rastegar, Kamran. *Literary Modernity between the Middle East and Europe: Textual Transactions in Nineteenth-Century Arabic, English, and Persian Literatures*. Routledge Studies in Middle Eastern Literatures. Edited by James E. Montgomery, Roger Allen, and Philip F. Kennedy. New York: Routledge, 2007.

Rawshanfikr, Kubrā and Sajjād Ismāʿīlī. "Barrasī-'i taṭbīqī-'i nūstālzhī dar shiʿr-i ʿAbd al-Wahhāb al-Bayātī va Shafīʿī Kadkanī." *Pazhūhash-hā-yi adabiyyāt-i taṭbīqī* 2, nos. 2–4 (Pāyīz va Zamistān [Fall and Winter] 1393 [2014-2015]): 27–55.

Al-Samarrā'ī, Mājid. *Rasā'il al-Sayyāb*. Bayrūt: al-Mu'assasah al-ʿArabiyyah li-l-Dirāsāt wa-l-Nashr, 1994.

Sanīr, Ru'ūbīn [Reuven Snir]. *Rakʿatān fi al-ʿishq: dirāsah fi shiʿr ʿAbd al-Wahhāb al-Bayātī*. Bayrūt: Dār al-Sāqī, 2002.

Sartre, Jean-Paul. *"What Is Literature?" and Other Essays*. Introduction by Steven Ungar. Cambridge, MA: Harvard University Press, 1988 [1947].

S̱arvatiyyān, Bihrūz. *Sharḥ-i ghazaliyyāt-i Ḥāfiẓ*. Daftar-i Duvvum. Tihrān: Pūyandagān-i Dānishgāh, 1380 [2001].

Al-Sayyāb, Badr Shākir. *Al-Aʿmāl al-shiʿriyyah al-kāmilah*. Baghdād: Dār al-Ḥurriyyah li-l-Ṭibāʿah wa-l-Nashr, 2008.

Al-Sayyāb, Badr Shākir. *Kuntu shuyūʿiyyan*. Aʿaddahā li-l-nashr Walīd Khālid Aḥmad Ḥasan. Kūlūnīyā [Cologne]: Manshūrāt al-Jamal, 2007 [1959].

Schimmel, Annemarie. *Mystical Dimensions of Islam*. Chapel Hill: University of North Carolina Press, 1978.

Schimmel, Annemarie. *A Two-Colored Brocade: The Imagery of Persian Poetry*. Chapel Hill: University of North Carolina Press, 1992.

Semaan, Khalil I. "'Al-Ḥallāj': A Poem by ʿAbd al-Wahhāb al-Bayātī." *Journal of Arabic Literature* 10 (1979): 65–69.

Shafīʿī-Kadkanī, Muḥammad Riżā. *Bā chirāgh va āyinah: dar justijū-ʾi rīshah-hā-yi taḥavvul-i shiʿr-i muʿāṣir-i Īrān*. Tihrān: Sukhan, 1390 [2012].

Shakespeare, William. *William Shakespeare: The Complete Works*. Edited by Alfred Harbage. Baltimore, MD: Penguin Books, 1972.

Shamīsā, Sīrūs. *Nigāhī bih Furūgh Farrukhzād*. 1st ed. Tihrān: Intishārāt-i Murvārīd, 1382 [2003].

Shāmlū, Aḥmad. *Āhang-hā-yi farāmūsh shudah*. 2nd ed. Tihrān: Intishārāt-i Murvārīd, 1386 [2007].

Shāmlū, Aḥmad. *Qaṭʿnāmah*. 4th ed. Tihrān: Intishārāt-i Murvārīd, 1364 [1985 (1951)].

Shāmlū, Aḥmad. *Quqnūs dar bārān: 1344–1345*. 1st ed. Tihrān: Intishārāt-i Nīl, 1345 [1966].

Shams, Fatemeh. *A Revolution in Rhyme: Poetic Co-Option under the Islamic Republic*. Oxford: Oxford University Press, 2021.

Shūlūkhūf, Mīkhāʾīl. *Dun-i ārām*. Bargardān-i Aḥmad Shāmlū, tarjamah az bargardān-i farānsavī-ʾi Āntwān Vītiz. Tihrān: Intishārāt-i Māzyār, 1391 [2012/2013] (1382 [2003/2004]).

Simawe, Saadi A. "The Lives of the Sufi Masters in ʿAbd al-Wahhāb al-Bayātī's Poetry." *Journal of Arabic Literature* 32, no. 2 (2001): 119–141.

Sin: Selected Poems of Forugh Farrokhzad. Translated by Sholeh Wolpé. Foreword by Alicia Ostriker. Fayetteville: University of Arkansas Press, 2007.

Smeaton, Winifred. "Tattooing among the Arabs of Iraq." *American Anthropologist* 39, no. 1 (January–March, 1937): 53–61.

Snir, Reuben. "A Study of 'Elegy for al-Ḥallāj' by Adūnīs." *Journal of Arabic Literature* 25, no. 3 (1994): 245–256.

The Stanford Encyclopedia of Philosophy. https://plato.stanford.edu/.

Al-Ṭaḥāwī, Mīrāl. *Brūklīn Hāyits*. Al-Qāhirah: Dār Mīrīt, 2010.

Tanke, Joseph J. "What Is the Aesthetic Regime?" *Parrhesia* 12 (2011): 71–81.

Ṭāqah, Shādhil. *Shādhil Ṭāqah: al-majmūʿah al-shiʿriyyah al-kāmilah*. Jamʿ wa-iʿdād Saʿd al-Bazzāz. Silsilat Dīwān al-Shiʿr al-ʿArabī al-Ḥadīth 77. [Baghdād]: Manshūrāt Wizārat al-Iʿlām, al-Jumhūriyyah al-ʿIrāqiyyah, 1977.

Thackston, Wheeler M. *An Introduction to Persian*. 4th ed. Bethesda, MD: Ibex Publishers, 2009 [1978].

Thiesen, Finn. *A Manual of Classical Persian Prosody: With Chapters on Urdu, Karakhanidic and Ottoman Prosody*. Wiesbaden: Otto Harrassowitz, 1982.

Thompson, Levi. "An Iraqi Poet and the Peace Partisans: Transnational Pacifism and the Poetry of Badr Shākir al-Sayyāb." *College Literature*. Special issue on poetry networks. Edited by Kamran Javadizadeh and Robert Volpicelli, 47, no. 1 (2020): 65–88. doi:10.1353/lit.2020.0008.

Thompson, Levi. "Review of Waed Athamneh, *Modern Arabic Poetry: Revolution and Conflict*." *Journal of Arabic Literature* 48, no. 3 (2017): 340–344. https://doi.org/10.1163/1570064x-12341352.

Thompson, Levi. "A Transnational Approach to ʿAbd al-Wahhāb al-Bayātī's ʿUmar Khayyām'." *Transnational Literature* 11, no. 1 (2018): 1–14. https://dspace.flinders.edu.au/xmlui/bitstream/handle/2328/38761/Thompson%20_A_Transnational_Approach.pdf.

Transnationalism from Below. Edited by Michael Peter Smith and Luis Eduardo Guarzino. London: Transaction, 1998.

The Transnational Unconscious: Essays in the History of Psychoanalysis and Transnationalism. The Palgrave Macmillan Transnational History Series. Edited by Joy Damousi and Mariano Ben Plotkin. New York: Palgrave Macmillan, 2009.

Vadde, Aarthi. *Chimeras of Form: Modernist Internationalism beyond Europe, 1914–2016*. Modernist Latitudes. Edited by Jessica Berman and Paul Saint-Amour. New York: Columbia University Press, 2016.

Wahba, Magdi. *A Dictionary of Literary Terms (English, French, Arabic)*. Beirut: Librairie du Liban, 1974.

Wild, Stephen. "*Zur Geschichte der Arabischen Metrik*." Abū 'l-Ḥasan ʿAlī b. ʿIsā ar-Rabaʿī an-Naḥwī. *Kitāb al-ʿarūḍ*. Edited by Muḥammad Abū'l-Faḍl Badrān. *Bibliotheca Islamica*. Vol. 44. Berlin: Das Arabische Buch, 2000.

Williams, Raymond. *Marxism and Literature*. Marxist Introductions. Edited by Stephen Lukes. Oxford: Oxford University Press, 1977.

Women and the Family in Iran. Edited by Asghar Fathi. Leiden: E. J. Brill, 1985.

Wright, Richard. *The Color Curtain: A Report on the Bandung Conference*. Foreword by Gunnar Myrdal. Cleveland, OH: The World Publishing Company, 1956.

Wright, W. *A Grammar of the Arabic Language*. Revised by W. Robertson Smith and M. J. De Goeje. 2 Vols. New Delhi: Munshiram Manoharlal Publishers, 2004 [1862].

Wu, Shengqing. *Modern Archaics: Continuity and Innovation in the Chinese Lyric Tradition, 1900–1937*. Cambridge, MA: Harvard University Press, 2013.

Yāḥaqqī, Muḥāmmad Jaʿfar. *Jūybār-i laḥẓah-hā: jaryān-hā-yi adabiyyāt-i muʿāṣir-i fārsī, naẓm va nas̱r*. Tihrān: Jāmī, 1388 [2009/2010].

Yushij, Nima. *The Bird of Sadness (Selected Poems)*. Translated by Munibar Rahman. Aligarh: Aligarh Muslim University, Institute of Persian Research, 2010.

Yushij, Nima. *The Neighbor Says: Nima Yushij and the Philosophy of Modern Persian Poetry*. Translated with an Introduction and Addendum by M. R. Ghanoonparvar. Bethesda, MD: Ibex Publishers, 2009.

Yushīj, Nīmā. *Arzish-i iḥsāsāt. Tawżīḥāt va ḥavāshī az Duktur Abū al-Qāsim Khubbatī ʿAṭāʾī*. Tihrān: Bungāh-i Maṭbūʿāt-i Ṣafīʿalīshāh, 1335; 1956.

Yushīj, Nīmā. *Arzish-i iḥsāsāt (va panj maqālah dar shiʿr va namāyish)*. Tihrān: Intishārāt-i Gūtinbirg, 2535 [1976/1977].

Yushīj, Nīmā. *Ḥarf-hā-yi hamsāyah*. 5th ed. Tihrān: Insishārāt-i Dunyā, 1363 [1984; 1939–1955].

Yushīj, Nīmā. *Majmūʿah-ʾi kāmil-i ashʿār-i Nīmā Yūshīj: fārsī va ṭabarī*. Tihrān: Intishārāt-i Nigāh, 1370 [1991].

Zubizarreta, John. "The Woman Who Sings No, No, No: Love, Freedom, and Rebellion in the Poetry of Forugh Farrokhzad." *World Literature Today* 66, no. 3 (Summer, 1992): 421–426.

Zurayk, Constantine. *The Meaning of the Disaster*. Translated by R. Bayly Winder. Beirut: Khayat's College Book Cooperative, 1956.

Zurayq, Qusṭanṭīn. *Maʿnā al-nakbah*. Bayrūt: Dār al-ʿIlm li-l-Malāyīn, 1948.

Index

1921, 6, 53
1922, 1–3, 6, 48, 50, 53, 68
1926, 50
1934, 86, 102
1938, 50
1945, 7, 76, 99
1946, 52
1947, 3, 27, 80, 167
1948, 36, 100, 103
1949, 34, 36, 100
1950, 21, 30, 77, 98, 106
1951, 73, 90, 116
1952, 100, 113, 115
1953, 7, 21–22, 41, 77, 79, 94, 96–97, 99, 103, 115–116, 118, 140, 166, 168
1954, 97, 118, 125
1955, 74
1956, 135
1957, 135
1958, 117, 125, 169
1959, 98, 118, 135
1960, 135
1961, 44, 74, 76, 98, 100
1962, 44, 135–136
1963, 146–147, 159
1964, 124, 135, 151
1965, 124–125, 135, 143
1966, 14, 135, 163, 165
1967, 3, 7, 22, 42, 136, 144
1968, 128, 135, 139
1988, 169
1989, 76

Abbasids, 27, 65, 131
Abd al-Sabur, Salah, 65, 68, 104
Abū al-Khaṣīb, 99, 114, 116
Abū Tammām (Ḥabīb ibn Aws al-Ṭā'ī), 28
academia, 12–13, 18, 73–75, 120, 125, 170
Ādāb, al-, 41
Adorno, Theodor, 1–2, 52
  "On Commitment," 44–45
Adūnīs, 4–5, 65, 68, 100, 104
  Dīwān al-shi'r al-'arabī (Anthology of Arabic Poetry), 4
  Thābit wa-l-mutaḥawwil, al- (*The Static and the Dynamic*), 19, 54
aesthetics, 12, 37, 101, 108, 119, 148, 167
  aesthetic regime, the, 45
Africa, 76
Aḥmadī, Aḥmad Rizā, 150
Akhavān S̱āliṡ, Mahdī, 144
Aleppo, 138
Āl-i Aḥmad, Jalāl, 9
al-ʿĀlim, Maḥmūd Amīn, 42
Amazigh (Berber), 167
America, Spanish, 14, 75, 86
Āmidī, al-Ḥasan ibn Bishr al-, 28
al- 'amūd ("poetry's back"), 27–28, 167
Anā al-ḥaqq ("I am the Truth"), 131, 134
anaphora, 93, 148
Andalusia, 29, 85, 167
Anderson, Benedict, 20
Anīs, ʿAbd al-ʿAẓīm, 42
Anjuman-i as̱ār-i millī (The Society for the National Heritage of Iran), 53–54
Arabian Nights, The, 103
Arabic, 7, 13
  colloquial, 29
  fuṣḥā, 29
Arabism, 117
Arānī, Taqī, 93–94
archaics, modern, 8
art, 158
al- 'arūḍ (prosodic science). *See* prosody
Asia, 76, 91, 97
Assassins, 137–138
atheism, 137
al- ʿAṭṭār, Farīd al-Dīn, 14, 55, 125, 131, 140, 154
  Manṭiq al-ṭayr (*The Conference of the Birds*), 55, 58, 62, 64, 66, 123, 129
  Taẕkirat al-awliyā' (*Biographies of the Saints*), 65

Aufhebung. *See* sublation
authenticity, 9, 127
authoritarianism, 124, 140, 166
Avicenna. *See* Ibn Sīnā
Awad, Louis, 20, 38, 41, 125, 166
  Blūtūlānd (*Plutoland*), 27, 46, 167
Azm, Sadik al-, 9
  Naqd al-dhātī baʿda al-hazīmah, al- (*Self-Criticism after the Defeat*), 9

Baathism, 139
Badawi, M. M., 11, 42
Badawī, ʿAbd al-Raḥmān, 126–128
Baghdad, 101, 110, 113, 131, 140, 169
Baghdad Pact, 118
Baghdad Teachers College (*Dār al-Muʿallimīn*), 99, 115, 125
Ban the Bomb Movement, 98
Bandung Conference, 74, 77, 85, 94–96, 168
Baraheni, Reza, 40, 144
  Ṭalā dar mis dar shiʿr va shāʿirī (*Gold in Copper on Poetry and Poesy*), 42
barzakh ("isthmus"), 128
Bashshār ibn Burd, 28
Basra, 99, 104, 150
Baudelaire, Charles, 1, 22, 149
  "*À une passante*," 147
  flâneur and, 145–149
Bayātī, ʿAbd al-Wahhāb al-, 21, 65, 67–68, 85, 118, 120, 153–154, 168
  Abārīq muhashshamah (*Broken Pitchers*), 125, 129
  "*ʿAdhāb al-Ḥallāj*" ("The Passion of al-Ḥallāj"), 123, 131–136
  "*ʿAnqāʾ, al-*" ("The Phoenix"), 129
  Ashʿār fī al-manfā (*Poems in Exile*), 125
  "*Bukāʾiyyah ilā Ḥāfiẓ al-Shīrāzī*" ("A Lament for Hāfiẓ al-Shīrāzī"), 126, 140
  existentialism and, 127–128
  "*Ghurāb*" ("The Raven"), 135–136
  Kitābah ʿalā al-ṭīn, al- (*Writing on Clay*), 126
  Mamlakat al-sunbulah (*Kingdom of Grain*), 126
  Mawt fī al-ḥayāh, al- (*Death in Life*), 128
  Muḥākamah fī Nīshābūr (*A Trial in Nishapur*), 136–139
  Nuṣūṣ sharqiyyah (*Eastern Texts*), 140–141
  Qamar Shīrāz (*Shiraz's Moon*), 126
  Tajribatī al-shiʿriyyah (*My Poetic Experience*), 135
bāzgasht (neoclassicism), 54
Beirut, 166, 169
Benjamin, Walter
  "Paris, the Capital of the Nineteenth Century," 147
  "The Paris of the Second Empire in Baudelaire," 147
Berlin Wall, 76
Bhagavad Gita, 8
Bint al-Shāṭiʾ (ʿĀʾishah ʿAbd al-Raḥmān), 100
blank verse, 151
bomb, atomic, 7–8
Brooks, Cleanth, 46
Buḥturī, -al, 28
Buwayb, 99, 155

Cairo, 43, 125, 169
Camus, Albert, 128
capitalism, 17, 44, 60, 74, 101, 103–104, 106, 110–111, 165
  time and, 156
Caspian Sea, 155
Chekhov, Anton, 115
China, 93, 97
Christianity, 29, 85, 117, 165
CIA, 100, 144
cinema, 158
close reading, 36
Cold War, 3, 17, 76, 94, 139, 166
colonialism, 3, 7, 15, 18, 23, 33, 70, 80, 103–104, 118, 167, 169
  anti, 42, 76, 98
communism, 21, 38, 52, 75, 98, 111, 116–117, 139, 166
Communists, 21, 43, 78, 93, 95, 97, 105, 114
Congress for Cultural Freedom, 100
consciousness
  Third World, 80
  transnational, 10, 70, 166
contrafaction. *See muʿāraḍah* (contrafaction)
Corbin, Henry, 126
cosmopolitanism, 76
coup d'état
  1952 in Egypt, 38
  1953 in Iran, 7, 79, 94, 97, 99, 116–117, 140–141, 144, 166, 168
  1958 in Iraq, 117, 125
craft (*ṣanʿat*), 49
  Nīmā's poetry and, 50
criticism, literary, 12
crow, 155
Cygnus cygnus. *See* swan: whooper

Daily Worker, The, 101
Dakrūb, Muḥammad, 115
Damascus, 125, 140
Darío, Rubén, 86
Darwin, Charles, 4
Darwīsh, Maḥmūd, 85
Dasein, 127

decolonization, 11, 70, 76, 80, 123, 166
Dial, The, 6
dissensus, 45
Don River, 118
drama, 105, 136–139
dunyā (material world), 132, 141

Eastern Bloc, 118
effendi, 115
Egypt, 29–30, 34, 37–38, 42–43, 126, 167
Ehrenburg, Ilya, 115
Einstein, Albert, 3–5, 8
  "On the Electrodynamics of Moving Bodies," 5
  relativity, theory of, 7–8, 166
Eliot, T. S., 1, 28, 44, 99, 146, 168
  "The Hollow Men," 154, 159–160
  "Tradition and the Individual Talent," 49
  The Waste Land, 1, 13, 22, 40, 48, 61, 101, 104, 145, 151, 154
    Burial of the Dead, The, 157
    Death by Water, 161–162
    Unreal City, 60, 149, 158, 160
England, 158
English, 11, 13, 17–18, 48, 58–59, 73, 75, 89, 102, 104, 137, 151, 154, 159
  meter, 151
enjambment, 129
enlightenment, 2, 7, 51, 160, 167
Enlightenment, Dialectic of, 1, 52
etymology, 50, 58
Eurocentrism, 3, 16
Europe, 7, 16–18, 30, 93, 168
  encounter with, 5
Even-Zohar, Itamar, 17
existentialism, 123, 126, 133, 141, 144, 166, 168

Fardīd, Aḥmad, 9
Farrukhzād, Furūgh, 22, 35, 43, 70, 128, 141, 168
  "*Dilam barā-yi bāghchah mīsūzad*" ("I Feel Sorry for the Garden"), 155
  "*Fatḥ-i bāgh*" ("The Conquest of the Garden"), 155
  flâneuse and, 146–149, 156–159
  Īmān biyāvarīm bih āghāz-i faṣl-i sard ("Let Us Believe in the Beginning of the Cold Season"), 143, 146–163, 168
  prosodic innovation and, 149–154
  T. S. Eliot and, 159–160
  Tavalludī dīgar (*Another Birth*), 146, 153, 155, 159
  turning garden into graveyard, 154–158

fascism, 52, 92
  Iran and, 85
  Spain and, 87
Fāṭimī, Ḥusayn, 140
Fertile Crescent, 23
Firdawsī, Abū al-Qāsim, 53, 73
  Shāhnāmah (*The Book of Kings*), 93
Fish, Stanley, 47
FitzGerald, Edward, 137–138
flâneuse, 145
form, 3, 11, 13, 16, 20, 22–23, 34–35, 46, 49, 63, 75, 120, 142, 144, 166–167
  Arabic poetry and, 27–32, 36–37, 102–104, 112, 129–131
  content, in relation to, 46
  Persian poetry and, 32–33, 37, 57–59, 68–69, 79, 149–154
Foucault, Michel, 3, 10
France, 110
Franco, Francisco, 84
Frazer, James
  The Golden Bough, 104
French, 18
Freud, Sigmund, 4

Ganges, 118
Garcia Marquez, Gabriel, 125
garden, 145, 149
  Persian poetry and, 154–158
genre, 14
geographies, modernist, 47–48
geographies, significant, 14, 16, 22–23, 33, 37, 48–49, 74, 76, 103, 120, 132, 142, 145, 149, 155, 166–167, 170
  in the Third World, 96
Germany, 93, 159
Gharbzadagī, 9
Ghazālī, Abū Ḥāmid Muḥammad ibn Muḥammad al-, 138
global, 12, 15, 47, 77, 97, 105, 120
Global North, 7, 13, 168
Global South, 16, 18, 35, 77, 80, 86, 124, 133, 139, 166
globalization, 3, 8, 12, 15, 17, 167
glocality, 98
God That Failed, The, 85
Gorky, Maxim, 115
  Mat' (*The Mother*), 102
Granada, 85
Guevara, Che, 128
Gulistān, Ibrāhīm, 158
  Golestan Studios, 159

Ḥāfiẓ, Shams al-Dīn Muḥammad, 53, 66, 73, 131, 154

Nīmā's *Afsānah* and, 54
Ḥakīm, Tawfīq al-, 125
Ḥallāj, al-Ḥusayn ibn Manṣūr al-, 13, 50, 64–69, 124, 128, 131–136, 140
Ḥaqqī, Yaḥyā, 125
Harlem Renaissance, 86
hashish, 138
Ḥāwī, Khalīl, 21, 104, 125
Ḥaydarī, Buland al-, 35
Hebrew, 169
Heidegger, Martin, 6
  Sein und Zeit (*Being and Time*), 39, 126–128
Hidāyat, Ṣādiq, 14, 136
  Būf-i kūr (*Blind Owl*), 14
Hikmet, Nâzım, 75, 115, 125
Hitler, Adolf, 92
Horkheimer, Max, 1–2, 52
Hughes, Langston, 94
Ḥusayn, Ṭāhā, 9, 38, 40–41
  iltizām and, 127
  Mustaqbal al-thaqāfah fī Miṣr (*The Future of Culture in Egypt*), 9
Husserl, Edmund, 126

iambic pentameter, 151
Ibn al-Rūmī, Abū al-Ḥasan ʿAlī ibn al-ʿAbbās ibn Jurayj, 28
Ibn Sīnā, 55
Idrīs, Suhayl, 41–42
Illumination, Philosophy of, 126
iltizām (literary commitment), 20, 37, 98, 106, 112, 115, 124, 126, 128, 149, 165
  al-adīb (the writer's commitment), 41
imperialism, 7, 15, 18, 33, 75, 92, 118, 140
Indonesia, 74
internationalism, 73, 76, 98, 102, 124
intertextuality, 9, 58, 65, 69, 87, 95, 106, 108, 123, 128, 146, 159
Intifāḍah
  1952 in Iraq, 113
Iran, 3, 7, 10, 16, 20, 31, 73, 80, 88, 115, 148, 154, 158, 166
  literary criticism in, 37
Iraq, 3, 7, 16, 21, 29–30, 69, 98, 112, 120, 123, 136, 166, 169
Iraqi Communist Party, 75, 97, 105, 107–108, 113–115, 118, 125
Isbir, ʿAlī Aḥmad Saʿīd. *See* Adūnīs
Iṣfahān, 126, 138
Isfandiyārī, ʿAlī. *See* Yūshīj,Nīmā
Islam, 28, 49, 53, 64, 66, 70, 85, 137, 167
Islamism, 166
Ismāʿīlis, 138
Israel, 36, 42, 144

Jabrā, Jabrā Ibrāhīm, 100
Jakobson, Roman, 6
Jāmī, Nūr al-Dīn ʿAbd al-Raḥmān, 125
Jawdat, Ṣāliḥ, 125
Jaykūr, 99, 101, 105, 108, 115, 155
Jayyūsī, Salmā al-Khaḍrā' al-, 100
Jesus, 135, 156, 165
jihād, 119
jinās (paronomasia), 112
Joyce, James, 2
  Ulysses, 2
Judaism, 29, 117
Jurjānī, ʿAlī ibn ʿAbd al-ʿAzīz al-Qāḍī al-, 28

Kaaba, 65, 116, 131
Kātib al-Miṣrī, al-, 38, 127
Khāl, Yūsuf al-, 104
Khalīl ibn Aḥmad al-Farāhīdī, al-, 31, 59, 69, 150
Khayyām, ʿUmar, 14, 53, 73, 124–125, 131, 133, 141
  Bayātī's *A Trial in Nishapur* and, 136–139
  rubāʿiyyāt, 14, 128, 137
Khurāsān, 141
Khūrī, Ra'īf, 42
Khurramshahr, 99, 115–116
Korea, 91, 154
Korean War, 21, 75, 77, 90, 94, 110
Koyré, Alexander, 126
kufr (blaspheming), 137
Kurdish, 169
Kuwait, 115

Lamb, Harold, 137
Latour, Bruno, 51
  We Have Never Been Modern, 51–52
Lawrence, D. H., 99
  Lady Chatterley's Lover, 115
Lebanon, 115
Left, 43, 73, 166
  Arab, 140
  Iranian, 21, 95
liberalism, 21, 98, 100, 123, 166
literature
  Arabic, 4, 19, 128
  comparative, 14, 75, 167–168
  less-commonly taught, 13
  minor, 12, 17, 74, 168, 170
  Persian, 3–4, 14, 73, 124, 143
  politics of, 12, 45
  Third World, 74, 95
  Western, 151
local, 12, 47, 97, 105, 120
London, 77, 149
Lorca, Federico García, 74, 77, 83–88

Lowell, Robert, 125
lyric "I," 77, 79–80, 88, 90, 94, 145, 149, 156

Madrid, 125
Maḥfūẓ, Najīb, 14, 125
  Nobel Prize, 169
Makkāwī, Sayyid, 140
Malā'ikah, Nāzik al-, 30, 57, 166
  Shaẓāyā wa-ramād (*Shrapnel and Ashes*), 34
Mallarmé, Stéphane, 1
Mantua, 108
map, 7, 9, 11, 16, 23, 47, 166, 170
  projection, Mercator, 7
Marx, Karl, 4, 37
  Kapital, Das, 117
  Manifesto of the Communist Party, 95
Marxism, 38, 43, 129, 139
Marzūqī, Abū ʿAlī Aḥmad ibn Muḥammad ibn al-Ḥasan al-, 28
Massignon, Louis, 67
  The passion of al-Hallāj mystic and martyr of Islam, 68
Masʿadī, Maḥmūd al-, 43, 100
materialism, 20, 61, 132, 136, 141
Mayakovsky, Vladimir, 6
Maʿarrī, Abū al-ʿAlā' al-, 129, 140
memoir, 118
Mesopotamia, 50, 55, 98, 104, 140, 167, 169
metaphor, 51, 66, 78, 88, 165
meter, 32, 58, 103, 108, 123, 130, 143, 150–151
Middle East, 2, 133, 171
Mīnah, Ḥannā, 115
misogyny, 148
Mississippi, 118
modernism, 12, 16, 170
  American, 17
  Arab, 19, 30, 35, 60, 69
  Arabic, 3–4, 23, 37, 130, 134
  canon formation, 13–14, 16, 96
  European, 17, 30, 68, 146, 168
  French, 145, 154
  global, 4
  Iranian, 3, 11, 23, 35, 37, 53, 60
  late, 166
  literary, 3, 86, 167
  Persian, 48, 95, 143, 149, 151
  planetary, 4, 11, 13, 16, 23, 28, 73, 120, 168
  poetic, 22, 46
  reorienting, 11, 16, 18, 77, 167, 169
  studies, modernist, 7
  Western, 11, 14, 101, 104
modernismo, 86
Modernist Latitudes, 13
modernity, 4, 8, 10, 20, 73
  attitude of, 3, 8, 10–11, 19, 38, 52
  discourse of, 9
  European, 8
  faith in, 11
  Pahlavi, 51
  secular, 51
  Western, 67
modernization, 11, 49–50, 68
monorhyme, 27, 30, 33, 35
Moscow, 115, 118, 125, 139
Mossadegh, Mohammad. *See* Muṣaddiq, Muḥammad
Muḥammarah, al-, 99, 115–116
muḥdath (modernist), 27
Mulk, Niẓām al-, 137
multilingualism, 15
Muruwwah, Ḥusayn, 42
Muṣaddiq, Muḥammad, 7, 21, 79, 95, 116, 119, 140, 168
Mutanabbī, Abū al-Ṭayyib Aḥmad ibn al-Ḥusayn al-, 100, 117, 129
muwashshaḥāt, 29
muʿāraḍah (contrafaction), 20, 50, 58, 69, 123, 129
mysticism, 131, 137
myth, 1–2, 13, 16, 19, 23, 34, 62, 80, 98, 104, 112, 124, 128, 167, 169

Nakbah, 36, 38, 103
nation state, 12, 17, 20, 124
nationalism, 43, 46, 75, 82, 119
  Iraqi, 97–100, 102–103, 110, 113, 116–117, 119, 139, 168
  Pahlavi, 43, 50, 74
Nazism, 92
neocolonialism, 74, 167
neoimperialism, 95, 98
Neruda, Pablo, 115
Netherlands, The, 158
New Criticism, 46
New Poetry. *See shiʿr-i naw*
New York, 86
Newton, Isaac, 5
Nietzsche, Friedrich, 4
nightingale (*al-bulbul*), 107
Nishapur, 126, 136–139
Nobel Prize
  Literature, 14
  Physics, 6
Non-Aligned Movement, 35, 74, 76, 85, 96
noria. *See* waterwheel (*nāʿūrah*)
North Africa, 28, 104
novel, 14, 86

Oppenheimer, J. Robert, 8
Orientalism, 17, 23

Osiris, 104
Ottoman Empire, 169

pacifism, 98, 102–103
Pahlavi dynasty, 20, 49, 51, 68, 93, 117, 140, 166
Pahlavī, Muḥammad Riżā, 42, 74
Pahlavī, Riżā Shāh, 53, 93
Palestine, 9, 36, 85, 103
Pan-Arabism, 97, 120
Paris, 77, 147, 149
Peace Partisans (*Anṣār al-salām*), 97, 113
Persian, 7, 13–14
  Middle, 32
  New, 32
  philosophy, 126
  pronouns, 146
  relational past (grammar), 89
phoenix, 13, 34, 50, 55, 57–69, 128, 165
poetry, 10, 14, 158
  Arabic, 27, 120, 141, 167
  French, 154
  German, 159
  modernist, 40, 120, 169
  Persian, 51, 123, 126
  premodern, 22–23, 50, 166
  prose, 29, 79
  Spanish American, 86
  Western, 23, 167
polysystem, 4, 17–18, 167
populism, 140
Portsmouth Treaty, 100
postcolonial studies, 18
postcolonialism, 166
Pound, Ezra, 1
  "Make it new!," 48
prose, 39–40
prosody, 3, 11, 13, 16, 20, 22–23, 50
  Arabic, 20, 27, 33, 49, 53, 55, 57–58, 103, 130, 142–143, 149, 167
  foot, metrical. *See taf ʿīlah*
  Persian, 32, 49, 69–70, 145, 149, 154
Proust, Marcel, 2
  À la recherche du temps perdu (*In Search of Lost Time*), 2

qaṣīdah (ode), 35, 86, 166
Qurʾān, 28, 106, 108, 136

Rabat, 97
Rabaʿī, ʿAlī Abū al-Ḥasan al-, 31
Radiolab, 5
Ramaḍān, 106
Ramādī, al-, 100
Rancière, Jacques, 45
rationalism, 137
raven, 136
relativity, theory of. *See* Einstein,Albert
religion, 16
Renaissance, 160
revolution, 138, 144
Revolution, Islamic, 166
rhyme, 29, 60, 63, 78–79, 94–95, 98, 109, 123, 133, 150, 168
rhythm, 30–31, 35, 104, 112–113, 150
Robespierre, Maximilien, 97
Romanticism, 73, 80, 88, 94
Rome
  Conference on Modern Arabic Literature, 44, 98, 100–101
rubāʿiyyāt (quatrains). *See* Khayyām,ʿUmar
rukn (poetic foot), 57, 59
Rūmī, Jalāl al-Dīn Muḥammad, 73, 80, 125, 140
Russia, 117
Russian, 6, 102, 126

Ṣabbāḥ, al-Ḥasan al-, 137–138
Ṣāliḥ, al-Ṭayyib, 14
  Season of Migration to the North, 14
Saljuq dynasty, 137
ṣanʿat (craft), 64
Sartre, Jean-Paul, 38, 41, 43–44
  Qu'est-ce qu'écrire? (*What Is Writing?*), 37–39, 127
Sasanians, 32
Sayyāb, Badr Shākir al-, 21, 30, 35, 38, 43, 57, 85, 128, 139–140, 155, 166, 168
  1952 *Intifāḍah* and, 113–115
  "*Asliḥah wa-l-aṭfāl, al-*" ("Weapons and Children"), 97, 103–113, 123
  Communists and, 99–103
  "*Fajr al-salām*" ("The Dawn of Peace"), 106
  Kuntu shuyūʿiyyan (*I Was a Communist*), 98, 101–102
  Kuwait and Iran, in, 115–117
  Mutanabbī, al- and, 100–101, 117
  Sindbad and, 104–105
  T. S. Eliot and, 43, 100
  William Shakespeare and, 100, 106–109
Saʿdī Shīrāzī, 73
Saʿīd, Nūrī al-, 118
scansion, 59
sectarianism, 138
self-determination, 77
sexism, 148
Shakespeare, William, 97, 99, 101
  Romeo and Juliet, 107–109
Shamirān, 116

Shāmlū, Aḥmad, 21, 35, 43, 70, 128, 139–141, 168
Āhang-hā-yi farāmūsh shudah (*Forgotten Songs*), 74, 80
Kitāb-i kūchah (*The Book of the Alley*), 94
lyric "I" and, 80–83
"*Marg-i Nāṣirī*" ("The Death of the Nazarene"), 165
"*Parchamdār!*" ("Flag-bearer!"), 82
"*Qaṣīdah barā-yi insān-i māh-i Bahman*" ("Ode for the Man of the Month of Bahman"), 93–94
Qaṭʿnāmah (*The Manifesto*), 21, 73, 154, 160
Quqnūs dar bārān (*Phoenix in the Rain*), 165
"*Surūd-i buzurg*" ("The Grand Anthem"), 90–93
"*Surūd-i mardī kih khudash rā kushtah ast*" ("Song of a Man Who Killed Himself"), 78–80, 88–90, 144
"*Surūd-i nīzahdārān-i ʿPārtʾ*" ("The Anthem of the Parthian Spearmen"), 82
"*Tā shikūfah-ʾi surkh-i yak pīrāhan*" ("Until a Shirt Blossoms Red"), 78–80
World War II, during, 82
Shaṭṭ al-ʿArab, 99, 103, 111
Shawqī, Aḥmad, 28
Shia, 138
Shīrāz, 126
Shiʿr (*Poetry*), 104, 166
shiʿr ḥurr (free verse), 30, 35, 49
shiʿr-i naw (New Poetry), 2, 20, 49
shiʿr-i sipīd (blank verse), 150
Sholokhov, Mikhail, 94
Shuʿūbiyyah, al-, 117
Silone, Ignazio, 95
simile, 51
Sindbad, 104
Sisyphus, 139
Six-Day War, 22, 42, 144
socialism, 124, 140
socialist realism, 42, 101, 103, 113, 119
Society for the National Heritage of Iran, The. *See Anjuman-i āsār-i millī*
South America, 76
Soviet Union, 82, 93, 97, 103, 116, 118, 165, 168
transnationalism from above and, 75
Spain, 85
Spanish Civil War, 83
Spender, Stephen, 85, 95
Sphinx, 58
Stalin, Joseph, 22, 96
Stockholm Appeal, 98, 100
sublation (*Aufhebung*), 20, 49, 53, 58, 69, 76, 128
Sufism, 14, 64, 66–69, 126, 137, 168
Ḥallāj, al- and, 131–136
Insān al-Kāmil, al- (The Perfect Man), 128
Suhrawardī, al-, 126, 131, 140
Sunni, 137–138
swan, 69
whooper, 55
symbolism, 3, 19, 50–51, 56, 69, 135, 144
Syria, 29, 115, 125

ṭabīʿat (nature), 48, 51–52
taḍmīn (poetic quoting), 22, 108, 123–124, 128–131, 133, 141, 168
tafʿīlah (poetic foot), 16, 31, 57–58, 103, 129, 150, 152, 168
tajnīs. See jinās (paranomasia)
takhalluṣ (mention of a pen name), 80
Tammūz, 2, 13, 65, 104
Ṭāqah, Shādhil, 35
Ṭarīq, al- (*The Way*), 115
tarṣīʿ (isocolon), 63, 110
tażādd (antithesis). *See ṭibāq* (antithesis)
taʿahhud (literary commitment), 42, 74, 80, 149, 165
Tehran, 2, 99, 116, 126, 140
Thaqāfah al-waṭaniyyah, al- (*National Culture*), 115
theory, 13
affect, 10
feminist, 132
polysystem, 4
world-system, 13, 15, 76
Third World, 10, 17, 35, 46, 74–75, 80, 88, 96, 128, 165, 168
Third Worldism, proto-, 73
definition, 74–78
literature and, 96
Qaṭʿnāmah (*The Manifesto*) and, 78–83
ṭibāq (antithesis), 112, 134
Tigris River, 113
time, 4–5, 7–8, 14, 149, 155
capitalism and, 156
Torah, 117
totalitarianism, 22, 96
traditionalism, 12, 28
translation, 18, 27, 54, 58, 73, 79, 85, 89, 94, 102, 104, 108, 129, 137, 159, 163
transnationalism, 4, 12, 18, 23, 37, 41, 47, 68, 76, 103, 166, 169
from above, 17, 75, 98, 111, 118–119, 168
from below, 17, 75
optic, transnational, 7
Tudeh Party, 43, 75, 98, 119
Sayyāb, Badr Shākir al- and, 116–117
Tunisia, 97

Turkish, 169
unconscious, 10
  transnational, 3, 8–10, 19, 49, 60, 70, 73, 133, 141, 166

United Kingdom, 21, 90, 93
United States, 21, 90, 93, 100, 118
Urmia, 82

Valéry, Paul, 28
Venice, 97
Verona, 107
voyeurism, 147

Wall Street, 118
waterwheel (*nāʿūrah*), 111–112
Wathbah (The Leap), 100
Westoxification. *See Gharbzadagī*
world literature, 14, 17, 21, 34, 73–74, 96, 103, 170
World War I, 1, 158
World War II, 21, 35, 82, 165
worldmaking, 77

Yūshīj, Nīmā, 1–2, 11, 16, 20, 35, 47, 73, 79, 123, 141, 144, 146, 155, 158, 166, 168
  Afsānah (*Myth*), 1, 48–49, 53–54
  Iranian Writer's Congress (1946), 52–53
  metrics and, 58–59
  "*Murgh-i amīn*" ("The Amen Bird"), 80
  prosodic innovation and, 59, 149–150
  "*Qū*" ("The Swan"), 55–57, 79, 165
  "*Quqnūs*" ("The Phoenix"), 57–69, 79, 128, 133, 149

Żaḥḥāk, 93
zajal, 29
Zoroastrianism, 64
Zurayq, Qusṭanṭīn, 9
  Maʿnā al-nakbah (*The Meaning of the Disaster*), 9

Printed in the United States
by Baker & Taylor Publisher Services